Why can't all Christians just get along? *Divided We Fall* explains how we got to where we are—with an amazing mix of tears, anger, and hope.

—**Leith Anderson**, President, National Association of Evangelicals

Some of the best writing that a Christian author ever does is the result of a seasoned, lifelong perspective learned by God's grace through humbly walking in the truth. Luder Whitlock gives us such a perspective in *Divided We Fall*. He presents the biblical truth of the church with great care and then shows how schism has soiled the bride's faithful witness to Jesus. He honestly addresses the challenges of our time and gives some of the finest action steps I've read. I am constantly asked for thoughtful, constructive ways to pursue unity. *Divided We Fall* will become a highly recommended book for everyone I mentor in Christian unity.

—**John H. Armstrong**, President, ACT3 Network

If Christian unity is such a big deal for Jesus, why isn't it a big deal for the contemporary church? If Jesus thinks it so vital to the church's witness, why doesn't the church take it more seriously? These are the questions that have haunted Luder Whitlock for years and impelled him to write *Divided We Fall*. Inspired by thinkers such as Francis Schaeffer, Dietrich Bonhoeffer, and Tim Keller, Whitlock makes the case that the church's greatest witness to the watching world is our observable love for and unity with one another. Our lack of unity and love destroys our witness and testimony to the world. Whitlock not only deftly shows how we have lost this unity and why recovering it is so important, but provides eight insightful ways to move toward more unity in the church. This is a challenging book, one that the church needs to read and heed. I found myself inspired and more passionate about unity and love after reading it. I can't commend it more highly.

—**Jim Belcher**, President, Providence Christian College

Sometimes one reads a book that is so clear, so wise, and so profound that one wants everybody to read it. *Divided We Fall* is that kind of book. Luder Whitlock is probably the only person I know who could have written this book and spoken its truth so clearly. He's been there, done that, and been a significant part of the story about which he writes. This is a book for every Christian. Its prophetic message must be heard lest we remain divided and really do fall. Read it and share it with everybody you know.

—**Steve Brown**, Radio broadcaster; author, *A Scandalous Freedom: The Radical Nature of the Gospel*; founder, Key Life Network

A prominent Christian historian has observed that some evangelical leaders have too often indulged in "their fair share of back-stabbing, power-mongering, petty-minded polemicizing, gratuitous boundary-marking and schismatic devilment." As a veteran leader of contemporary evangelicalism, Luder Whitlock has seen the damage that so much of this unnecessary fragmentation has done to the larger evangelical witness. His book is a bold cry of sincere lament and a clarion call for repentance, healing, charity, and visible unity before an unbelieving watching world. It should become required reading for pastors, teachers, and seminary students preparing for future ministry.

—**Michael Cromartie**, Vice President, Ethics and Public Policy Center

In *Divided We Fall*, Luder Whitlock demonstrates why he is considered one of the most widely respected leaders in the evangelical world. Clear, lucid, and balanced, this volume provides us with a compelling and much-needed vision for the unity of God's people, grounded in the Trinitarian gospel and the historical pattern of Christian truth. Recognizing that how we apply, implement, celebrate, and live out the Christian faith is as important as what we together confess, this important and timely publication calls God's people to repentance and renewal in fresh, constructive, and inviting ways. It is a joy to recommend this deeply hopeful and welcomed appeal to the Christian community.

—**David S. Dockery**, President, Trinity International University

Too often Christians have been divided over issues that are less than gospel essentials. What are the causes of and cures for these divisions? Luder Whitlock is more qualified than most to plead for the unity of the church. Without yielding one inch on matters of principle, he entreats the modern reader to consider the urgency of the communion of the saints. The appeal of this book is its biblical basis, combined with a very good survey of church history (including the more recent Presbyterian episodes), sociological insights, and his own most valuable and poignant personal accounts. His lucid writing style masks the deep learning and research behind these pages. Dr. Whitlock does not shrink back from some of the tough questions that he rightly anticipates: Was Luther a schismatic? What about denominations? What are the limits of tolerance? Some of the answers will surprise you. Others may disturb you. All of them will edify you. This is essential reading for our times.

—**William Edgar**, John Boyer Chair of Evangelism and Culture, Professor of Apologetics, Westminster Theological Seminary, Philadelphia

My good friend Luder Whitlock has written an excellent book on a subject that has long been dear to my heart—the unity of the church. It covers biblical principles, historical and theological issues, and practical means of achieving reconciliation and love in Christ. His understanding of the issues is deep and right on target, and his presentation is well ordered to foster the unity he urges us to seek. I hope this book receives a very wide readership.

—**John M. Frame**, J. D. Trimble Professor of Systematic Theology and Philosophy, Reformed Theological Seminary

Jesus did not come to establish a dismembered church or a disunited body. He prayed for his disciples, and for us, that we would be one, as he and the Father are one, so that the world may believe. That prayer is still operative, and this book, from one of our wisest evangelical leaders, is an urgent plea for its fulfillment. Let us hear and heed.

—**Timothy George**, Founding Dean, Professor of Divinity History and Doctrine, Beeson Divinity School

Luder Whitlock has been acknowledged as a major leader in American and global evangelicalism for more than thirty-five years. Writing from this distinctive perspective, he makes a simple argument: to mark the five hundredth anniversary of the Reformation, it is time for Protestant Christians to affirm and take seriously the rich and energetic ecumenicity of those who led that Reformation. While not calling for an organizational unity like the failed mainline ecumenical attempts in the twentieth century, he does believe it's time for evangelicals to focus more closely on what they hold in common, especially in the face of increasing cultural opposition to the gospel that they all hold dear in the twenty-first century.

—**Jeffrey J. Jeremiah**, Stated Clerk, Evangelical Presbyterian Church

Luder Whitlock's *Divided We Fall* seeks to revive a dormant conversation about why and how Christians and churches must pursue ways to display our unity in Christ visibly to the watching world, as Jesus prayed (John 17:21–23). Building on solid biblical foundations, Whitlock explores the history of the visible church's unity and brokenness, and the complexities entailed in efforts to restore our communion in biblical truth. Some of his diagnoses of causes and prescriptions of remedies are self-evident, whereas others are provocative and controversial. In either case, Whitlock's voice rouses followers of Jesus from our complacency in a status quo in which Christ's church is, sadly, "by schisms rent asunder, by heresies distressed." This book merits reading with humble self-examination, as well as theological discernment.

—**Dennis E. Johnson**, Professor of Practical Theology, Westminster Seminary California

Luder Whitlock's book is something of a *cri de coeur* for greater unity in the church. At a time when Christian leaders are almost obsessed about the culture, this book rightly argues that we will shape the broader society only to the degree that we make the Christian church what it should be. And in our present moment, the unity of the church is both a witness to the world and a necessity for its strength and vitality. Luder's appeal comes from long experience and membership in several denominations. He marshals evidence for his contentions from the Bible, theology, history, and organizational literature. Not everyone will agree with every proposal or every argument, but overall the book makes a compelling case.

—**Timothy Keller**, Senior Pastor, Redeemer Presbyterian Church, New York City

If you know Luder Whitlock, you can almost hear his audible voice as you read *Divided We Fall.* He illuminates the reality that although we often experience the church as a fractious mess, that is not the spiritual reality of the body of Christ. Whitlock calls the church to manifest the unity of the Spirit in the bond of peace even in the absence of consensus on particular issues. As the culture continues to shift and the relevance of the church is increasingly called into question, visible unity becomes essential to the fruitful witness of Christ's people. This is a must-read for all those interested in the church's bearing a unified witness to the world and experiencing the joy of real community with fellow believers.

—**Carmen Fowler LaBerge**, President, Presbyterian Lay Committee; Host, *The Reconnect* radio show

If you've ever wondered why the church is so fragmented, Luder Whitlock, one of America's premier ecclesiastical statesmen, provides a compelling answer. If you've longed for greater unity in the body of Christ, here is balm for your soul. Whitlock's *Divided We Fall* issues a gracious plea for renewed concern for biblical unity. His thoughtful analysis of the church's ages-long proclivity for disunity is convicting yet encouraging as it challenges us to pursue a fresh commitment to Christian community. This is a much-needed study for both leaders and congregants, especially for us in the Reformed and Presbyterian traditions. *Divided We Fall* will help you to reassess and address the spirit of partisanship, independence, and schism that lurks within our hearts and the culture of our churches.

—**Peter A. Lillback**, President, Westminster Theological Seminary

Jesus thought and taught that the unity of those who call themselves by his name was and is extremely important. He prayed in John 17 that Christians might be one, just as he is one with the Father. He specified that a key goal of his entire ministry was that believers might be brought to complete unity. Why that specific goal? Because *then* "the world may know that you sent me." Luder Whitlock's superb book explores the full biblical basis for such unity, it traces the challenges to that unity throughout church history, and it makes very practical suggestions about how we might move toward accomplishing that for which our Savior prayed.

—**Samuel T. Logan Jr.**, Professor of Church History, Biblical Theological Seminary; Former President, Westminster Theological Seminary

Sometimes it seems that the greatest enemy of the church's work is the church itself, with its propensity for division, backbiting, and even downright unchristian behavior. We should not be surprised that fallen human beings behave as badly as we do, since Christian theology predicts it. But how can the church become a stronger force for counteracting those tendencies and begin to more closely resemble the community of redemptive love that it is meant to be—and that it needs to be, today more than ever before? Luder Whitlock's book is a resounding call for us to do better, delivered not in the hectoring tone of a would-be prophet but in the generous and encouraging tone of a learned and experienced friend, who offers us not only exhortations but also concrete and constructive suggestions. It is most welcome, and highly recommended for all, especially pastors and lay leaders.

—**Wilfred M. McClay**, G. T. and Libby Blankenship Chair in the History of Liberty, University of Oklahoma

Luder Whitlock is a trusted voice for Christians because he evidences deep wisdom, compassion, and maturity, as well as intellect and skill. This book calls the church to gospel unity in ways that will provoke you to think, ponder, and pray.

—**Russell Moore**, President, Ethics & Religious Liberty Commission of the Southern Baptist Convention

This book speaks deeply into my soul. I know that Jesus calls us to work for Christian unity, but I am very distrustful of what people have in mind when they offer plans for pursuing that goal. Luder Whitlock understands all my misgivings, but he pushes beyond them with his profound call—backed by careful biblical thought, historical explorations, and moving personal confessions—for new efforts at healing and reconciliation. I want to belong to the kind of church he hopes for!

—**Richard J. Mouw**, President Emeritus and Professor of Faith and Public Life, Fuller Theological Seminary

From a full lifetime of Christian service, Luder Whitlock has written an unusually insightful assessment of the contemporary American church and an unusually helpful challenge to follow Christ as head of the church. Biblically rooted, historically informed, and pastorally helpful, this book gracefully fulfills its purpose of strengthening unity and community in Christ's church.

—**Mark A. Noll**, Research Professor of History, Regent College

The church of Jesus Christ exists in a perilous time, especially for those living out of a broad Reformed evangelicalism. More and more out of step with the values of culture, churches and denominations should consider it imperative to live and serve in a manner of unity, yet that often seems only a hoped-for reality. Dr. Luder Whitlock's book shines a thought-provoking and informative light on this subject. With years of experience across a variety of cultural and denominational lines, he brings wisdom, clarity, and practical ideas for turning the tide back toward the unity of the body.

—**David D. Swanson**, Senior Pastor, First Presbyterian Church of Orlando

A powerful case for evangelical ecumenism (based on grace and truth), with special reference to Reformed Christians, from an esteemed insider.

—**Don Sweeting**, President, Colorado Christian University

As a long-term president of a seminary that draws students from many denominations, and from his decades of experience as a minister, Dr. Whitlock realizes the difficulties for the various branches of the church in realizing organizational unity. He therefore wisely advocates a working unity based on the Apostles', Nicene, and Athanasian Creeds and a common commitment to fulfilling the Great Commission. Dr. Whitlock suggests cooperative ministry directed toward achieving common goals in areas such as evangelism, education, ministries of mercy, and Christian witness to an increasingly secularized culture. All branches of the church lament the divisions of the church and long for some sort of unity before Christ's return. Dr. Whitlock's proposal is a step in the right direction.

—**L. Roy Taylor**, Stated Clerk of the General Assembly of the Presbyterian Church in America

Luder Whitlock's *Divided We Fall* is a work of such tender conviction, such loving wisdom, that its words carried my heart closer to Jesus and the church he loves and leads. It meant all the more to me because I know that Luder's concern for the unity of the church is not merely an intellectual idea, but a deeply held desire that he shares with Christ. I've seen this work out in my interactions with Luder, and it is evident in these pages. *Divided We Fall* is honest about what has divided Christians, and about the challenges we have in healing those divides. It is my hope that through this book entire communities will be motivated to earnestly seek unity, and find in the church and the Savior that Whitlock describes so sweetly the resources needed to do so.

—**Michael Wear**, Founder, Public Square Strategies LLC

Divided We Fall is exquisitely timed. It comes into print when hundreds of evangelically oriented congregations race to exit their denominational encumbrances. But where will they go, and how will they relate to one another after their departures? An increasingly secularized environment in the United States and a virulent Islamic assault beyond its borders portend persecution for those who profess that Jesus Christ is "the way, and the truth, and the life" (John 14:6).

Author Luder Whitlock implores evangelicals to know that the time has come to cherish their common commitment to the Lord Jesus while graciously recognizing secondary differences.

—**Parker T. Williamson**, Editor Emeritus, *Presbyterian Layman*

Dr. Luder Whitlock is a seasoned, very well-respected leader in American evangelicalism. In this timely volume, he calls Christians "to live together as God has directed" and to repent of "unloving"attitudes toward each other (John 17). Dr. Whitlock's sage reflections prod and pinch, encourage and exhort. In these contentious days, Dr. Whitlock's volume constitutes a much-needed reminder that we as Christians should seek the unity of Christ's church and love the Lord our God with all our hearts, souls, and minds and our neighbors as ourselves.

—**John D. Woodbridge**, Research Professor of Church History and the History of Christian Thought, Trinity Evangelical Divinity School

DIVIDED WE FALL

DIVIDED WE FALL

Overcoming a History of Christian Disunity

LUDER G. WHITLOCK JR.

P&R
PUBLISHING
P.O. BOX 817 • PHILLIPSBURG • NEW JERSEY 08865-0817

Italics within Scripture quotations indicate emphasis added.

ISBN 978-1-59638-192-6 (pbk)
ISBN 978-1-62995-369-4 (ePub)
ISBN 978-1-62995-370-0 (Mobi)

Printed in the United States of America

Library of Congress Cataloging-in-Publication Data

Names: Whitlock, Luder G., author.
Title: Divided we fall : overcoming a history of Christian disunity / Luder G. Whitlock Jr.
Description: Phillipsburg : P&R Publishing, 2017. | Includes bibliographical references and index.
Identifiers: LCCN 2017002371| ISBN 9781596381926 (pbk.) | ISBN 9781629953694 (epub) | ISBN 9781629953700 (mobi)
Subjects: LCSH: Christian union--History. | Church--Unity.
Classification: LCC BX6.5 .W46 2017 | DDC 280/.042--dc23
LC record available at https://lccn.loc.gov/2017002371

This book is dedicated to

Jim Seneff
Tim Manor
David Lucas

Three friends who have shaped my life and ministry

CONTENTS

FOREWORD

AS I HAVE grown older and served longer as a minister in the church, I've come to believe that one of the blind spots in the recent history of my own denominational tradition has been a failure to devote as much attention and effort to promoting godly, biblical church unity as to preserving godly, biblical doctrinal fidelity. Few are good at both. Often those who are interested in doctrinal purity care little about church unity, and those concerned for church unity are prepared to sacrifice doctrinal fidelity for it. But this should not be the case.

For the last twenty years or so, I have been involved in a friendship that turned into a pastors' conference (the aim of which is to foster pan-Reformed pastoral friendships) called "Together for the Gospel." One of the things that we are trying to do is to foster *both* godly unity and doctrinal fidelity. The twentieth century has seen a number of failed strategies to promote unity among evangelical Christians. One is to unite around a mission and make theology a secondary matter. But the message and mission of the church are irreducibly theological, and so what eventually happens when this strategy is used is that the gospel itself gets thinned and diminished—or, worse, elastic.

Another failed strategy has been to try to unite around a few core theology affirmations and declare everything else secondary. For instance, "we all believe in the atonement, and so our differences on baptism shouldn't matter." But this view underplays the practical importance of much Bible truth in the everyday life of the church, and tends to promote an ambivalence about things on which we should be emphatic. It also fails to reckon with the fact that the

Bible's theology is systematic (whether people want to admit that or not!) and that truths are therefore interconnected with other truths. There are other reasons why Baptists, Lutherans, Presbyterians, and Catholics believe what they believe about baptism, so you can't just isolate their beliefs about baptism and declare them inconsequential when they entail other important theological assertions.

My friends in "Together for the Gospel" have tried to go a different direction in promoting unity. We have candidly acknowledged our theological differences, and have not attempted to downplay the importance of those disagreements, while at the same time celebrating the significance of the very important things to which we share mutual theological commitments. We are agreed on the gospel, and not a scaled-down gospel, but a robust, biblical, full depiction of the saving work of God in Christ. We are also committed to historic, orthodox Christianity and to Protestant, confessional, Reformed doctrine. Yet there remain major differences—differences that have separated ecclesiastical traditions and denominations for centuries. We don't try to paper over those or pretend that they don't matter. We both celebrate what we share in common and celebrate that we still care about our differences, because those principled differences are the result of the fact that we all believe in truth and its importance for the life and mission of the church (my friend Al Mohler often jokes that we are among the last people on earth who can have an honest disagreement because we still believe that truth matters!). And we also deliberately pursue friendship and cooperation, consistent with our theological convictions, for the sake of the gospel and the glory of Christ in the unity of his people, his body.

I'm not claiming that we've arrived, or figured this out, but we are trying. That is one reason why I am so thankful for this book and its author. Much of what I know in this area I've learned from him. Not just from what he says, but from how he lives and what he does.

The important (and difficult) topic that Dr. Luder Whitlock tackles in this book is not simply one that he has researched. He speaks from conviction and experience. He has not merely thought about the unity of the church, or studied the unity of the church, but spent a lifetime promoting and cultivating the unity of the church in a fractured and fragmented world. I have had the privilege of watching him do so for over three decades.

If you are a Christian leader, this book will push you hard and make you think. I have been reflecting a good bit of late on the contributions of Sam Patterson (founding president of Reformed Theological Seminary) and Luder Whitlock (his successor and the longest-serving president in the history of RTS) to the pandenominational Reformed resurgence that has been slowly building over the last fifty years (both men played a major role, though often unappreciated). Two things about both men were key to their ability to foster a movement as well as to promote unity across denominational lines: (1) their unwavering commitment to truth and (2) their convictional kindness in dealing with others.

Dr. Whitlock has put this twofold principle into practice in serving in a number of influential positions in graduate theological education and international ecclesiastical cooperation. We could learn a thing or two about the pursuit of unity and community in the church from such a man. I was challenged and edified by reading *Divided We Fall.* I think you will be, too.

Ligon Duncan
Chancellor/CEO, Reformed Theological Seminary
John E. Richards Professor of Systematic Theology, RTS Jackson
Past Moderator, General Assembly, Presbyterian Church in America

PREFACE

WHAT IF THE Christian church radiated unity and harmony, mutual understanding and cooperation? What if believers everywhere joyfully worked together to achieve the mission mandated by God, ensuring that all people would be attracted to Christ and believe in him?

Sadly, reality is completely different. Although many wonderful Christians are involved in thriving ministries, the church that Jesus established has been plagued from its beginnings with bad behavior, including disagreements and divisions. Most Christians are familiar with the great divisions that resulted in the Eastern Orthodox and Protestant churches, but they are usually unaware of the nearly continuous stream of rifts and ruptures, on a local and global scale, that have troubled the church throughout its existence.

These problems should not be a surprise. After all, the intimate circle of twelve apostles most closely associated with Jesus harbored a traitor willing to betray the Son of God for a mere thirty pieces of silver. Barnabas and Paul, who collegially engaged in early missionary activity, disagreed so strongly regarding John Mark that they were no longer able to be a team. Once seemingly inseparable, they never worked together again.

Other problems in the church were also not slow in surfacing. For example, the Judaizers insisted that keeping the law was essential for all followers of Christ, so they demanded the circumcision of all Gentile converts. They couldn't, in good conscience, be faithful to their Jewish heritage and keep the ceremonial law without requiring circumcision. But Paul condemned the Judaizers' position as another gospel that to him was *anathema*!

Paul's follow-up letters to the churches that he planted during his missionary journeys also reveal those churches' wide range of problems. He straightforwardly confronted the Corinthians about the divisions developing in their community. They seemed proud of their partisan cliques, bragging, "I follow Paul" and "I follow Apollos" (1 Cor. 3:4). One super-pious group even claimed to be "of Christ." Their interest was personality driven. Clustering devotedly around the most appealing leader, they did not realize that they were not just arguing among themselves but also seriously wounding the church that Christ died to establish. They were too wrapped up in themselves and mesmerized by their leaders.

Intervening centuries have failed to deliver the church from disagreement and division on personal, congregational, and denominational levels. If anything, problems may have worsened, although historical distance makes that difficult to judge. Today, new denominations and independent congregations sprout more quickly than weeds in springtime. And the pace shows no sign of slowing.

Hundreds of denominations and thousands of independent congregations dot the American landscape, with new ones constantly popping up. According to the latest information, there are about forty-five thousand denominations globally—a number difficult to justify.[1] It can be quite bewildering to non-Christian spectators who no longer recognize all the labels. They encounter churches everywhere in all sizes and shapes, from St. Luke's Episcopal to Faith World to First Baptist to Kairos Church to The Holy Ghost Missionary Fellowship of Mount Zion. Many congregations seem to be going their own way, uncaring about others except when they appear to pose a threat. The proliferation of denominations and independent congregations is ample evidence of excessive fragmentation. Add the disagreements and factions found in many—if not most—of them.

"Why can't we all get along?" was the infamous, plaintive protest of Rodney King after his beating by Los Angeles police. That question

1. Center for the Study of Global Christianity, "Christianity in its Global Context, 1970–2020: Society, Religion, Mission" (Gordon-Conwell Theological Seminary, June 2013).

pricks my Christian conscience as I survey the fragmented pieces of the church. Why can't those of us who believe in the authority of the Bible and the necessity of faith in Christ get along amicably? Why fuss and fight? Why refuse to associate with other believers? Is there anything we can do to heal our divisions?

There is always a reason behind discord, and that reason is usually the fault of someone else. But this is not the way it was meant to be nor the way it should be now. As Paul asked, "Is Christ divided?" (1 Cor. 1:13). Of course not! Then why are we so divided—especially when we know Christ prayed that we might be one as he and the Father are one?

This bothers me, and it should bother you. I belong to a denomination that is the result of a separation. I joined because I wanted to identify with a Reformed Presbyterian denomination that embraced the authority of Scripture and the necessity of faith in Christ for salvation. I have found a happy home here. But the longer I live, the more I realize that the most important identifying factor is not that I belong to this denomination but that I belong to my Savior Jesus Christ. I am a Christian first. That is what counts most. I resonate with "Just give me Jesus," because Jesus is the one who gave me a new life. Because I am united to him, I have become joined to everyone else who is united to Jesus. I am part of one new family, with many new brothers and sisters in the Lord.

Years ago, Carl Henry spoke of the "Uneasy Conscience of Evangelicals," referring to the way evangelicals avoided reaching out to meet the needs of others because they did not want to be identified with the "social gospel" of liberals.[2] Perhaps, in this twenty-first century, the Fundamentalist-Modernist Controversy and the conflict with liberal theology are sufficiently distant for evangelicals to develop an uneasy conscience about our lack of unity. Our consciences should be troubled as we survey the mess we have made of the church. We have wounded one another and limited our effectiveness as a witness to the unbelieving world.

2. Carl F. H. Henry, *The Uneasy Conscience of Modern Fundamentalism* (Grand Rapids: Eerdmans, 2003).

We can and should do better than this, asking how we can avoid the tragic mistakes of past generations. What does the Bible say? What steps should be taken? How can we become the church God wants his people to be?

My approach in the following chapters is to make that case as compellingly as I can. Chapter 1 describes the unity of the church in God's plan of redemption and its early expression. Chapter 2 builds on that by showing that there has always been an understanding that the church is one, although there may have been disagreements about who belonged and who didn't. Additionally, organizational differences and other expressions of diversity did not preclude that understanding or realization of unity. While division is repugnant to the Lord, diversity enriches God's people.

Chapter 3 emphasizes the importance of the communion of saints, especially in contrast to the loss of community during the final half of the twentieth century. Compounded by sectarianism and schism, various ecumenical efforts failed to heal the existing and added divisions, as chapter 4 explains. Chapter 5 mentions some of the well-known obstacles to achieving unity. The final chapter suggests some ways in which progress is possible and should be pursued.

Admittedly, the fragmented and partisan times in which we live are a challenge to any such uniting effort but provide all the more justification for it. Although it will quickly be apparent that this was written primarily for Presbyterian Reformed evangelicals, it should—and I hope will—be beneficial for a larger evangelical audience.

I don't expect this to ignite a new movement toward organizational unity, nor am I convinced we are ready for that. But we certainly need to learn to love each other and work together constructively for the gospel. There is room for more partnering, collaboration, and cooperation. Our increasingly partisan, polarized society needs such a model. The changing social and political circumstances make it necessary.

Some who hear this plea for unity, a call to a true communion of saints, will either see it as impossible and a waste of time or say, "Been there, done that." On the other hand, research has demonstrated that many Christians are weary of partisanship, politics, and polarization.

Making mountains out of molehills is distasteful to them. They yearn to ride the exhilarating wave of a missional movement that exalts Christ and brings believers together. They are open to constructive ways of joining together to do good and advance the work of the church. For many years, Billy Graham was the inspirational leader who brought about global cooperation in reaching people with the gospel. Who will assume that mantle now? And who will take up the baton at regional, denominational, and local levels?

Countless rejections and failures do not mean that it is impossible to come together and do great things for God. As our country grows less supportive of—and even hostile to—Christianity, it will be necessary to learn to listen to each other and work together for the common good. Negative attitudes toward evangelicals appear to be increasing, offering little encouragement for the future if the trend continues. These circumstances will pressure evangelicals to learn to love one another and live together constructively in spite of our deepest differences. If we can do that, we can also overcome many of the problems we have created for ourselves and open new doors of opportunity for the Lord's people to reach out redemptively to an unbelieving world.

This is a call to repentance for our failure to be the church God wants us to be. We tend to point fingers and shift blame to others. But many of the problems we face and challenges we have to overcome are our own fault. It is high time to admit it—sorrowfully. This is not only a call to repentance; it is equally a call for us to determine to live together as God has directed. It is not too late, but the clock is ticking. The time has come to tear down walls and build bridges.

ACKNOWLEDGMENTS

ANY EFFORT OF this nature always owes a debt to others who have helped make it possible. I am especially grateful to Jim Seneff for granting me some time to work on this book as well as for his encouragement along the way. Without him, I undoubtedly would have remained in earlier stages of writing. He has definitely been the friend that sticks closer than a brother (Prov. 18:24).

Lauren Geiger has served as my executive assistant for many years, and her involvement in preparing and editing the manuscript—including indices—as well as making other improvements has been invaluable.

In addition, numerous friends and colleagues have read the manuscript and offered advice that considerably improved the final version including John Frame, Bill Edgar, Tim Keller, Michael Allen, David Dockery, Don Sweeting, Michael Cromartie, Leith Anderson, Jeff Jeremiah, Wilfred McClay, Joel Carpenter, John Armstrong, David Swanson, Roy Taylor, and Mark Noll. I am especially indebted to Dennis Johnson and John Woodbridge, who read the draft several times and offered helpful suggestions that significantly improved the final version. My thanks also go to the following individuals for their encouragement and insight: Jim Belcher, Ligon Duncan, Timothy George, Carmen Fowler LaBerge, Peter Lillback, Sam Logan, Russell Moore, Richard Mouw, Michael Wear, and Parker Williamson.

The two churches that I pastored as well as the denominations to which I have belonged have shaped my understanding of the church and given me hope regarding God's ability to do far more than we can. I am grateful to them for their vital role in shaping my ministry.

My wife, Mary Lou, has provided steady encouragement, including reading the manuscript and providing helpful observations.

I also want to express my appreciation to John Hughes, who has been a constant encourager as well as a valuable consultant during this process.

1

BIBLICAL FOUNDATIONS

A divided church in the New Testament sense of the word "church" is something illogical and incomprehensible—as illogical and incomprehensible as human sin.
Lesslie Newbigin, *The Reunion of the Church*[1]

How good and pleasant it is when brothers live together in unity!
Psalm 133:1

May the God who gives endurance and encouragement give you a spirit of unity among yourselves as you follow Christ Jesus, so that with one heart and mouth you may glorify the God and Father of our Lord Jesus Christ.
Romans 15:5, 6

THE TINY CHRISTIAN church birthed at Pentecost shortly after Jesus ascended has become a vast global presence of diverse nationalities, gifts, and organizational expressions. It has been remarkably adaptive and resilient. The myriad identities of churches and denominations can be confusing, however, especially in their relentless change, which prompts people to ask, "What is the church? What is its purpose? How is it supposed to function? Where should we begin to best understand it?"

1. Lesslie Newbigin, *The Reunion of the Church: A Defense of the South India Scheme* (London: SCM, 1960), 24.

Inevitably, the question of unity arises. People ask, "Why are there so many different churches and denominations? How can you justify all these divisions in the church? How did it happen? How can you decide which church is right for you?" These are reasonable concerns. If we ever hope to resolve them, we must begin at the beginning—with God.

The Triune God

The Triune God revealed in the Scriptures is the basis and model for the church and its unity. That is not to say that you cannot begin elsewhere, but any attempt to understand or achieve unity among believers that doesn't begin with or ultimately find its basis in the doctrine of God is poorly grounded. In hindsight, it is now easy to see that John Calvin had the right idea when he began his *Institutes of the Christian Religion* with a treatise on the knowledge of God. He understood how foundational the doctrine of God is to all theological and biblical study. That is where all theological inquiry and the search for understanding must begin. For this reason, it makes good sense to consider the doctrine of God, and specifically the Trinity, as foundational to our understanding of the church and its unity.

Most Christians would agree that as our understanding of God is enlarged through a serious study of the Scriptures and a growing awareness of his work throughout human history, we gain a more accurate comprehension of our world, ourselves, and what God expects of us. A correlative intellectual and spiritual (or heart) awareness develops, giving us a sense of what is right. The same could be said regarding what God expects of the church and our place in it.

In reflecting on many years of ministry and observation of the church in its various ecclesiastical forms, I have frequently wondered why the Trinity, although so important, has been an oft-neglected key to rethinking ecclesiology.

Fortunately, during the twentieth century, a renewal of interest in the social significance of the Trinity has led to substantial theological research and writing, enriching the conversation about the church and its unity—particularly during the last half of the twentieth century. This interest in rebuilding spiritual communities—a reaction to the effects of social fragmentation that left people feeling alone or estranged—is understandable and has been a welcome development. The social or relational aspect of the church is often referred to as the "communion of saints" or "fellowship of believers." That communion has its roots in the Trinity.

The initial pages of the Bible clearly reveal the existence of the one true God, who has eternally existed as Father, Son, and Holy Spirit. Although the word *Trinity* is never used in the Bible, the Trinitarian message is consistently relayed to the reader: God is one, yet God is also three (Matt. 28:19; 2 Cor. 13:14). It is important to emphasize that as three persons, God is a relational being in whom unity and diversity are perfectly blended. Augustine put it well: "Each is in each, all are in each, each is in all, all are in all, and all are one."[2]

Not only does the Trinity give insight into the nature of God, it enables us to comprehend the significance of and the value of diversity in all human relationships. Because God exists in three persons—Father, Son, and Holy Spirit—we should quickly realize that he is just as much relational as he is sovereign, wise, just, or holy. Although it is not usually mentioned, the relational attribute of God deserves equal emphasis with his other frequently mentioned attributes. Although we cannot completely comprehend the profundity of the Trinitarian relationship, we may assert with confidence that God has eternally existed in an intimate, harmonious relationship as Father, Son, and Holy Spirit.

Tertullian was the first of the church fathers to use the word *person* to refer to the Father, Son, and Holy Spirit.[3] The doctrine of the Trinity was offered by the Council of Nicaea in A.D. 325, and the Council of Constantinople (A.D. 381). The latter explored it by stating: "There is one Godhead, Power and Substance of the Father and of the Son and of the Holy Ghost; the dignity being equal, and the majesty being equal in three perfect essences and three perfect persons."[4]

2. Augustine, *The Trinity*, vol. 45 of *The Fathers of the Church*, trans. Stephen McKenna (Washington DC: Catholic University of America Press, 2010), 214.

3. Tertullian, *Apology*, 39.

4. *NPNF*[2], vol. 3, 138.

The Trinity is a triunity of intimate understanding, perfect love, and seamless functioning, as the three persons of the Godhead eternally relate to and exist in one another. Moreover, their personal identities are revealed in their reciprocal relationships. As would be expected, God's relational perfection is revealed in this unity. This is significant for the church because as we grow spiritually, we are being remade in God's image in many ways, including relationally. Relational factors, including our ability to work together harmoniously in spite of our differences, play a significant role when assessing our sanctification. You might say that the closer we are to God, the closer we should be to one another. This has, or should have, a direct bearing on the unity of the church; you would expect the unity of the Trinity to be expressed in the unity of the church.

It is also important to note the diversity revealed in the very nature of the Trinity, which does not come at the expense of unity. The Father, Son, and Holy Spirit exist as distinct and different persons with distinct and different responsibilities. This is consistently presented throughout the Bible. Herman Bavinck, aptly noting the diversity that existed prior to sin, says that this should lead us to conclude that it is "good and important also for the church."[5] Differences can enrich relationships; diversity enriches the church. By contrast, it is hard to imagine life in a universe of clones.

Given our inclination to think of God as detached and impersonal, this is a timely corrective. The nature of God makes me the person I am: a person influenced by love—or its absence. God is personal and loving, longsuffering and forgiving. He is known by his love because "God is love" (1 John 4:16). That love has always existed within the Trinity. As Jesus said to the Father, "you loved me before the creation of the world" (John 17:24).

Love doesn't happen in the abstract; it needs an object. It is impossible to love nothing. Love needs someone to love and someone by whom we can be loved. Companionship, therefore, is essential to God's very nature because God is love. John's Gospel reminds

5. Herman Bavinck, *Reformed Dogmatics: Holy Spirit, Church, and New Creation*, vol. 4 (Grand Rapids: Baker Academic, 2008), 318.

us of this eternal relationship: "the Word was with God" (John 1:1) and "at the Father's side" (v. 18). Not only was the Word in the beginning and essential to the creation of the world, the Word was with God. Father, Son, and Holy Spirit were bonded together before the world came into existence.

Humans as Relational Beings

When you begin at the beginning—with Creation—the significance of the Trinity in the unity of the church becomes apparent. Let me explain how this is true. The first chapter of Genesis reveals that God created Adam and Eve in his image. In doing so, he created them as relational beings like himself. This becomes apparent in Genesis 2 as God observes Adam in the garden of Eden: "It is not good for the man to be alone" (Gen. 2:18). At first glance, this may appear to be a simple statement that Eve was needed for the human race to continue. While that is true, there is more to it.

This statement would not make any sense unless God wanted to call attention to the fact that Adam was a relational being made for love and companionship. Why else would he mention being alone as undesirable (v. 18)? There is nothing wrong with solitude or being alone. The problem was that permanent solitude did not fit Adam's nature because Adam was a relational being, just like his creator. Adam was created not only for a relationship with God but for a relationship with someone like himself. Without that human companionship, he was an incomplete person.

This is why God created Eve as Adam's soul mate, taken from his rib. They could share love and life together in the garden of Eden. Male and female, they were united as one (Gen. 2:24). Consequently, their Edenic experience mirrored the relational nature of the Triune God as they enjoyed a beautiful, harmonious relationship with him and with each other. It also provided a model for marriage and all other human relationships, because God gave them that responsibility as part of what is called the cultural mandate (1:26–28). As J. Richard Middleton observed, "Imaging God thus involves representing and perhaps extending in some way God's rule on earth through the ordinary communal practice of human socio-cultural life."[6]

Adam and Eve's subsequent disobedience—eating the forbidden fruit of the tree of the knowledge of good and evil—profoundly marred God's image in them. Little did they realize how much would change if they disobeyed. The ramifications were huge, injecting alienation and misery into all human existence. Adam and Eve were jarringly expelled from Eden, and the idyllic relationship they had shared with God and with each other evaporated. Banned from Eden in shame and disgrace, they and their progeny faced an unexpected life of hardship and misery.

As bad as that was, the immediate effect of this dramatic reversal of relationships marked the advent of the destructive human relationships that would result from sin. From that moment, hostility, enmity, and various divisive forces became a constant irritant and threat to human life on earth. As an example, not long after God expelled Adam and Eve from the garden, their son Cain murdered his brother Abel: a painful, unintended consequence of their sin. These torments multiplied swiftly among the expanding human race.

Sin in its various forms divides and destroys. Misery and pain are its companions. Prejudice, deceit, manipulation, and anger become its weapons. Looking back to what happened in Eden, we now realize that alienation, estrangement, loneliness, and all other forms of flawed and broken relationships find their origin in that first sin of Adam and Eve. The rest of the Bible is an unfolding commentary about the damage that sin inflicts on human relationships. God offered a remedy to Adam and Eve in clothing them with skins to cover their nakedness and shame, which required the shedding of blood: a harbinger of the gospel. God also promised that one of their descendants would crush the head of the serpent, although the serpent would wound him in the heel in that confrontation (Gen. 3:15).

We acknowledge the hunger for companionship and intimacy

6. J. Richard Middleton, *The Liberating Image: The Imago Dei in Genesis 1* (Grand Rapids: Brazos Press, 2005), 60.

that remains an endemic part of human nature. People are by nature relational. The inner desire to belong emanates from this. In spite of repeated wounds and disappointments, an underlying desire for satisfying, fulfilling relationships continues to nest in the human heart. This desire is not only the foundation for marriage, family, and friendships but also the basis for groups and communities of every kind, including work relationships, childhood friendships, and club memberships. After their playing days are over, athletes often nostalgically reminisce, concluding that the part they miss most is the camaraderie, the locker room.

The good news is that through the gospel, God offers a way of escape as an alternative to our broken, sinful world. According to his redemptive plan, God is remaking into his image all who trust in Christ. Though it is a slow process, he rebuilds the relational dimension of life as part of that process, providing an opportunity for the believer to experience the fulfilling joy and lasting reward of redemptive community. Close relationships that weather the storms of life, imparting good feelings and fond memories, are irreplaceable.

This gives clarity to the gospel. Christ came to end the hurt, enmity, and estrangement caused by Adam's sin. To accomplish that, he became despised and rejected, suffering God's punishment of sin during his crucifixion so that we could be forgiven and accepted into his family. Although he cried out, "Why have you forsaken me?" on the cross (Matt. 27:46), his promise to those of us who believe is that we will never be forsaken (Heb. 13:5). We are reminded that he was killed outside the gate so that we can come inside to be with the Father (v. 12).

When we come to faith in Christ, we join those whose names are written in the Book of Life. Not only are our sins forgiven, our relationship with God is restored. We become part of his family. It is critical to understand that not only forensic but relational reconciliation is integral to our salvation. When our relationship with God is restored, our relationships with people will inevitably be transformed. Through faith in Christ we experience an innate desire, as part of his family, to repair relationships and form new ones by reaching out to one another (Gal. 3:28–29).

This puts into perspective the well-known hymn,

Blessed be the tie that binds
Our hearts in Christian love:
The fellowship of kindred minds
Is like to that above.

We should expect to encounter happy, wholesome, enriching relationships among believers through the fellowship of the Holy Spirit, just as we expect to experience it within marriage and family. If our relationship with God enables us to establish wholesome, flourishing relationships, it should translate into our marriage and family and then to all other relationships in the church as well as in business and the community. The radical change in Charles Dickens's Ebenezer Scrooge as a consequence of his dreams is the type of change that should occur among believers, dramatically affecting all relationships for the better and giving life a new glow. The transformation may be gradual or swift, but it will come; and when it comes, it will have a beneficial effect on those who are touched by it.

Theologian John Owen (1616–83) said that our communion with God consists of his communication of himself to us and our reciprocal response flowing from the union we have with him in Christ.[7] We love him because he first loved us. This translates into our relationships with others. But it doesn't happen overnight, as is obvious from experience. By contrast, alienation and division, wherever they appear, are warning signs of spiritual deficiencies. Disagreements, anger, hostility, and estrangement are rooted in sin, and they are a persistent plague. The inevitable outcome, even among churches, is that relationships are constantly damaged and torn by deceitfulness, mean-spiritedness, and other bad behavior. Worse still, some days discord seems more prevalent among Christians and

7. John Owen, *The Works of John Owen*, ed. William H. Goold, vol. 2 of *Of Communion with God the Father, Son and Holy Ghost* (Edinburgh: Banner of Truth Trust, 1965), 8–9. Owen became a friend of Oliver Cromwell in 1647 and was appointed vice chancellor of Oxford University in 1652–58. He was one of several ministers summoned by Cromwell to a meeting on church union in 1653.

their churches than in secular organizations. It shouldn't happen that way, but believers are sinners too. Some Christians are less spiritually mature and especially vulnerable.

If there were no sin, all relationships would be idyllic. It will be that way in heaven, but that's not the way life is now. However, we are not excused from our responsibility to maximize relationships to the best of our abilities. Right now, if we truly are in Christ, we must do our utmost to bring love, healing, and hope to all relationships. This is our spiritual obligation. Any less cannot be justified. The degree to which we cause rifts or divisions demonstrates our failure. When that happens, we should acknowledge and correct the problem as quickly as possible so that relationships are restored. Consistent, genuinely grace-motivated responses can make a huge difference in redeeming relationships.

One Lord, One Church

The unity and triunity of God also enable us to understand what God intends the church to be: one church comprising many believers who are marked by diverse gifts, organized in many different ways to carry out the Lord's will, and reflecting the harmonious relationship of the Trinity as they worship and serve. Mindful that it mirrors the attributes of God, the church should be one—harmoniously so, as is true of God. How beautiful and appealing this would be to a broken, hurting world!

Before we consider the rich trove of information the New Testament offers, we should not forget the Old Testament roots of the church. When God selected Abraham, he did so to lavish his favor upon those he planned to make "into a great nation" that would become his instrument to bless all people (Gen. 12:1–3). God established a covenant with Abraham, promising that in time he would give him and his descendants their own land and make them a witness to all the nations (Gen. 15).

Abraham's descendants as God's chosen people became the Old Testament precursor to the church (Isa. 43:20–21). God said, "I will . . . be your God, and you shall be my people" (Lev. 26:12).

At Sinai, God promised, "you will be for me a kingdom of priests and a holy nation" (Ex. 19:6). When the church was formed, it was understood to be Abraham's seed (Rom. 2:29; Gal. 3:29). Peter explains it this way:

> But you are a chosen people, a royal priesthood, a holy nation, a people belonging to God, that you may declare the praises of him who called you out of darkness into his wonderful light. Once you were not a people, but now you are the people of God; once you had not received mercy, but now you have received mercy. (1 Pet. 2:9, 10)

There were twelve tribes but only one people of God. There was a divided kingdom but only one people of God. They lived in different lands, under different circumstances, but they were always one people of God. As G. W. Bromiley has observed,

> It is not for nothing that in the Old Testament the elect people of God, divided though it was into twelve tribes and later grouped into two kingdoms, consisted of a single race tracing its descent from a single progenitor. It is not for nothing that it was constituted the one nation by redemption out of Egypt, the deliverance at the Red Sea and the giving of the law at Sinai. There might be all kinds of breaches of this unity, from civil war on the one side to foreign marriages on the other. But nothing could shake the oneness of divine election, redemption, and overruling as focused in the common descent and national membership. The fact that Israel was a national unity clearly meant that it was to be one people.[8]

How is this expressed in the New Testament? When Jesus speaks of the church, the assembly, he uses a description rich with Old Testament meaning: the heavenly scene is a gathering from every tribe and language and people and nation, who are a kingdom and

8. G. W. Bromiley, *The Unity and Disunity of the Church* (Grand Rapids: Eerdmans, 1958), 9–10.

priests serving God (Rev. 5:9; 7:9, 10). One day, Abraham and all the other Old Testament saints will join together in heaven for a great celebration with Peter and Paul and all believers from every time and place.

While recognizing the scattered existence of many congregations in various stages of development, the New Testament acknowledges only one church, comprising all those who are in Christ. Peter, in his sermon to the amazed crowd at Pentecost, emphasized that everyone who called on the name of the Lord would be saved (Acts 2:21). If they turned to Christ in faith, they would be accepted by God and become identified with his people.

The apostles preached this message wherever they went. New converts gathered into congregations to worship, learn, and be guided into service. Although multiple congregations and house churches soon existed in many cities and new ones were constantly being added, it is apparent from Paul's letters that there was and is only one church, whether in Philippi, Antioch, Corinth, or Thessalonica. These congregations were part of the one and only church planned and brought into existence by God. As Robert Banks has pointed out,

> Scattered Christian groups did not express their unity by fashioning a corporate organization through which they could be federated with one another, but rather through a network of personal contacts between people who regarded themselves as members of the same Christian family.[9]

The Jerusalem Council (Acts 15) was a definitive early meeting of church leaders that offers an example of how this was understood and implemented among multiple congregations in various locations. Several major misunderstandings and disagreements regarding differences between Jewish and Gentile Christians prompted the leaders of the church to gather in Jerusalem to discuss and pray about these

9. Robert Banks, *Paul's Idea of Community: The Early House Churches in Their Historical Setting* (Grand Rapids: Eerdmans, 1980), 48.

issues, seeking a decision acceptable to all (vv. 1–2). They gathered to address the problem because they realized that, as much as possible, they needed to be in agreement regarding belief and practice as followers of Christ.

Once they reached a conclusion on which they all agreed, the church leaders immediately determined how best to communicate their decision to all the churches. As they did so, it is apparent that they expected compliance (vv. 22–35). We may assume this is because of the sense of unity that characterized them. Why would they have felt obligated to resolve disagreements and seek conformity of belief and practice unless all the congregations considered themselves part of the same church? It seems reasonable to conclude that, in spite of the problems and tensions that existed from the beginning, there was a clear sense that the church was one because of its identity in Christ.

From time to time, vigorous disagreements occurred regarding who was right or wrong and who belonged or did not, but a consensus remained that there was only one church, of which Jesus was Lord. The strong inner coherence is unmistakable. As Jesus said, there is "one flock and one shepherd" (John 10:16).

Edmund Clowney has summarized the matter succinctly:

> The abiding presence of the Spirit joins the church together into one. There is but one holy temple of the Lord, one body of Christ where the Spirit dwells. The Spirit binds the church together in the unity of a common life. In Paul's letters this unity is applied especially to the joining together of Jews and Gentiles (Eph. 2:11–22). In the power of the Spirit, the church went from Jerusalem to Judea, Samaria and the ends of the earth. . . . The temple of God was no longer local, on the Judean hillside, but universal, wherever the saints gathered to join in heaven's praise.[10]

A careful reading of the Bible inevitably leads us to conclude that there are essentially only two kinds of people, Christians and non-Christians, insofar as a relationship to God is concerned. If so, all

10. Edmund P. Clowney, *The Church* (Downers Grove, IL: InterVarsity Press, 1995), 53.

Christians belong to the one true church that has existed through all the centuries, and they will eventually be gathered around the throne of God in heaven. Their names are written in the Lamb's Book of Life (Rev. 21:27). They belong.

The single requirement for belonging to the one true church is faith in Christ. That alone is the determinant. A person's spiritual maturity, doctrinal discernment, giftedness, or cultural identity are not the determining factors, important as each of these may be. Neither are one's denomination or doctrinal distinctiveness—all those who genuinely trust in Christ, from the weakest to the strongest and the least to the greatest, belong to his church. How much they understand of God's Word and how well they obey are expressions of their spiritual maturity but not the basis for their inclusion in the church. As Peter said, "everyone who calls on the name of the Lord will be saved" (Acts 2:21).

Varying degrees of spiritual maturity and discernment cannot be avoided and should actually be expected. People are converted at different times, and they develop spiritually at different rates. This broad range of spiritual maturity, combined with a variety of gifts and contextual influences, will inevitably foster a wide spectrum of rich, colorful diversity. I am reminded of the experience of attending a Christian conference in Amsterdam that had representatives from more nations than any other event to that date, including the Olympics. That was diversity! That is the church!

On the other hand, as enriching and stimulating as it may be, this diversity can easily spawn misunderstanding and tensions that escalate into anger, hostility, and division, especially when confronted with adversity or sudden change. The periodic rifts and ensuing fragmentation of the church throughout the centuries illustrate this. From its inception, the church has never achieved more than an imperfect experience of its unity in Christ. Various problems and divisions have seemingly been perpetual. This has been painful and disappointing, but it is a reality that must be acknowledged. Yet it may also be argued that many of these conflicts were matched by equally endless and sincere—and sometimes sacrificial—efforts to restore unity.

Protestant churches of the Western world have proliferated and continue to grow incessantly, augmented by parachurch ministries and independent congregations. The multiplicity of denominations and Christian organizations does not, however, diminish that there is only one church of Jesus Christ, comprising all those who truly believe in him.

Finding appropriate ways to express the unity of the triune God remains the responsibility and challenge of the church in all its parts. Not only is it a responsibility, it is a priority. Those who desire to please the Lord cannot ignore their obligation to seek a joyfully united church until all believers are eventually united in praise around God's heavenly throne.

The High Priestly Prayer and Unity

As Jesus neared the end of his earthly ministry and the completion of his redemptive mission, he prayed for strength to finish the task for which he had been born, knowing that it necessitated his substitutionary atonement for sin. Yet as repugnant as it was to him as the sinless Son of God to suffer the full punishment of God the Father against sin, Jesus was willing to do it so that we could be forgiven and receive the gift of eternal life. He was willing to die on the cross to accomplish the purpose for which he had come. That much is well known.

It is also essential to notice that Jesus prayed that believers might, because of his atoning sacrifice, become one as he and the Father are one (John 17:21–22) and in doing so come to complete unity (v. 23). John had already mentioned Christ's desire for only one flock with one shepherd (10:16). This petition, particularly so near the end of his life on earth, conspicuously signaled the priority that Jesus placed upon the need for unity among all believers. This spiritual unity, transcending any kind of organizational unity, is paramount for believers who are one only in and through Christ and the truth revealed in him. This unity belongs to all believers in diverse nations, ethnicities, cultures, and church organizations. Apart from him, they are without God and without hope.

In John 10:11–18, Jesus referred to himself as the good shepherd who lays down his life for his sheep. His sheep will hear his voice, know him, and follow him so that there will be one flock. Although a wolf may attack the sheep and scatter them, the good shepherd will gather them back together to remain one flock. Anyone who has cared for animals, especially pets, is aware of the emotional attachment that develops. This attachment is reflected in the good shepherd's effort to gather his sheep. It is significantly different from, for example, gathering rocks.

Elsewhere in the Gospel, John uses metaphors that heighten the awareness of a believer's relationship to Christ and to other believers. One is the reference to the vine and the branches. The branches connected to him are fruitful; the others are thrown away (John 15:1–8). In this illustration, Jesus appeals to the command to love each other as he has loved them (v. 12). He also promises them a place in his Father's house so that they can be there together (14:1–3).

Given such an undeniably clear emphasis by Jesus on the importance of unity, how can his people afford to neglect it or treat it lightly? Isn't it appropriate to expect that the unity and harmony of the Godhead should somehow find similar expression in our lives and relationships, including in the church? If John 17:21 were the only reference to unity in the Bible, that alone would be sufficient to obligate us to pursue unity. But it does not stand alone. Copious Old and New Testament texts emphasize the importance God places on the unity of his people who are united to him and therefore to one another.

We should be asking, "Why doesn't the unity of the church have a higher priority among Christians?" To the degree that we fail to express our oneness in Christ, we fail him and his desire for us as part of his church. What will it take to give this matter higher priority, even urgency?

The Church in Acts

The beauty of biblical unity is captured brilliantly in the description of the birth and development of the church in Acts. This was, for all the newly converted Christians, undoubtedly the most exciting, wonderful experience of their lives; there was nothing else like it in the world. They had found faith and hope in Christ. In addition, they had discovered a powerful new *koinonia* that bound them together in love and service. It forged them into a dynamic community of renewed people that, through these unusual characteristics so different from any ordinary experience, compellingly appealed to those around them.

Acts 2:42–46 describes them as devoted to the teaching of the apostles and "to the fellowship." This fellowship of the Spirit is a dramatically different way to describe what they had become. Their devotion was so strong that they met every day to encourage and help one another, nurturing their fellowship through the observance of the Lord's Supper (or Communion) and prayer, as well as demonstrating the kind of generosity cited in Acts 4:32–35. They took care of the needy as if they were members of their own families. Incidentally, the word translated as "multitude" in verse 32 is also often used to designate "community," including a religious community.

The important observation is that the Christians were one of heart and soul: that is, they were united. This made them very different from everyone else in that, as a new group, they had such cohesiveness. This sense of bonding into a community of love and service was extraordinary. Others remarked about the way they loved one another, especially as they experienced adversity. This fellowship of disciples in covenant with one another was a compelling witness.

As more and more people—Gentiles in particular—became Christians, the unity of the church was tested. In retrospect, that was to be expected of people from such different cultural backgrounds who were suddenly clumped together. Very early in the development of the church, Greek Jews complained that Hebraic Jewish widows were being favored when food was distributed. The response was quick, and apparently seven Greek men were appointed to help. There is no record that the problem continued (Acts 6:1–7). Cultural differences can impose many relational challenges, as those with experience will attest.

Peter provides a good example of a typical Jew relating to

Gentiles in the first century. He soon became convinced that if God forgave the Gentiles and accepted them as his people, then he too was obligated to accept them (Acts 10). It may seem a simple matter to us today, but because of their strong faith and the identification of that faith with Israel, accepting Gentile believers was a difficult hurdle for Peter and all the Jewish Christians in Jerusalem to overcome. But after hearing what had happened among the Gentile believers, the leaders at the Jerusalem Council—after much discussion and prayer—decided that it was right to accept Gentile converts. Given the convincing evidence, they had to acknowledge and accept what God was doing. As described earlier, once the church leaders had made a decision about the matter, they prepared an official communication for all the churches, including any new ones, about the conversion of the Gentiles. They communicated their acceptance of Gentile Christians and their expectation that all believers everywhere would welcome Gentiles as part of the church (15:1, 2, 22–35; 16:4).

As Paul notes, the right hand of fellowship was extended by the Jewish Christians to the Gentile Christians. It was a symbol of belonging (Gal. 2:9). This clearly communicated to everyone who was interested that they considered themselves to be one new believing community, followers of the risen Christ. Unless all these Christians scattered around the Mediterranean considered themselves to belong to one church, why would they be concerned to resolve disagreements, seeking conformity of belief and practice? The only answer that makes sense is that they *did* understand themselves to be bound to one another, just as they were now bound to the Lord by faith. Therefore, how they resolved these disagreements was of utmost importance.

Another testimony to the sense of community that characterized the new church is the offering that Paul began to collect during his missionary travels. The offering was intended to help the Christians in Jerusalem, who were being persecuted by Jewish citizens who regarded them as heretics and were determined to punish them for abandoning their faith. Paul thought it was necessary for all other Christian congregations to help them. He expected new believers from all the churches, including Gentile Christians, to pitch in generously to provide relief and encouragement to their fellow Christians in Jerusalem, helping them cope with the persecution and impoverishment they were experiencing. Their generosity demonstrated the bond of unity in the church that was so reminiscent of the generosity offered to all believers immediately after the church was born at Pentecost (Acts 2:42–47).

On that day, people had gathered in Jerusalem from at least fifteen countries of the Eastern Mediterranean world, speaking an assortment of languages typical of the regions where they lived. They had returned to Jerusalem to celebrate Pentecost, one of the three great annual feasts of Israel. Suddenly they were attracted—or perhaps distracted—by an unusually loud noise caused by a small group of people who were, under the influence of the Holy Spirit, speaking their *languages*. Surprised, some of the foreign visitors wondered if the members of the group were intoxicated. That was soon determined to be an inadequate explanation of their linguistic abilities, which were too different and extraordinary for the initial explanation to suffice.

Peter gave them a quick explanation of what was unfolding by referring to Joel 2:28–32 and relating this phenomenon to the miraculous death and resurrection of Jesus. So stunning was the incident that about three thousand people were converted through Peter's sermon, including some of the visitors and others who were listening. This dramatic Pentecostal occurrence and its mass conversions undoubtedly helped stimulate the rapid spread of the Christian faith. It brought a variety of languages and cultures into one new church and made it possible to transcend all the differences that otherwise would have separated them.

The church continued to flourish and grow until Stephen was killed (Acts 7:54–60). At that time, however, believers began to encounter a backlash of vicious persecution. Saul, in his Pharisaic zeal, was bent on destroying the church before it could become more of a threat to the historic Judaism that dominated Jerusalem. He was determined to perpetuate the faith of their fathers and the God of Israel.

This and later persecutions failed to destroy the church, however, although they continued for many years wherever the gospel bore fruit. An unintended consequence was persecution's contribution to the rapid spread of the faith throughout the Mediterranean world as well as the conversion of Saul himself, who would be transformed from chief persecutor to the greatest missionary of the church. Early Christianity quickly became a formidable missionary force that moved inexorably forward, regardless of adversity. In some instances, anti-Christian forces resisted or overwhelmed Christian advances, as with Muslim victories in North Africa. These followers of the Way, though a small group initially, would dramatically change the course of history as the church of Christ expanded everywhere.

Acts describes the birth and expansion of the church, highlighting important milestones and identifying marks. This book is critical to understanding the transition from the faith revealed in the Old Testament to that of the New Testament. There remained one people of God. Now the focus was on Christ as the fulfillment of all the promises to the people of God, starting from when God called Abraham to leave everything and follow him.

Ephesians and the Church

In addition to the highly informative narrative provided in Acts, the apostle Paul's letter to the Ephesians contributes to our understanding of the church and its unity. Remember that Paul spent three years establishing the church in this important Mediterranean city. His letter's primary emphasis is the church. Paul wants the Ephesian readers to know what a pivotal role the church has in God's plan to glorify himself in human history, which is his principal purpose. As God establishes the new community of faith, he uses it to point others to himself so that they can begin to comprehend the wonder and beauty of his character.

Of course, the question is: How will God accomplish this grand plan? By transforming each believer into his likeness. The more a person grows spiritually, the more he or she will become like him. God reveals his goodness and other attributes to the world wherever those attributes are apparent in the lives of individual believers and in the community of believers. God will be glorified as this happens because it will enable the world to catch a glimpse of what he is truly like.

Paul, in helping the Ephesians understand the witness God intends for the church and for them individually, emphasizes unity among believers as an essential expression of genuine faith and vital component to achieving God's plan. He underscores the significance of relationships in the church, where our experience of unity both becomes an important measure of our faith and glorifies God.

That the unity of the church is a major motif in Ephesians is not surprising given Paul's history. After all, he was there when the church was born and soon became a major player in its growth. He personally witnessed the power of fellowship and unity among believers, and he painfully experienced the downside of disunity and divisions. For Paul, unity in Christ and the implications of that unity are not minor concerns or an afterthought.

Paul explains God's plan: to use the church as his instrument to glorify himself in the world by calling a people to love and serve him, and in doing so to be different from everyone else. This difference becomes apparent as his people grow spiritually and are conformed to his image in Christ, revealing his attributes to an unbelieving world.

Foundational to this spiritual transformation is the powerful experience of unity in all its richness and beauty. It is a unique sense of belonging that—similar to falling in love—is difficult to explain unless you have experienced it. The abiding presence of the Holy Spirit bonds believers to one another and bonds the church into one unified community.

Because this is true, Paul urges the Ephesians to live in a way that is worthy of their calling to follow Christ (Eph. 4:1). He uses similar phrases elsewhere regarding their obligation (Phil. 1:27; Col. 1:10; 1 Thess. 2:12). Their lives should align with the goal God intends for them. Their calling as ambassadors of God is, therefore, one of responsibility as well as privilege and blessing as they call others to reconciliation—which is all the more reason they should prioritize seeking and maintaining the unity of the Spirit (Eph. 4:3). Paul urges believers to do so because it is fundamental to their identity as Christians.

> There is one body and one Spirit—just as you were called to one hope when you were called—one Lord, one faith, one baptism; one God and Father of all, who is over all and through all and in all. (Eph. 4:4–6)

When we are unified, loving and supporting one another, we act worthy of our calling as Christians. This is exactly what God wants us to do. But it will not happen unless we love each other and work hard "to keep the unity of the Spirit through the bond of peace" (v. 3), so Paul urges the Ephesians to develop the needed characteristics: humility, gentleness, patience, and bearing with one another in love (v. 2). They are to serve so that "the body of Christ may be built up until we all reach unity in the faith and in the knowledge of the Son of God and become mature, attaining to the whole measure of the fullness of Christ" (vv. 12–13). Paul's comments about husbands and wives, parents and children, and slaves and masters make more sense in this larger context.

In chapter two, Paul points out that the gospel not only removes the barrier between us and God, it also tears down the wall separating us from one another. Through his atonement, Christ smashed the barriers dividing us from God and one another, restoring us to fellowship with the Lord and creating a new fellowship of believers.[11] The point: as our distinctive community of faith mirrors God's character, especially his oneness, it glorifies him. The experience of this loving, accepting community of believers is an easily underestimated dynamic, as Rodney Stark points out in *The Rise of Christianity*.[12]

Paul helps us see the result: a new identity and unity for all

11. Markus Barth titled his study of Ephesians as *The Broken Wall: A Study of the Epistle to the Ephesians* (Chicago: Judson Press, 1959).

12. Rodney Stark, *The Rise of Christianity: A Sociologist Reconsiders History* (Princeton: Princeton University Press, 1996), 73–94.

Christians, which transcends all earthly relationships and barriers such as family, church, and state (Eph. 2:14–22). Gentiles who did not have Jewish citizenship were foreigners to the covenants of promise (v. 12). Jews were well aware of the barrier that separated them from the Gentiles. The dividing wall that Paul mentions is a reference to the temple and the Gentiles' exclusion from it. Gentiles could be put to death if they attempted to enter the Holy Place, and of course only the high priest could enter the Most Holy Place. The law, with all its regulations, would have served as a similar wall of separation. The reference to Gentiles as being "without God" in other Greek writings typically refers to those who do not believe in God or are forsaken by God.[13] Certainly, they did not worship the true God.

In an unexpected and wonderful way, Jew and Gentile become one new body in Christ, who destroyed the barrier and reconciled them (Eph. 2:14–16). The mystery of the gospel is that these two formerly estranged, hostile groups are now brought together as one body. Moreover, the Gentiles became joint heirs with Israel (3:5–6) when they became fellow citizens with God's people, members of God's household, and a church in which God lives by his Spirit. In Galatians, Paul adds: "There is neither Jew nor Greek, slave nor free, male nor female, for you are all one in Christ Jesus. If you belong to Christ, then you are Abraham's seed, and heirs according to the promise" (3:28, 29). This was a shocking message for Jews—as dramatically powerful as saying to Protestants that Buddhists and Christians are one. That just isn't true, and apart from Christ it was impossible for Jews and Gentiles too. The gospel changed all these relationships.

It may not be obvious, but it is important to notice that in describing the oneness or unity of the church, Paul mentions the three basic institutions of society: family, church, and state. Each offers a powerful identity.

For example, I am an American. I often take that for granted, without much reflection on its significance. But the reality that I am

13. Andrew T. Lincoln, *Ephesians*, vol. 42 of the WBC (Dallas: Word, 1990), 138.

an American is strikingly apparent when I travel to other cultures where people speak and behave differently. I become aware that I am in a different environment that is perhaps not a comfortable fit.

When cultural or economic differences are pronounced, the basic requirements of everyday living become quite challenging and tiring. I usually enjoy the experience of being away, but I am always glad to return home again. I still recall how, many years ago upon returning home from a month-long trip to Asia, that first long-awaited sip from a frosty glass of iced tea was one of the most refreshing experiences I'd had in a long time. I was comfortable being back home where I belonged.

I am also a Presbyterian and have been one for many years. Over time, I have learned from and grown to admire many other Christians, along with their denominations and organizations. In doing so, I have become aware of many differences and learned to appreciate them. This has also enabled me to appreciate and embrace all the more heartily the richness that is mine in the Presbyterian Reformed tradition. I love the confessional heritage, the emphasis on biblical authority, and the theological clarity. Additionally, I value the prominent role Presbyterianism has played in American history because I understand and appreciate the singular contribution it has made to our government, culture, and education. Because of this long association and the memories that attend it, I would find a change extremely difficult. I now realize that being Presbyterian is an important way that I define myself.

Family is also important. One's genes and family lineage cannot be disregarded; family ties and experiences are a defining factor in a person's identity. Parents and grandparents comment that a child looks just like some older member of the family. But it is not only the physical traits that are conveyed to successive generations; the influence of family on one's thinking and behavior can be even more pronounced. Family heritage, stories told about or by relatives—all become a part of the narrative. The varied experiences that come from growing up and living together in a family combine to form a distinct identity. As the years have passed, I've gradually realized that there is no way I can understand myself apart from my family ties.

Family gatherings and holidays help cement that realization. Hence the old saying, "Blood is thicker than water."

When considering the fundamental importance of family, church, and state, it is easy to understand why Paul uses these three institutions to introduce us to our radical new identity as the family of God. You are, Paul insists, fellow citizens with God's people, members of God's household, and a church in which God lives by his Spirit (Eph. 2:19–22). As I have traveled to different places and engaged people in all parts of the world, I have come to understand how my identity in Christ creates a bond that, in many instances, would not have otherwise occurred.

Paul says that this new identity and sense of belonging displaces a former enmity and in the process transcends the unifying identity that is found in the three basic institutions of society mentioned above (vv. 19–22). God's grace conquers estrangement and alienation, replacing it with a higher, stronger sense of identity and unity than would have otherwise been thought possible. Because of the gospel, Jewish and Gentile believers have unexpectedly become the new community of faith, the fellowship of believers. As we observe the difference in this new community, we recall how the wolf and the lamb lie down together in the New Jerusalem (Isa. 11:6; 65:25).

This provides Paul with the leverage he needs to urge all the Ephesian Christians to "make every effort to keep the unity of the Spirit through the bond of peace" (Eph. 4:3). As he taught the Galatians, all who believe in Christ are children of Abraham and belong equally (Gal. 3:6–14). Paul's argument is straightforward: God has rescued you from the hostilities and divisions of this sinful world to meld you into one new community—the church. Putting any unpleasant experiences behind you, Paul insists, you must demonstrate the reality of God's love and grace as the one church of the one Lord through an expression of unity so common and consistent that it will be evident to all the world.

This unity does not require cloning or anything approximating it. Paul is well aware of the many ways in which we differ from one another, including our variety of personalities and gifts (Rom. 12:4–8; 1 Cor. 12:4; Eph. 4:7–12); he sees diversity as a benefit. His emphasis in Ephesians, however, is on unity rather than diversity, while the Romans and Corinthians passages emphasize the value of diversity to unity. Paul's point is that diversity should not militate against the achievement of unity among believers. Rather, "as each part does its work" (Eph. 4:16), the complementary, harmonious blending of gifts and efforts should propel the body of believers toward the realization of "unity in the faith" as an expression of their spiritual development (vv. 13, 15).

While this kind of experience leads to a higher, richer grasp of the reciprocal fellowship and sense of belonging that occurs under the headship of Christ, the synergistic benefits are apparent. These in turn foster greater motivation to keep the unity of the Spirit to maintain—or possibly strengthen—the benefits. This also encourages those who discover the joy of this new fellowship to anticipate its full and final realization with all the saints in glory.

Unity and Diversity

If faith in Christ was the essential factor in forming the church, the fellowship of believers was next in importance. When a believer was joined to Christ, he or she also experienced a dynamic new relationship with other Christians—especially those they knew and lived with, as is clear from the description of the early church in Acts. They knew that they were now tied to one another regardless of their differences in background or gifts, which was important because there were indeed differences.

This fits quite well with Paul's metaphor of the body (Rom. 12:4–8; 1 Cor. 12; Eph. 4:16). He notes that the human body is composed of many different parts with different functions and sizes, yet they are all one body, each part offering a beneficial function for the whole. The diversity is obvious but necessary. Ears are for hearing and eyes are for seeing. Speaking and thinking require other parts. If any part is impaired or lost, this has a negative effect on the rest of the body. Even the loss of a little toe affects a person. You are well aware if you have a toothache, an injured hand, or impaired hearing.

Granting that each part of the body is important, does it make sense for someone to say, "We don't need this body part, so let's get rid of it" (cf. 1 Cor. 12:12–26)? Paul also adds that as each part does its work—that is, when it functions as expected—it benefits the whole body. This leads us to conclude that when believers are functioning as they should, it contributes to a harmonious unity of the whole body in Christ.

The diversity of gifts is a wonderful truth that should enrich and strengthen the church. Unfortunately, differences can also create tensions. Musicians, for example, don't usually think like accountants or athletes, whose interests and priorities can be so different that they find it hard to relate to one another. When this happens, it can be difficult to work together. Paul was aware of the potential of different gifts to drive people apart. In the case of the Corinthians, this was a real challenge. The consequent divisions were unacceptable to Paul because they hurt the church and were a bad witness publicly.

Gifts should be harnessed and guided so that they are not only productive but contribute to both the development of the whole body and a greater sense of belonging or unity. Romans 12, 1 Corinthians 12, and Ephesians 4 emphasize the unity of the church while acknowledging its rich, mutually beneficial diversity. In Ephesians, diversity appears to receive greater emphasis as a contributing value to unity. Whether unity or diversity receives the greater emphasis, the truth remains that unity in diversity marks the church of Christ.

Love, Paul also notes, is the vital factor that binds the church in unity (Rom. 12:9: Col. 3:14). As Schaeffer rightly insisted, love is the mark of the Christian.[14] It motivates Christians to bear with each other and forgive each other rather than allowing mistakes and misunderstandings to drive them apart. Love forges an enduring bond of unity that enables believers to transcend differences. In his first letter, John emphatically advocates that it is the major influence that binds believers to God and to one another. Without that bond of love in Christ, they don't belong (1 John 4:7–21). They are outside, looking in.

14. Francis A. Schaeffer, *The Mark of the Christian* (Downers Grove, IL: InterVarsity Press, 1970), 35.

Divisions

The first Christians possessed a unity that could never be achieved through mere human structures. This unity and the *koinonia* that marked the apostolic church were powerfully reinforced every time believers gathered in a communion of hearts and minds to observe the Lord's Supper. This common bond was reinforced in many ways. As believers willingly faced death from disease and persecution to help one another, the bond was strengthened. They also heard multiple warnings not to divide what God had joined together.

At least some of those warnings fell on deaf ears. A couple of examples are worth noting here. The first is the deceitful sin of Ananias and Sapphira that occurred soon after the exhilarating Pentecost experience and birth of the church, resulting in swift and dramatic judgments of death. Their unexpected deaths brought a stern warning to the nascent church to maintain the *koinonia* with integrity—a warning that sharply focused everyone's attention, apparently. Other disagreements and divisions followed nonetheless, as they have throughout the ages. The well-known disagreement between Paul and Barnabas that pushed them to go in different directions is another example (Acts 15:36–41).

Sadly, the prevalence of divisions in the Corinthian church threatened to rip it apart, jeopardizing its future. Paul, upon writing his first letter to the Corinthians, mentions it immediately, signaling its importance. In doing so, he refers to the report he had received from Chloe's household. Evidently, he was warned that the situation there had become so threatening that it could blow the church apart.

Although he had no firsthand knowledge of the situation, Paul took the message at face value, writing directly to the church to confront this serious problem. As he explained, he wrote "out of great distress and anguish of heart and with many tears, . . ." (2 Cor. 2:4). They were preoccupied with their concerns about each other: who was right and who was wrong. They certainly weren't putting the Lord first. Moreover, their disagreements were many, intense, and persistent. There were disagreements about worship, the Lord's Supper, sexual immorality, the gift to believers in Jerusalem, and several other matters.

Paul wanted to persuade them to lift their eyes beyond these current issues to the Lord, leaving no doubt in their minds that these divisions, including the party strife that he cites, were scandalous and repugnant to the Lord (1 Cor. 1:10ff). Upset by their bad behavior, he scolded them with these words: "Was Paul crucified for you? Were you baptized into the name of Paul?" (v. 13). As far as he was concerned, there was no way they could please the Lord with such attitudes and behavior. Summoning the most powerful illustration he could, he reminded them that when they observed the Lord's Supper, they confessed a unity in Christ. "Because there is one loaf, we, who are many, are one body, for we all partake of the one loaf" (10:17). He admonished them that divisions between believers who are one in Christ are anathema to God, regardless of the reasons they may use to justify them.

Divisions such as those at Corinth obviously troubled the church and distracted it from its primary calling (1:10–17; ch. 3). The Corinthian Christians were an extraordinarily gifted, elite group. They had tremendous potential for good, but they succumbed to pride. As a result, there was no way their diverse gifts and other differences could be used to justify harmful divisions. Not only did they fail to enrich the church, they tarnished its reputation in the city.

Paul sharply criticized their divisive attitudes, demanding that they quickly rid themselves of divisions and contentiousness. He bluntly challenged them: "Is Christ divided?" (1:13). The expected response was, of course, that Christ is not divided, and there is only one church. Paul insisted that the wounds they had caused be healed quickly so that unity could be restored. They were in danger of destroying the church in Corinth, and he was attempting to confront them with the irreparable harm that was imminent (3:17). Addressing the numerous issues that needed attention, Paul eventually pointed them to love—a love for the Lord and for each other—as the answer that would enable them to restore *koinonia* (ch. 13). Love would help rebuild trust and healthy relationships. But without genuine love for one another, regardless of their gifts and great accomplishments, they would have nothing.

In his letter to the Philippians, Paul addressed other problem relationships—notably between Euodia and Syntyche, urging them to resolve their differences and reconcile with one another (Phil. 4:2–3). They were apparently women of great influence; the longer their estrangement continued, the more harmful it was to the church, threatening its peace and unity. Paul urged them to shift their focus from themselves and to become more interested in the good of others than in their own good (2:1–4). Their union with Christ was expected to carry over into their relationships with others who were united with Christ. If only they could agree with each other and be reconciled, it would be a wonderful example and encouragement to the whole congregation.

Selfishness and pride are frequent causes of friction. Thinking only about yourself and ignoring others leads to trouble. Unselfish, sacrificial love is the antidote. To that end, Paul reminded his beloved Philippians of their Savior, who remains the greatest example of humility and sacrifice. Pointing them to Jesus, he encouraged them to have similar attitudes of humility and willingness to serve. This would bring them closer together and give them a great reward. This is Paul at his best in modeling pastoral discipline. He reminds them that discipline should be pastoral and primarily to preserve the unity of the body. When that fails, then expulsion or excommunication follows.

Jesus established the sacrament of the Lord's Supper, sometimes called Communion, just prior to his arrest and crucifixion. This sacrament reminds us of our need for continued forgiveness, humility, and reconciliation with God and one another until we gather together as one family in heaven. James K. A. Smith writes:

> The Supper is a gracious communion with a forgiving God; but it is also a supper we eat *with one another*, and that too will require forgiveness. God's design for human flourishing cannot be satisfied in isolation. As dependent, social creatures we are created for community.[15]

15. James K. A. Smith, *Desiring the Kingdom: Worship, Worldview, and Cultural Formation* (Grand Rapids: Baker Academic, 2009), 201.

It is impossible to observe this sacrament with a hardened heart and be pleasing to God. Paul warned the Corinthians that if they participated in an unworthy way—as they had been—they sinned against the body and blood of the Lord and in doing so brought judgment upon themselves (1 Cor. 11:17–29). The ancient Didache also warned similarly, "Let no one who has a quarrel with a companion join you until they have been reconciled, so that your sacrifice may not be defiled."[16] When we receive the sacrament, it is a time to confess sins and seek forgiveness, acknowledging how much we need the grace of God and one another. Together as one, we depart to serve the Lord with glad hearts, looking forward to the great communal feast in the kingdom that will come according to his promise.

This brief survey of the biblical record should leave no doubt regarding God's gracious work in calling out a people for himself: the people of God. As we have seen, the body of Christ, the temple of God, and the fellowship of the Spirit are some of the ways the Bible identifies those who belong to God through faith in Christ. Found in different times and places, they are the one community of faith that we call the church.

16. Ibid., 202. *The Didache* (first or early second century) is the oldest written catechism, and it shows how Jewish Christians viewed themselves and adapted their practices for Gentile Christians. Eusebius called it the "Teachings of the Apostles."

2

HISTORICAL CONSIDERATIONS

I believe in one holy catholic and apostolic church.
Nicene Creed

Whoever tears asunder the church of God, disunites himself from Jesus Christ, who is the head, and who would have all his members united together.
John Calvin[1]

Christian community is more than just a supportive fellowship; it is an alternate society. And it is through this alternate human society that God shapes us into who and what we are.
Timothy Keller[2]

The Apostolic Church

The birth of the Christian church was an absolutely exhilarating development for those who experienced it. Following immediately upon the arrival of the promised Holy Spirit, the apostles and new converts were swept along in a rapidly spreading flame that quickly numbered thousands of new believers (Acts 2:41, 47; 5:14; 6:7; 9:31; 11:21). Never before had they experienced anything like this

1. John Calvin, *Commentaries*, Christian Classics Ethereal Library, accessed December 2, 2016, https://www.ccel.org/ccel/calvin/commentaries.i.html.

2. Timothy Keller, *Serving a Movement: Doing Balanced, Gospel-Centered Ministry in Your City* (Grand Rapids: Zondervan, 2016), 133.

astonishing movement, easily making it the most exciting time in their lives. The enthusiastic band of new believers aggressively evangelized wherever opportunity presented itself, spurring additional growth; the gospel that had brought them to faith in Jesus Christ had to be shared with others.

Consequently, the church quickly became a phenomenon in the Mediterranean world. Its leadership was soon forced to assume unanticipated organizational responsibilities to keep up with and care for all its new adherents.

A dynamic new arrival always generates resistance from those who are threatened by it or do not understand it. This was the case with early Christianity, whether it was resistance from the Judaizers, Rome, or others. Not everyone loved—or even liked—the church. The more they flourished, the more opposition and hostility increased. All efforts to repress or extinguish the new Christian movement failed spectacularly. Repeated brutal persecutions on a large scale were unsuccessful in halting its incessant advances.

Another distinctive feature of the nascent church was its sense of belonging, marked by an unusual level of caring and sharing. New believers welcomed additional opportunities to express their joy and delight in the Christ-centered faith that had captured their hearts and given them new identities. Their personal spiritual transformation and desire to share the good news clearly marked them as not only a new but also a dramatically different kind of religious group. But they also wanted to demonstrate their solidarity with other believers, reaching out to care for them in extraordinary ways. This was the long-awaited day of salvation, and they were making the most of it.

> They devoted themselves to the apostles' teaching and to the fellowship, to the breaking of bread and to prayer. Everyone was filled with awe, and many wonders and miraculous signs were done by the apostles. All the believers were together and had everything in common. Selling their possessions and goods, they gave to anyone as he had need. Every day they continued to meet together in the temple courts. They broke bread in their homes and ate together

> with glad and sincere hearts, praising God and enjoying the favor of all the people. And the Lord added to their number daily those who were being saved. (Acts 2:42–47)

Luke points out that these new Christians were "one in heart and mind" (Acts 4:32). Their sense of oneness prompted an extraordinary generosity to meet the needs of everyone in the church. They were willing to do this at significant personal cost. Undoubtedly this unmatched generosity affected how they were perceived by others as well as how they viewed themselves. As the church spread around the Mediterranean, the sense of oneness continued; expansion did not diminish it. There were the usual differences of opinion, even sharp disagreements on various matters, but those did not detract from their perceived unity in Christ.

When the inclusion of Gentiles came into question—an issue that threatened to seriously damage the burgeoning movement, if not blow it apart—the concerns of Jewish believers were honestly discussed in a council at Jerusalem that included the key Jewish leaders, and they were satisfactorily resolved. Once the Jewish believers became aware of and understood the significance of the conversion of Gentiles through the work of the Holy Spirit, they readily accepted the Gentile converts (Acts 10:44; 11:1, 18; 14:27). The potential rupture had been squarely faced and resolved.

As mentioned earlier, the Jerusalem Council communicated its decisions to the churches in Antioch, Syria, and Cilicia: a clear indicator of inclusion. Paul also communicated the decisions of the Jerusalem Council to the churches, acknowledging them as part of the church (Acts 16:4). This continuous flow of information among the churches assured their awareness of new developments—whether good news to celebrate or concerns to be addressed, such as the collection Paul made to relieve the poverty of Christians in Jerusalem. The steady communication also brought eagerly awaited news of God's activity and drew the churches closer together as parts of the exciting new movement.

Clement of Rome, writing toward the end of this period, encouraged the believers in Corinth—already confronted by Paul for their factious spirit—to be filled with God's love so that they might become "blameless in love, standing apart from the factiousness of men."[3]

The idea of God loving people was as foreign to pagan religion as the idea of people loving God. This emphasis on pleasing God by loving one another and being willing to sacrifice for one another distinguished Christianity from other religions in a compelling way. Tertullian spoke of this uniqueness by observing how the pagans referred to Christians, exclaiming, "Look how they love one another." This unexpected affection in the face of persecution and epidemics drew believers closer together and distanced them from the pagans.

But the more the church grew, the greater the likelihood that problems would arise somewhere—especially given the impediments of slow communication, challenges to the faith, and persecution. Various internal problems are typical of organizations, especially rapidly growing ones. And problems seemed to occur with monotonous regularity, whether among the sparring parties in Corinth, erring brethren elsewhere that needed correction, or the unscrupulous who took advantage of the euphoria among new Christians to deceive and defraud. Reading the New Testament letters makes one acutely aware of the incessant challenges the church faced. Nonetheless, the undeniable experience of the unity of the Spirit at Pentecost—transcending racial, national, and linguistic barriers—became a hallmark of the New Testament church.

The Early Church

The early church continued to possess a strong sense of unity as the one holy, catholic, and apostolic church of the Lord Jesus Christ, whether in Judea, Samaria, or far beyond. The distinctive community with strong inner coherence was centered on belief in Jesus Christ—who was the fulfillment of God's promises—and expressed through love, faith, and worship. These dominant characteristics

3. 1 Clement, 50.

were decidedly fundamental to the existence of the church; they were a great strength that spurred the flourishing movement. They also contributed to a sense of unity during this period that was indisputable, although problems and tensions of one kind or another were clearly evident, continuously stretching and straining the community's fabric.

Historical documents on this period of the early church do not evade or attempt to hide troubling issues, such as Clement's letter to the Corinthian Christians. Clement wrote in response to a serious problem that was caused when a group of younger men removed certain older presbyters from office. A short time later, Ignatius—the Bishop of Antioch—had to deal with doctrinal problems.

This became typical. As the church expanded, new needs and challenges emerged. Communication was far more difficult than we are accustomed to today. Agreement and cooperation were not always offered as happily as might be desired. Generational and cultural differences sometimes led to disagreements and intense conflict, just as they do today. Then came the more significant doctrinal clashes with Docetism and Gnosticism. Donatists, Montanists, Arians, and Nestorians stirred up even more controversy. When passions became inflamed, accusations flew.

In spite of all the disagreements and disruptions, however, there was a general, unspoken sense that the church was one. Vigorous—occasionally violent—disagreements regarding who was right and who was wrong, who belonged and who did not, seemed to continue unabated, yet there was a consensus in acknowledging only one church. It may have resembled a family with serious problems: occasionally dysfunctional, but still a family. Irenaeus describes his understanding of it this way:

> The church, having received this preaching and this faith, although scattered throughout the whole world, yet as occupying but one house, carefully preserves it. She also believes these points just as if she had but one soul, and one and the same heart: and she proclaims and teaches them, and hands them down with perfect harmony, as if she possessed only one mouth. For although the

> languages of the world are dissimilar, yet the import of the tradition is one and the same.[4]

In A.D. 251, Cyprian, Bishop of Carthage, wrote *The Unity of the Church* in response to a schism in his diocese caused by the Decian persecutions. He said, "Nor is there any other home to believers but the one church," adding, "He that holds not this unity of the Church, does he believe that he holds the faith?"[5] In this same document Cyprian stresses that although the church is one, it has also by virtue of its expansion become a plurality. In his opinion, bishops were a key factor in providing the glue that held the church together.

Consider Cyprian's statement in light of a trying experience: to avoid persecution, thousands of North African Christians renounced their faith. But when the danger passed, they asked to be readmitted to the church. Cyprian, who had fled to avoid being captured, opposed readmitting them unless they demonstrated earnest repentance. It became a messy situation. Three other schisms resulted from this period of persecution, including the Novatian church. Cyprian, who continued to refuse to sacrifice to pagan deities, was eventually executed at the order of the Roman Proconsul, Galerius Maximus. His death, along with the deaths of many other believers, did not lessen negative feelings toward those who capitulated to avoid hardship or death.

During and after the Constantinian era, there was a fresh emphasis on achieving organizational unity, just as the great ecumenical councils—beginning with the Council of Nicaea in the fourth century—pressed toward doctrinal consensus. Although statements, or creeds, were approved and became standard, only an imperfect experience of the desired unity was achieved. An example is the Monophysite church, which came about because of major disagreement.

The Council of Nicaea, meeting in A.D. 325 and regarded as the first of four great ecumenical councils, was Constantine's attempt to achieve consensus regarding Christian doctrine, particularly the deity

4. Irenaeus, *Against Heresies*, 1.2.
5. Cyprian, *The Unity of the Church*, ix, iv.

of Christ and the relationship of the Son to the Father. His political sensitivities may have prompted his interest in achieving an outward unity among the churches, but his faith cannot be discounted as a key motivator. Nicaea remarkably achieved an assembly of diverse leaders and regional expressions of the Christian faith, largely because of Constantine's influence.

Nicaea and the ecumenical councils that followed it contributed to the building up of a single religious community. An institutional framework was slowly established that permitted the development and protection of truth and rejected of alternative formulations or expressions of the Christian faith.

A contemporary English version of the Nicene Creed reads as follows:

> We believe in one God, the Father, the Almighty, maker of heaven and earth, of all that is seen and unseen. We believe in one Lord, Jesus Christ, the only Son of God, eternally begotten of the Father, God from God, light from light, true God from true God, begotten, not made, one in Being with the Father. For us and for our salvation he came down from heaven, by the power of the Holy Spirit he was born of the Virgin Mary and became truly human. For our sake he was crucified under Pontius Pilate; he suffered, died and was buried. On the third day he rose again in fulfillment of the Scriptures; he ascended into heaven and is seated at the right hand of the Father. He will come again in glory to judge the living and the dead, and his kingdom will have no end.
>
> We believe in the Holy Spirit, the Lord, the giver of life, who proceeds from the Father [and the Son]. Who with the Father and the Son is worshiped and glorified. Who has spoken through the prophets. We believe in one holy catholic and apostolic Church. We acknowledge one baptism for the forgiveness of sins. We look for the resurrection of the dead, and the life of the world to come. Amen.[6]

6. "Nicene Creed," Theopedia, accessed February 23, 2016, http://www.theopedia.com/nicene-creed. Prepared by the International Consultation on English Texts, this version

The Apostles' Creed is another ancient creed that has been used by Christian churches through the years and continues to be used in several traditions today. It served well as a consensus statement of faith.

> I believe in God, the Father Almighty,
> the Creator of heaven and earth,
> and in Jesus Christ, His only Son, our Lord:
> Who was conceived of the Holy Spirit,
> born of the Virgin Mary,
> suffered under Pontius Pilate,
> was crucified, died, and was buried.
> He descended into hell.
> The third day He arose again from the dead.
> He ascended into heaven
> and sits at the right hand of God the Father Almighty,
> whence He shall come to judge the living and the dead.
> I believe in the Holy Spirit, the holy catholic church,
> the communion of saints,
> the forgiveness of sins,
> the resurrection of the body,
> and life everlasting.
> Amen.[7]

Failures, such as the schisms at Carthage, did not deter church leaders from persistent efforts to discover acceptable, peaceful solutions to their continuing problems. But it must have seemed like as soon as one problem was solved, another popped up to replace it. As ecumenical scholars Rouse and Neill observed, "If this great age of the church was marked by endless division, it was marked also by endless efforts for the restoration of unity."[8] It is important to grant the validity of their observation.

is used by many mainline communions in the United States and other English-speaking countries.

7. "Apostles' Creed," Theopedia, accessed February 23, 2016, http://www.theopedia.com/apostles-creed.

8. Ruth Rouse and Stephen Neill, eds., *1517–1948*, vol. 1 of *A History of the Ecumenical*

Admittedly, some of the prolonged controversies of the fifth century were not successfully resolved and continued into succeeding centuries as "a source of unhealed division."[9] Interference—and sometimes domination—by emperors such as Constantine, as well as personality clashes between leaders, contributed to the tensions and conflicts. Often misunderstandings and disagreements were caused by linguistic or cultural differences. Given the dramatic growth of the church during these centuries, it is amazing how cohesive and unified it remained in spite of all its challenges. "One Lord, one faith, one baptism" was the heritage of the early catholic church.

The Medieval Period

During the medieval period the church continued its global expansion, extending beyond Europe and the Middle East into Asia, India, and Africa. In *The Lost History of Christianity*, Philip Jenkins provides a wealth of information on the growth and influence of Christianity and its offshoots during this era. He includes the tragic loss of vast numbers of believers and churches in the Middle East and North Africa to the brutal onslaught of Islam, reminiscent in some ways of recent purges in Africa by Muslims.[10] For example, around A.D. 750 the situation worsened to the point that local Muslim rulers in Africa were apologizing that they could no longer supply Christians for slaves because of their scarcity.[11] And in 1200–1400 some of the most ancient Christian communities were almost completely annihilated.[12] These losses—being as serious and substantial as they were—changed the face and future of the church, as areas of its greatest strength historically were severely diminished and in some instances eliminated.

Movement (London: SPCK, 1954), 11, 12.

9. Ibid., 12.

10. Philip Jenkins, *The Lost History of Christianity: The Thousand-Year Golden Age of the Church in the Middle East, Africa, and Asia—and How It Died* (New York: HarperCollins, 2008), 5, 6, 24–26, 97, 98.

11. Ibid., 228.

12. Ibid., 115.

Also to be considered is the magnitude and lasting significance of the Great Schism in 1054, which occurred when the papal legate, Cardinal Humbert, laid on the altar of the cathedral in Constantinople a document of excommunication against Cerularius, the patriarch. Cerularius replied in similar fashion, excommunicating Cardinal Humbert and the other legates. This schism—resulting from theological, political, linguistic, and geographical issues—divided the eastern and western wings of the church. The rift was never repaired in spite of countless attempts to do so, including the Second Council of Lyon in 1274 and culminating with the Council of Florence in 1438–39. In the aftermath of the Council of Florence, any lingering hope for reunion between the two wings of the church faded.[13]

For hundreds of years, the Greek- and Latin-speaking wings of the church had their disagreements and spats. Upon the loss of many churches in the Middle East and Africa, and spurred by increased strength in Rome, the Pope pressed steadily to become the supreme power who would determine the faith of the church and its boundaries of ecclesiastical control. Pope Leo I did much to consolidate centralized power in Rome. The establishment of the Holy Roman Empire was a major factor in its accumulation of solidified power and control, but linguistic and cultural differences seemed to contribute significantly to recurring controversies.

The major issue apparently centered on the Pope's claim to be the universal head and ruler of the church. This was unacceptable to the patriarchs of the eastern churches, who refused to acknowledge any status other than *primus inter pares*, or "first among equals."[14] During the fourth Crusade, Constantinople—the greatest Christian city in the world—was sacked by Crusaders. This infamous act inflamed animosity toward the west as never before. Moreover, it permanently and fatally weakened the eastern churches in their struggle against Islam, for the Crusaders had birthed a hatred among Muslims for all things western.

13. Steven Runciman, *The Eastern Schism: A Study of the Papacy and the Eastern Churches During the Eleventh and Twelfth Centuries* (Oxford: Clarendon, 1955), 159ff.

14. Rouse and Neill, *Ecumenical Movement*, 11, 12.

Transcending these conflicts and other differences was a sense that both east and west belonged to Christ and were a part of his church. But by now there were seemingly irreconcilable differences so that all attempts to heal the deep wounds and reunite east and west became ineffective. The divorce was final. Even a fifteenth-century effort, driven by the realization that Constantinople could survive only with the support of the west, also failed. The Christian church appeared to be hopelessly divided.

That division—combined with the overwhelming losses to Islam—painfully remains, yet receives scant attention from Western Christians. This troubling reality perhaps reveals a focus on our own history at the expense of the greater Christian story with its divergent traditions.

At the height of the medieval era, the western wing of the primarily European church (the Roman Catholic Church) appeared to be united. A principal factor in their unity was the prevailing coherent worldview and system of values based on the Christian faith. The church was the dominant influence in society, especially given the power of the state to support and enforce that influence. Church unity now centered in ecclesiology, primarily in obedience to or compliance with the authority of the Pope. Unfortunately, one of the consequences of the Great Schism was an imposition of the undisputed authority of the papacy of the Roman Catholic Church rather than the ultimate authority of God's Word. If and when dissent occurred, papal force was used to ensure submission. Persuasion was preferable, but force was acceptable.[15] Ongoing conciliar efforts became similarly subject to papal authority, limiting their effectiveness.

Not to be ignored is the shameful reality that the Roman Catholic Church had become a bloated, bureaucratic money machine by the end of this period. Ubiquitous and dominating, it grew insensitive and unresponsive to repeated appeals for reform from John Wycliffe, John Hus, Girolamo Savonarola, and others. That lamentable spiritual declension, combined with various destabilizing political and economic factors, including the rise of the city state (all of which

15. Ibid., 21.

need not be explained here), fanned a restive spirit within the church. Disappointment morphed into disillusionment.

This unsettling state of affairs prompted late medieval theologians to a fresh concern about the identity and authority of the church. Soon they found themselves caught up in a "passionate inquiry into the nature of the true church."[16] The divided papacy—resulting from Clement V moving the papal court from Rome to Avignon, with theological and political ramifications—intensified these concerns. Passions ran high because the fundamentals of the Christian faith were perceived to be at risk. After many years of disillusionment and unrewarding struggles, the pressure for change was building to an unstoppable level. The situation had become intolerable for those who wanted to have a Christian church with integrity. Given these circumstances, a special kind of courageous and intelligent leader with strong allies was needed to step forward and become the catalyst for genuine reform.

The Reformation

Martin Luther (1483–1546), the primary catalyst for the Reformation, never intended to leave the church or divide it. That was the furthest thing from his mind. He loved the church in which he ministered and wanted only to reform it.

Luther passionately embraced the gospel of God's grace and the church that was the instrument of transmitting that gospel. He was disappointed in his experience at Rome and with many church doctrines and practices such as the indulgences. Luther hoped that these current disputes could be resolved by convening a Free Christian Council: that is, a council that would not be controlled by the Pope. In his opinion, a council could be effective only if it were unfettered by papal authority. Otherwise, regardless of their discussions and decisions, nothing would change. Mindful of the conciliar tradition, including the Council of Constance (1414–18), Luther believed that

16. Hans J. Hillerbrand, ed., *Oxford Encyclopedia of the Reformation*, vol. 1 (Oxford: Oxford University Press, 1996), 324.

such a council of Christian leaders, free from papal control, had the requisite competence to deal with the issues at hand given the opportunity to do so. In his opinion, this could unlock the door to the biblical and spiritual fidelity that is pleasing to God. This was the best—perhaps only—hope for the future.

Luther's level of seriousness, and perhaps his hopefulness for positive change, can be measured by his suggestion that it would be better for all parties—including himself—"to compromise, even on weighty issues, so long as they are not against God," rather than to allow the church to perish, as it seemed in danger of doing.[17] This was a major concession, clearly demonstrating that he was more concerned about finding an agreeable way forward than insisting on having his way. He was prepared to engage in honest, substantial discussions with Roman Catholic leaders and showed a genuine willingness to make whatever reasonable compromises would be required to preserve the unity of the church.

The Emperor Charles, sensing the urgency of the moment, urged the Pope to call a council to deal with this matter. The Pope refused, and by blocking a council meeting, he essentially destroyed the last chance of maintaining the unity of the Western church.[18] Undoubtedly the Pope failed to grasp the profound, unintended consequences of his decision. Problems of this nature seem to have been continuous for several centuries, but they had not yet resulted in division.

Although Luther clearly did not wish to cause or perpetuate a separated church, once Pope Leo X drove him from the church by excommunication, the consequences were beyond anything that the Pope might have imagined. No simpering wimp, Luther was now a wounded, roaring lion—fierce and unyielding in conflict. The lines were drawn. For Luther, there was no church without the gospel, for Christ had given birth to the church, and he was the center of its existence. There was no turning back. Realizing that unless he

17. Jaroslav Pelikan, *Obedient Rebels: Catholic Substance and Protestant Principle in Luther's Reformation* (New York: Harper & Row, 1964), 58.

18. Heiko A. Oberman, *The Reformation: Roots and Ramifications* (Grand Rapids: Eerdmans, 1994), 151.

capitulated he had no other choice but to denounce the papacy, Luther resolutely moved forward to uphold the gospel and the authority of Scripture, uniting much of Northern Europe behind him. Once again, a cataclysmic division shook the church that would dramatically shape its future.

A newly birthed Protestantism, energized and focused because of the separation from Rome, emerged as a mighty spiritual, social, and political force in Europe. No longer part of the Roman Catholic Church, Protestants gradually lost any attachment to it, becoming increasingly estranged and hostile. But the Reformers, with gratitude for their Christian heritage, continued to prize the concept of one holy, catholic (universal), and apostolic church, notwithstanding the pain of their separation from Rome. They may have been ejected from the Roman Catholic Church, but they had been pushed closer to God as a result. Moreover, God's favor was far more important to them than the Pope's approval. Without a doubt, they loved the church that had birthed and nurtured them spiritually, but they loved their Lord even more and saw themselves becoming the greatest possible blessing to the church by being supremely faithful to him.

To be sure their new identity was not misunderstood, the Reformers insistently asserted their catholicity, as John McNeill has observed:

> They were far from regarding themselves as heretics, schematics or sectaries. Among their deepest convictions was the assurance that they were the perpetuators of the catholic church of which Rome had become the betrayer.[19]

Luther and One Church

Luther is portrayed by some as a destructive schismatic and by others as a reluctant separatist, so it is worthwhile to observe him

19. John T. McNeill, *Unitive Protestantism: The Ecumenical Spirit and Its Persistent Expression* (Richmond: John Knox, 1964), 63. See also the detailed explanation provided by Heiko A. Oberman in *Luther: Man between God and the Devil* (New Haven: Yale University Press, 1982), 232–45.

more closely to understand him accurately. The first thing to note is that although the body of Christ had been broken and torn by the breach with the Roman Catholic Church, the unity of the church was still so important to Luther that he insisted that he was willing to sacrifice his life for it. Yet he was also willing to take whatever appropriate steps might be required to maintain its unity. What changed? Luther could not bear the thought of compromising the commitments that caused the break with Rome. These commitments were the bedrock of his understanding of the gospel and his obligation to obey God rather than men—even the Pope. His relationship to Christ by faith was the most important thing in his life. Essential to the life of faith and the church was the gospel: salvation through faith in Christ alone.

Consider the Colloquy of Marburg in 1529 as a source of insight into developments in German Europe and the way in which those developments affected Luther. Philip of Hesse called the meeting in an effort to unify Protestants against Catholics. Marburg was the first formal conference for achieving unity among Protestants and, as such, offered an important opportunity for achieving a united Protestant future in the face of Roman Catholic opposition. Despite its potential, however, Luther and Zwingli could not agree on the nature of the presence of Christ in the Eucharist. It appears that Luther himself torpedoed the union that might have been achieved. Whatever his motivation, a wonderful, timely opportunity was tragically lost.

Given the chance to create a powerful, united front highly effective in opposing Roman Catholic error—especially in view of his statements about the importance of accomplishing such—why wasn't Luther more flexible? Many assume that his steadfast refusal to consider any compromise in what he believed the Scriptures taught about the Eucharist prevented the formation of a united Protestantism.

Upon closer investigation, however, there is more to it than Luther's unyielding position regarding the presence of Christ in the Eucharist. One easily overlooked explanation for Luther's behavior that merits more serious consideration is his antipathy toward the politically driven factors that contributed to the convocation of the

Colloquy of Marburg.[20] These factors turned on the significance of the growing power of the city state. Philip of Hesse wanted to build an anti-Hapsburg coalition to oppose Rome, which also fed his desire to have independent political strength. This ultimately could have been more important to him than the theological and ecclesiastical factors. Knowing this about Philip might have negatively affected Luther's attitude and actions.

Melanchthon may have also had a greater influence on Luther and the results at Marburg than was realized at the time. Ironically, Melanchthon's reason for persuading Luther to take the position that he did seems to have been his concern that if the compromise was tentatively agreed upon at Marburg, it would scuttle any hopes of future reconciliation with the Roman Catholic Church. Melanchthon was convinced that reconciliation with Rome needed to precede an agreement with Zwingli, making his primary goal reunification of all parties, including the Roman Catholic Church. So he persuaded Luther to disagree at Marburg. Whether that was a wise decision or not, it is quite different from the common perception of Luther as bullheaded and stubborn, making a decision regardless of the consequences.

Admittedly, the final results at Marburg were disappointing. Although unintended, they drove a lasting wedge between Protestants while weakening their efforts to reconcile with Roman Catholics. The potential union of Protestants may have failed because of Melanchthon's persuasive influence on Luther in his desire to eventually achieve an even greater union.

Although Luther continued efforts toward union among Protestants for another ten years, they were essentially fruitless, conferring a divided Protestantism upon future generations. The greatest moment of opportunity had been squandered, although influenced by the best of intentions.

A major consequence of this failure to achieve a united Protestantism—one that has received insufficient attention—is that it

20. McNeill, *Unitive Protestantism*, 148. Philip of Hesse was pressing for a united Protestantism, but Luther did not want a political federation.

essentially abandoned hundreds of thousands of Protestants to persecution.[21] The tragic, unnecessary loss of Protestant lives—and the consequent weakened influence of the Reformation movement because of their failure to unite—should not be underestimated. It can easily be argued that they could not have anticipated those consequences at that time, which is probably true. Ironically, Luther's unambiguous position was as follows:

> It is a dangerous and terrible thing to hear or believe something contrary to the one witness, faith, and doctrine of the entire holy Christian church, which has been maintained harmoniously from the beginning, that is, for more than fifteen hundred years, through the whole world.[22]

Luther insisted privately and publicly, including during his debate with Johannes Eck, that the church must not be restricted to those who were Roman Catholic because the church necessarily included all those who believe in Christ—whether of the Greek Orthodox Church, Bohemia, or any other church. All who were in Christ belonged to the one, true church, although they belong to different Christian ecclesiastical organizations. Furthermore, believers and unbelievers coming to or associating with the church did not lessen Luther's sense of its oneness. In this respect, Luther considered himself to be in accord with the great church councils and church fathers.[23]

Another way of gaining insight into Luther's views on church unity is possible through analyzing his experiences with the Anabaptist movement—particularly the Peasants' Revolt that caused more than one hundred thousand deaths and indescribable misery. Luther judged such social revolutionaries and radical reformers to be fanatics who threatened to destroy the Reformation and its benefits. In his opinion, they were separatists "with no sense or feeling of responsibility for Church and Society, disobedient to the temporal

21. Oberman, *Luther*, 243–44.

22. Donald Nugent, *Ecumenism in the Age of the Reformation: The Colloquy of Poissy* (Cambridge: Harvard University Press, 1974), 1.

23. McNeill, *Unitive Protestantism*, 66, 67.

authorities and the Holy Scriptures."[24] As such, they were a threat, not a benefit. Luther adamantly opposed initiating any military action to advance the gospel because, as far as he was concerned, such aggressively violent action was the work of the devil. The full force of his feelings is vividly stated: "Before I would have mere wine with the fanatics, I would rather receive sheer blood with the pope."[25] His statement is a reminder of the danger of converging socio-political concerns and theological issues.

Luther also disagreed with other Reformers regarding the sacraments, yet he expressed his appreciation for John Calvin and graciously courted the goodwill of Heinrich Bullinger for years, engaging him in substantial conversations and communication. On the other hand, it is clear that Luther's strength was not consensus building or unifying divergent parties. That simply did not fit his personality. The Herculean task of rallying the forces for reform into a massive movement had fallen upon his shoulders. He accomplished that mission masterfully, as the Reformation attests. Given that achievement, Luther's failure to become the unifying force among Protestants should not be held against him. Nor does his failure to unify Protestants diminish our appreciation for his commitment to the oneness of the church.

John Calvin

Although he is typically associated with Geneva because of his writings and ministry there, John Calvin (1509–64) was born in France and educated at the University of Paris. Introduced to Luther's writings during his early teen years, he became a Christian. Unfortunately for him, France was inhospitable to Protestants. Protestant Christians were persecuted, with many killed or exiled. Calvin found it necessary to move to a safer place: Basel. After a brief ministry there, during which he was influenced heavily by Martin Bucer, he settled permanently in Geneva.

24. Oberman, *Luther*, 229.
25. Ibid., 232.

While Calvin is primarily known for his intellectual prowess—aptly displayed by his prolific, enduring, and influential writings—less attention has been directed to his concern for unity among the fragmented Protestantism of his time. There is every reason for that neglect to be remedied because the unity of believers was of paramount importance to him, as his writings attest. Schism was repugnant to Calvin because he had experienced its bitter fruit. Therefore, the unity of the church was more than a doctrine he believed to be true; it was a cause to champion, and a cause he embraced experientially.

From the time of his early ministry under Bucer's influence, Calvin was ecumenically oriented. He became zealously committed to achieving the unity of the church in Europe to restore its apostolic character. In the opinion of T. H. L. Parker, the noted Calvin scholar, "The concept of unity is at the very heart of Calvin's doctrine of the church."[26] There is a logical compulsion to Calvin's thought, Parker claims, that makes it consistently oriented to unity. Parker continues:

> We think of his insistence on the unity of God, on the unity of Christ, on the initial unity of creation, on unity with Christ, and therefore on unity in Christ. He regarded nothing so unchristian, ungodly, and against the true order of things as disunity.[27]

It should be no surprise then, that although he was an enduring champion of the Reformation and a huge influence on its international expansion, Calvin maintained his ardor for the union of one holy, catholic, and apostolic church. He found diverse ways to express his zeal and desire that "the union between all Christ's churches upon earth were such that angels in heaven might join their song of praise."[28]

Because of his deep commitment to the unity of the church,

26. T. H. L. Parker, *John Calvin: A Biography* (Oxford: Lion Publishing, 1975), 159.
27. Ibid.
28. T. H. L. Parker, *Portrait of Calvin* (London: SCM, 1960), 122.

Calvin expended considerable energy toward resolving differences, especially doctrinal ones, within Protestantism. He realized that unless he did this as a prominent leader, the church would continue to fragment. In a telling letter to Archbishop Cranmer, Calvin stressed his willingness to cross ten seas for the sake of unity if necessary.

> God grant that there may be brought about in some place a meeting of learned and serious men from the principal churches, to define the main points of the faith, and hand down to posterity a solid, scriptural doctrine framed by common counsel. Amongst the greatest evils of our century must be counted the fact that the churches are so divided from one another that there is scarcely even a human relationship between us; at all events there is not the shining light of that holy fellowship of the members of Christ, of which many boast in word, but which few seek sincerely in deed. In consequence, because the members are torn apart, the body of the church lies wounded and bleeding. So far as I have it in my power, if I am thought to be of any service, I shall not be afraid to cross ten seas for this purpose, if that should be necessary."[29]

In the *Institutes*, Calvin is equally explicit, as can be ascertained from the title to the first chapter of Book IV: "Concerning the True Church, with which we must maintain unity, because it is the mother of all the faithful." He states that it is a highly dangerous matter to separate from the church because we are bound to all who are in Christ, and apart from the church there is no salvation. Therefore, to separate from the church is to deny Christ. Who could justify doing that? Calvin reiterated this concern about the dangers of schism in his Geneva Catechism, with the stern warning that "those who disrupt the body of Christ and split its unity into schisms are quite excluded from the hope of salvation, so long as they remain in dissidence of this kind."[30]

29. G. E. Duffield, ed. *John Calvin* (Appleford: Sutton Courtenay Press, 1966), 127.

30. J. K. S. Reid, ed., *Calvin: Theological Treatises*, vol. 22 of *The Library of Christian Classics* (London: SCM, 1960), 256.

Calvin's high view of the catholicity of the church convinced him that it was best to acquiesce one's own rights and desires for the benefit of other believers to assure the greatest degree of unity.[31] In his opinion, those who insist on having it their way to the detriment of others are in the wrong and do lasting harm to relationships with other believers. An accurate way to judge a person's convictions is by comparing actions to words. Doing is more powerful than saying, and it is a truer index to that person's standards.

In this respect, Calvin demonstrated a willingness to work for reunion with Roman Catholics by participating in conferences that were called for that purpose.[32] He exhibited an open spirit at the conferences in 1540 and 1541, before the parties became too entrenched in their positions and permanently polarized. He pleaded with Roman Catholics to recognize Protestants as part of the true Christian, Catholic church. Reciprocally, he was willing to recognize the various churches of Roman Catholicism as the true church in spite of the spiritual and doctrinal declension in the organization as a whole. A letter written to Bullinger in 1540 reveals his sentiments:

> It concerns not our church alone, but all Christianity, that all to whom the Lord has entrusted any charge in his church should agree in true concord; we must therefore purposefully and carefully cherish association and friendship with all ministries of Christ. . . . As for me, as far as in me lies, I shall always labor to this end.[33]

During his Strasbourg years, Calvin was approached by leaders from Geneva who needed his help in responding to a letter from Bishop Sadoleto who, upon hearing that Calvin and other pastors had been asked to leave Geneva, asked them to return to Roman Catholicism. Calvin was early in his ministry—thirty years old—but his reply, a classic defense of the Reformation, also reveals his high view of the church and its unity:

31. Jacob T. Hoogstra, ed., *John Calvin: Contemporary Prophet* (Grand Rapids: Baker Books, 1959), 152.

32. Ibid., 154.

33. Rouse and Neill, *Ecumenical Movement*, 49.

> Now, therefore, if you will accept and submit to a truer definition of the church than yours, call it henceforth the assembly of all the saints, spread over the whole world, dispersed in every age, yet bound together by one doctrine of Christ and by one Spirit of Christ, holding and maintaining the unity of the faith with a brotherly concord and charity. Now we deny that we are at variance with this church; rather, honoring her as our mother, we wish to remain in her embrace.[34]

In addition, Calvin pressed the issue with Sadoleto by emphasizing his desire to serve and glorify God by being faithful to God's expectations of the church, not to enrich himself. Moreover, he reminded Sadoleto that Protestants actually had a better claim to apostolic heritage because it was Rome, not the Protestants, who had broken communion. Reformers were also more closely aligned with the apostolic church than Rome because of their reliance on the full and firm assurance of justification by faith alone as commended by the apostle Paul.

As late as 1560, Calvin was still hoping to heal the existing divisions of Christianity through a new council called for that purpose and attended by representatives from all parts of the divided church.[35] In his communications with Protestants, Calvin was persistent and conciliatory in his efforts to develop a unified front, especially in regard to Rome. He was also outspokenly appreciative and supportive of Luther, for whom he professed great admiration. For example, regarding the disagreement on the Lord's Supper at Marburg, Calvin years later (1541) described the difference as a dynamic spiritual encounter between Christ and the communicant during the sacrament rather than a matter of substance. Emphasizing presence rather than substance appears to have been a brilliant move by Calvin, well regarded by Luther. When Luther read Calvin's analysis, he said that if Oecolampadius and Zwingli had taken a similar approach at Marburg, their dispute would not

34. Hoogstra, *John Calvin: Contemporary Prophet*, 119.
35. Ibid., 154; Duffield, *John Calvin*, 121.

have been so long and bitter.[36] As Bruce Gordon observes in his biography of Calvin,

> When he entered the gates of Geneva in 1541 Calvin saw himself as part of the wider European Reformation, a member of the Protestant fraternity. . . . They stood united in their commitment to the Word of God. What remained to be achieved was to make that unity real among the Protestant churches. Calvin's audacious plans to spearhead the evangelizing of France from Geneva required the support of the Lutheran and Reformed churches. But his eye was not just on France. With the failure of the religious colloquies, Catholics and Protestants had parted ways; the divisions between them had proved insurmountable. To Calvin the whole endeavor had been a delusion. The path forward was to Protestant unity, and in this, he believed, his spiritual brother was Philip Melanchthon.[37]

As his lieutenant, Melanchthon pressed Luther to compromise on some doctrinal matters, especially as they might heal the breach with Rome. Nonetheless, Calvin became deeply attached to him and often made excuses to others for Melanchthon. His feelings and attitude are bared in his admission that, "I have wished a thousand times that it had been our lot to be together."[38] In 1545, Calvin wrote to Luther expressing his desire to come to Wittenburg to visit with him. It didn't happen, but who knows what might have resulted from a sincere, substantial discussion between the two of them? In one of the ironies of history, it appears the visit was thwarted by Melanchthon, who withheld Calvin's letter from Luther.[39] Good intentions, coupled with bad results like these, are strewn across the pages of history.

It is informative to observe that when misunderstandings arose between Reformed leaders, Calvin was frequently the one who was called upon to be the reconciling agent. In retrospect,

36. Duffield, *John Calvin*, 125.

37. F. Bruce Gordon, *Calvin* (New Haven: Yale University Press, 2009), 161.

38. Hoogstra, *John Calvin: Contemporary Prophet*, 155.

39. Rouse and Neill, *Ecumenical Movement*, 50.

he appears to have been far more active in fence-mending than is usually surmised. Calvin was always ready to work for unity among Protestants. Whether through correspondence or in person, he repeatedly emphasized the need for tolerance of differences to achieve a greater measure of peace and to facilitate an emphasis on advancing the gospel, the priority. Through his persistent efforts—at first with Bullinger, later with the ministers at Berne—the churches of Switzerland were united around the Consensus of Zurich.[40] This was a major accomplishment, and Calvin's involvement was pivotal to its success.

Because Calvin took an unyielding position on certain doctrinal issues, reconciliation and unity seemed to be unrealistic hopes—probably of secondary importance. In most instances, dogmatic positions usually ended up negating the appeal for unity. But Calvin's integrity and staunch commitment to certain doctrinal positions never diminished his desire for the unity of the church, which was also a doctrinal issue with high priority. Schism, by contrast, was so abhorrent to Calvin that he was convinced one should do everything possible to avoid it, including compromise. If the marks of the church are present, he concluded, you should not break its unity even though disagreements on other matters might continue:

> nor need it be any hindrance that some points of doctrine are not so pure, seeing that there is scarcely any church which does not retain some remnants of former ignorance. It is sufficient for us if the doctrine on which the church of God is founded be recognized and retain its place.[41]

All doctrines were not of equal importance to Calvin. He acknowledged a hierarchy of doctrines, beginning with the primacy of God and salvation only in Christ. He deemed some doctrines to be nonessential, disagreement on which did not offer sufficient grounds for schism.

40. Ibid., 57.
41. Hoogstra, *John Calvin: Contemporary Prophet*, 161.

> Does this not sufficiently indicate that a difference of opinion over these nonessential matters should in no wise be the basis of schism among Christians? . . . But I say we must not thoughtlessly forsake the church because of any petty dissensions.[42]

On the other hand, having emphasized his desire for unity, it must also be acknowledged that his willingness to accommodate doctrinal differences had limits. For example, Calvin was equally concerned that indiscriminate doctrinal compromises could do more harm than good, weakening the church and exposing it to error. Because he was aware of the danger of such compromises, he was reticent to accommodate doctrinal differences unless absolutely necessary.

Regardless of who was involved in the discussion, Calvin could not and would not abandon the final authority of the Word of God; he unflinchingly stood his ground. His respect and affection for others was undiminished, but he insisted that it would be wrong "to become indifferent to the duty we owe to the honor of God and the preservation of His church."[43] He could not yield on that which he understood to be essential to membership in the true church, and was absolutely unbending regarding the authority of the Scriptures, the gospel, and the sacraments.

But Calvin was equally committed to pursue such concerns prudently, avoiding unnecessary disagreement. Given the temper and spirit of the times, he should be seen in a much more favorable light for his efforts and commitment to the unity of believers. Unfortunately, at the height of his influence in Geneva, Calvin reduced his activities toward achieving unity among Protestants, delegating that role to Beza. Considering his health and many other weighty responsibilities including the challenging circumstances

42. John Calvin, *Calvin: Institutes of the Christian Religion*, ed. John T. McNeill, trans. Ford Lewis Battles, vol. 21 of *The Library of Christian Classics* (Philadelphia: Westminster, 1960), 4.1.12. See also John Calvin on Eph. 4 in Calvin, *Commentary on Galatians and Ephesians*, accessed on November 6, 2016, https://www.ccel.org/ccel/calvin/calcom41.iv.v.i.html.

43. John Calvin, "Writings on Pastoral Piety," in *Classics of Western Spirituality*, ed. and trans. Elsie Anne McKee (New York: Paulist Press, 2001), 309.

in which he ministered, his decision can be considered reasonable. Divisions remained and an unfinished task beckoned, but he decided it was appropriate to give other needs his attention.

Consequently, Calvin did not become the catalyst for Protestant unity that he might have been and probably hoped to be, but there remains no doubt about his attitude and efforts. In spite of all that had happened, especially the intense hostility that developed between Catholics and Protestants, he still reached out to bridge the chasm. Would that he had been more successful.

Other Reformers

The need for a united front against Roman Catholicism was not far from the minds of other Reformation leaders either, and many of them did what they could at different times and places to achieve maximum unity. For example, Heinrich Bullinger's moderation and conciliatory spirit—not especially popular qualities during that period—were undoubtedly a significant factor in the unity that was achieved among the Swiss Protestants, beginning in Geneva and Zurich.[44]

But the most zealous and influential advocate for Protestant unity during the first half of the sixteenth century may have been Martin Bucer who, as noted earlier, also had a significant influence on Calvin. A tireless advocate for Christian unity, Bucer recognized one church made up of all believers in Christ, and he insisted that all Christians should place themselves within the communion of the institutional church.[45]

Although Bucer and Melanchthon were both active on behalf of unity, Bucer was able for a time to interact more effectively with all the major Protestant groups. From 1530 to 1535, he persisted in achieving an agreement with Luther that culminated with the Wittenberg Concord. He was also instrumental in achieving union

44. Geoffrey W. Bromiley, ed., *Zwingli and Bullinger*, vol. 24 of *The Library of Christian Classics* (London: SCM, 1953), 283ff.

45. McNeill, *Unitive Protestantism*, 144.

among Geneva Protestants.[46] This achievement became an initial stepping-stone toward a wider Protestant union. Bucer was even convinced that it was possible to persuade Roman Catholics to join the Reformation. For a time those prospects appeared favorable, but eventually they faded away—partly because the Swiss churches, led by Bullinger, became impatient with Bucer.[47] Unfortunately, Bucer's strenuous exertion to achieve agreement was devastating to his health, and consequently he died in England.

Melanchthon did not possess the upbeat personality and persuasiveness of Bucer, but he also fervently desired and worked for unity in his own way. As has been intimated above, Melanchthon was concerned about the Protestant church's relationship with Rome while Bucer's primary concentration was achieving Protestant unity. Melanchthon's liberality of spirit and irenic personality equipped him well for this task, and he became extremely popular. One of his final attempts to reconcile with Rome was through Francis I, but various complications and opposition from all sides—especially from French church leaders—squelched that initiative.

Thus far we have observed the Continental Reformers, but similar observations could be made regarding the English Reformers from Cranmer to Hooker. These leaders benefitted substantially from the Continental Reformation and its theological writings, which they carefully read. John Jewel, Bishop of Salisbury, rigorously defended the Anglican Church from Rome's charge of schism, asserting the catholicity of Anglicanism.[48] Archbishop Cranmer, whose views on unity were similar to those of Bucer and who had married Andreas Osiander's niece, drew even closer to the Continental Reformation leaders. Attempting to find a suitable way to unite the Protestant churches, Cranmer invited the major leaders of Europe to an all-expenses paid council meeting in England. He thought it might be possible to achieve a doctrinal basis for union if all the key Protestant leaders from Europe could be assembled at the same table.

46. Ibid., 158.
47. Ibid., 160, 161.
48. Ibid., 79.

Melanchthon was, in Cranmer's judgment, the pivotal figure to ensure the meeting's success, so he made every effort—including several solicitous letters—to get him to attend. Unfortunately, Melanchthon chose not to do so—perhaps because of political factors in Germany, perhaps for other reasons. When it became apparent that Melanchthon would not participate, Cranmer abandoned his efforts to host the council since, in his opinion, it would have been unable to achieve its objective without Germanic participation.

Interestingly, Calvin—writing to Cranmer of his support for uniting the divergent forces of the Reformation—expressed his opinion that the Germanic princes were primarily responsible for the failure of the union efforts because they were more interested in their own regional security than anything else.[49] This observation is worth greater attention because it is too easy to focus on theological issues and ignore other important contextual factors that could have determined the outcome. In retrospect, it appears that the rise of city states and national churches brought unintended good and bad consequences for the Reformers—a development that they never envisioned but found necessary to endure because they knew no effective means to overcome it.

Without a doubt, Cranmer believed in the existence of one church from which the Church of England should not be separated. Despite a succession of efforts to achieve greater organizational unity among Protestants, the clear, undeniable fact is that Luther, Calvin, Melancthon, Bullinger, and Cranmer never met together. Had they done so, Reformation unity among Protestants might have become a reality.

A Brief Evaluation of the Reformers

The paramount concern of the Reformers was to be right with God through genuine faith in Christ. They reverently bowed to the authority of God's Word and pledged themselves to protect and proclaim the gospel essential to salvation. Assuming leading roles

49. Ibid., 247.

in the Reformation and the formation of a Protestant church, they exemplified courage, tenacity, and an unshakeable commitment to the authority of God's Word. They wanted everyone else to share their faith.

Often they planned and held conferences; they sought to discover "fundamental articles"; they looked to general or national councils for help. These were honorable methods, not despicable or censurable, but they proved inadequate to overcome the zeal and passions of special loyalties or to call forth a commitment to ecumenical unity. Though beneficial, conferences were inadequate to meet the overarching needs of the time; heroic leadership and wise decisions were of greater importance.

Meanwhile, the European scene was shifting ominously. A long and devastating war was in process. The drift toward religious disintegration had grown too strong to be reversed. Although the ecumenical spirit never failed altogether, the opportunities that had been lost or rejected in the first century of the Reformation could not be recovered, and it would be a long time before the climate became so favorable to ecumenical enterprise and achievement again.[50]

The Reformers were correct in insisting that the church should be understood in terms of who trusts in Christ alone and therefore who is right with God. By centering on justification by faith alone rather than on organizational alignment and compliance to church authority, they captured the true catholicity and unity of the church: all who ever were or would be right with God through faith in Christ are a part of it. This was the defining essence of the true church. They also stressed the faithful preaching of the Bible and the proper administration of the sacraments as necessary for a true church of Christ. Other concerns, however important, were secondary.

As they themselves admitted, the Reformers were inclusive, making room for Orthodox Christians and other Christian bodies within the one true church. Organizational unity, though desirable and sincerely pursued, was not essential. For Roman Catholicism, however, the identity of the church was attached to the primacy of Rome—its

50. Rouse and Neill, *Ecumenical Movement*, 69.

authority and power. If you were outside of the Roman Catholic Church, you were outside of the church, and there was no salvation outside of the church. By contrast, the Reformers insisted that through their conformity to Scripture and the doctrine of the early church, they were definitely part of the one, holy, catholic, and apostolic church.

With this identity in view, the Reformers readily acknowledged the need to seek organizational unity. They were always supportive of the unity of the visible church, which would honor Christ and the gospel. This is why they launched multiple efforts to achieve a united Protestantism and to resolve the conflict with Rome. Unfortunately, their efforts failed, leaving a divided Protestantism that was unable to transcend these divisions. The unintended consequences created vulnerabilities that linger to this day. The rupture with Rome and ensuing fragmentation of Protestantism did not please the Reformers, who never wanted or expected it. Had they been able to reconcile and form a united front, they would have done so. Given their circumstances, it simply wasn't possible.

Looking back we can clearly see that, from the beginning, Protestantism was never a homogeneous entity. Once the churches separated from Rome, their lack of homogeneity militated against an easy reunion, especially when they were influenced by secular political interests and other external issues. The same political, nationalistic, and economic factors that added fuel to the Reformation movement initially militated against a completely unified Protestantism. In addition, the personalities and egos of the Reformers often heightened the walls of division. Their bruises and scars from the painful experience of division probably made them cautious about efforts toward unification lest they create a new set of problems as bad as or worse than those that precipitated the Reformation. They certainly had no desire to repeat painful experiences unnecessarily.

Finally, it should be acknowledged that the radical realignment of political allegiances and the ensuing reorganization of the churches was added to the ferment and innovation that marked the Renaissance. The Reformation that followed released, but also absorbed, tremendous energy and emotion for church leaders. The most important and pressing things had to be dealt with first, so any concern to create a united front among Protestants was often and understandably of secondary importance when other responsibilities and challenges appeared far more urgent. Yet as time passed, the united front became less and less a real possibility. Looking back, it is easy for us to suggest alternative strategies that might have proved helpful, perhaps even successful, but the choices facing the Reformers in the white heat of controversy and the acrimony of dissent and division undoubtedly appeared quite different.

Post-Reformation Protestant Churches

The story of the Protestant church after the Reformation is also one of multiple church bodies that continued separately—and in some instances continued to divide. John Knox planted Presbyterianism in Scotland, but further south the Church of England was dominant. There were also nonconforming and independent churches. The Westminster Assembly was one effort to bring unity among disparate parties in Britain. It failed in that respect, but the Westminster Confession of Faith and Catechisms were a monumental accomplishment that continues to have influence today. These documents greatly influenced the early settlers in North America, whose leaders initially were primarily Puritan and Reformed.

Baptists, Quakers, Anglicans, and Catholics established congregations early and, in time, denominations. Lutherans, Moravians, and others soon followed. As would be expected, the Christianity transplanted in America was clearly related to its European heritage because most of the developing churches and denominations had European roots. Where the French and Spanish dominated, Roman Catholicism became the primary religion. Apart from Maryland, Protestants were the overwhelming majority in the colonies, and by the mid-seventeenth century they outnumbered the Catholics. Because the northeastern and middle colonies were primarily English, the predominant religious bodies were Protestant and of Puritan influence. They were mostly congregational because of sparse population, small towns, and relatively poor transportation. Winthrop Hudson, a highly regarded church historian, has observed that,

> Whether in Virginia or in New England, the same books of religious edification were read, the same doctrines were taught from the pulpits, and the same laws were passed to enforce religious duties.[51]

At the same time, it is apparent that most churches were zealous to perpetuate their particular beliefs and worship, as they differed in certain details. Because of the oppression that had occurred in Europe and Britain, the churches wanted to ensure freedom to practice their faith according to their desires. If someone held different beliefs, they preferred for that person to conform to the church's pattern or move to practice their religion elsewhere; this is how Roger Williams came to live in Rhode Island. Many of these churches organized into denominations as the number of people and congregations grew. A few state-controlled churches were established after the pattern of their old countries.

As time passed, the large canopy of common faith and doctrine with minimal concrete differences experienced a copious measure of disagreement and feuding that led to divisions. Organizationally, pluralistic diversity became the prevailing pattern. One fear that united many colonists was the Church of England gaining control, making Anglicanism the established, state religion. This was resisted fiercely on all fronts—especially by Presbyterians.

In spite of the prevalent pluralism, the Great Awakening of the 1700s became a major unifying influence that gave nearly four-fifths of the churches a common understanding of the Christian life and faith. So many people from various congregations and denominations were converted or spiritually influenced by it that denominational distinctions were minimized and a new basis for respect, appreciation, and cooperation was established—to the point that G. K. Chesterton referred to America as the "nation with the soul of a church."[52]

The catholicity of John Wesley and George Whitefield permeated

51. Winthrop S. Hudson, *Religion in America: An Historical Account of the Development of American Religious Life*, 3rd. ed. (New York: Scribner's Sons, 1981), 9.

52. Sidney E. Mead, *The Nation with the Soul of a Church* (New York: Harper & Row, 1975), 48.

the religious landscape. Preaching in Philadelphia, Whitefield famously exclaimed:

> Father Abraham, whom have you in heaven? Any Episcopalians? No! Any Presbyterians? No! Any Independents or Methodists? No, no, no! Who have you there? We don't know these names here. All who are here are Christians. . . . Oh, is this the case? Then God help us to forget party names and to become Christians in deed and truth.[53]

As Leonard Trinterud has noted, the Great Awakening roused the average lay Presbyterian to the common faith and sense of unity shared by so many other Americans.[54] A new national consciousness and cohesiveness swept across all boundaries. Samuel Davies, a leading Presbyterian minister from Virginia, reflected similar sentiments in the straightforward advice contained in one of his sermons:

> My brethren, I would now warn you against this wretched, mischievous spirit of party. . . . A Christian! A Christian! Let that be your highest distinction; let that be the name which you labor to deserve. God forbid that my ministry should be the occasion of diverting your attention to anything else. . . . It has . . . been the great object of my zeal to inculcate upon you the grand essentials of our holy religion, and to make you sincere, practical Christians. . . . unless I succeed in this, I labor to very little purpose, though I should presbyterianise the whole colony![55]

Consequently, because of this functional catholicity, no single denomination could claim to be "the church." As the country continued to grow, spreading westward, it attracted an ethnic and religious mix of people who were gradually and happily Americanized. The American character represented a blend of republicanism

53. Hudson, *Religion in America*, 80, 81.

54. Leonard J. Trinterud, *The Forming of an American Tradition: A Re-Examination of Colonial Presbyterianism* (Philadelphia: Westminster, 1949), 197.

55. Hudson, *Religion in America*, 81.

and Christianity that would carry into the twentieth century.[56] In addition, the wave of popular religious revivals and related movements that followed the formation of the new nation "did more to Christianize American society than anything before or since, representing a new form of religious populism that remains among the oldest and deepest impulses in American life."[57]

Two major religious earthquakes would unexpectedly shake the church during the twentieth century. The first full-blown crisis that shook American Protestantism was the Fundamentalist-Modernist Controversy. Ferocious in intensity because the stakes were so high for both groups, the clash erupted into vitriolic vehemence that permanently scarred and irrevocably polarized them all. The key issue for Fundamentalists was the authority of the Bible as God's Word. Did it determine what Christians believed and how they lived? The Modernists, attuned to the rising influence of the natural and social sciences, wished to accommodate Christianity to the new discoveries of philosophy and science. Communicating convincingly to a broader, well-educated constituency, they publicly made their case. They were concerned that a failure to make appropriate adjustments to new knowledge and changing times would cause them and the Christian faith to lose credibility. For them it was a matter of prudent necessity to protect the Christian faith.

The Fundamentalists were, by contrast, committed to upholding the ultimate authority of the Bible and its supernatural message regarding salvation. In the Presbyterian world, for example, years of tensions and troubles culminated in an attempt to assure a minimal standard of orthodoxy within Presbyterianism, represented by the affirmation of five key doctrines: the inerrancy of the Scriptures, the virgin birth and deity of Christ, his substitutionary atonement through his death on the cross, his bodily resurrection, and the authenticity of his miracles.

In 1924, 1,274 Presbyterian ministers declared that they did

56. Mark A. Noll, *America's God: From Jonathan Edwards to Abraham Lincoln* (New York: Oxford University Press, 2002), 64ff.

57. Nathan O. Hatch, *The Democratization of American Christianity* (New Haven: Yale University Press, 1991), 3, 5.

not accept these five fundamentals. Prior General Assemblies had required all ordained ministers to accept them and subscribe to the Westminster Confession of Faith and Catechisms. These ministers signed a document called the "Auburn Affirmation," claiming the additional support of hundreds of other ministers who did not sign. They referred to the five key doctrines as "particular theories" among others taught from the Bible, but not the only theories that were acceptable. Their affirmation was essentially a rejection of the demand that all ministers affirm the five key doctrines, and therefore it was understood as a rejection of biblical authority and the gospel.

Not only Presbyterianism but also other denominations were divided by this controversy, resulting in thousands of Christians separating from the "mainline" or traditional denominations. These Fundamentalists, or evangelicals as many of them came to be called, started new congregations and denominations. Fundamentalists had a more sectarian identity while evangelicals, in general, tended to be more cooperative and continued to recognize the validity of other evangelical ministries. Many evangelical Christians, clergy and laity, remained in the mainline denominations but became increasingly uneasy as the years passed. Some found it desirable—if not necessary—to leave and join with evangelical churches, whether of the same denominational tradition or not.

Because this religious disruption coincided with the Great Depression, it placed a huge financial hardship on those congregations at the worst possible time, especially those who lost their buildings. In addition, those who separated discovered that they were now marginalized because they were disconnected from the major culture-shaping influences of which they had been a part. Bruised, diminished, and stripped of massive resources, it would take years for these churches to regain strength. In the 1940s, however, evangelicals began to regroup with the formation of the National Association of Evangelicals (NAE). Since that time, they have increasingly thrived. As George Marsden has observed,

> Certainly one of the most remarkable developments in American religion since 1930 has been the reemergence of evangelicalism as a

> force in American culture. Probably it is the one least likely to have been predicted in 1930.[58]

During the 1960s and 1970s, the second earthquake hit. Americans of all ages were deeply troubled by moral, political, and religious developments. Key researchers declared that, "Nothing changed so profoundly in the United States during the 1960s as American religion."[59] As a consequence, evangelical organizations and denominations grew rapidly during the 1970s and 1980s, finally slowing in the 1990s. The numbers and recognition that evangelicals had hoped for and expected in the1920s and 1930s finally materialized in the latter part of the century.

The NAE's vision of a united evangelicalism or evangelical alliance was fading, however. During this time, the membership of the mainline denominations dropped precipitously as they were torn by the increasingly hostile struggle between liberals and evangelicals.[60]

Ironically, in spite of the various divisions and strife, Americans have continued to be deeply religious and sensed themselves to be one nation under God. This quality has had a uniting rather than a dividing effect, especially among laity. Some claim it is merely civil religion, not genuine Christianity, but it does have a unifying influence. Another factor to consider: Americans are religiously diverse, and one half of them are married to someone who came from a different religious denomination or tradition.[61] Most Americans are intimately acquainted with people of other faiths, contributing to religious fluidity and acceptance.[62] This religious bridging has helped foster a sense of commonality or belonging.[63]

58. George M. Marsden, *Understanding Fundamentalism and Evangelicalism* (Grand Rapids: Eerdmans, 1991), 63.

59. Maurice Isserman and Michael Kazin, *America Divided: The Civil War of the 1960s* (New York: Oxford University Press, 2008), 249.

60. Robert Wuthnow, *The Struggle for America's Soul: Evangelicals, Liberals, and Secularism* (Grand Rapids: Eerdmans, 1989), 178.

61. Robert D. Putnam and David E. Campbell, *American Grace: How Religion Divides and Unites Us* (New York: Simon and Schuster, 2010), 521–22.

62. Ibid., 523, 526.

63. Ibid., 531.

Even among evangelicals, about 40 percent believe that theirs is the one true faith, with that number decreasing among younger members.[64] For the most part, American evangelicals continue to think that all are believers regardless of label. By contrast, a small percentage of Americans—perhaps 10–13 percent, who are very evangelical and morally conservative—are less comfortable with religious pluralism and diversity. Surprisingly, 75 percent of evangelicals do not fit into this category.[65]

Looking back on the history of Christianity in America, its overwhelming cultural influence is evident. This pervasive influence gave Christians a general sense of unity regardless of denominational affiliation. During the twentieth century, however, evangelical Christianity came into increasing conflict with the liberal Christianity of the mainline denominations. When the authority of the Bible, the gospel, and miracles were rejected, many evangelicals concluded that these denominations no longer represented the true church and found it necessary to separate and form their own, much after the pattern of the Reformation.

The process of evangelicals disassociating from the mainline denominations continued in waves, usually triggered by denominational crises throughout the twentieth century. Evangelicals formed new networks and new denominations as they continued to concentrate their efforts on spreading the gospel, affirming the authority of the Bible, and doing the spiritual work of the church rather than on attempting to organize the church into one institution. The principal area in which they most easily cooperated was missions.

64. Ibid., 538.
65. Ibid., 547.

3

THE COMMUNION OF SAINTS

What life have you if you have not life together? There is no life that is not in community, And no community not lived in praise of God. Even the anchorite who meditates alone . . . Prays for the Church, the Body of Christ.
T. S. Eliot[1]

The communities of God, to which Christ has become teacher and guide, are, in comparison with communities of the pagan people among whom they live as strangers, like heavenly lights in the world.
Origen[2]

In the battle against evil, especially against the evil in one's own culture, evangelical personality needs ecumenical community.
Miroslav Volf[3]

THE WORLD CHANGED so much during the last half of the twentieth century that it is difficult for those who did not

1. T. S. Eliot, *Complete Poems and Plays* (New York: Harcourt Brace, 1952; London: Faber and Faber, 1969), 101. Used by permission of Faber and Faber Ltd. Excerpt from "Choruses from 'The Rock'" from COLLECTED POEMS 1909–1962 by T. S. Eliot. Copyright © 1936 by Houghton Mifflin Harcourt Publishing Company. Copyright © renewed 1964 by Thomas Stearns Eliot. Used by permission of Houghton Mifflin Harcourt Publishing Company. All Rights reserved.

2. Origen, *Against Celsus*, III, 29, quoted in John Hardon, *The Catholic Catechism* (Garden City, NJ: Doubleday, 1975), 215.

3. Miroslav Volf, *Exclusion and Embrace: a Theological Exploration of Identity, Otherness, and Reconciliation* (Nashville: Abingdon Press, 1996).

live through that era to comprehend what used to be. If in doubt, talk to any teenager. When I describe party line phones and snowy black-and-white TVs with only four channels and no remote, they express surprise that this was true during my lifetime. The reality that everyone didn't have indoor plumbing is an even greater shock.

In retrospect, however, the 1950s were a great time to grow up in America. World War II was past, leaving America strong and a major global influence. The Korean War soon ended, and although the Cold War was a major concern and the atomic bomb a menace, America seemed equal to any challenge. Toward the end of the decade, dissidents led a successful revolution in Cuba, ousting the corrupt dictator Fulgencio Batista. This would provoke dramatic consequences, including bringing Fidel Castro to power, yet at the time it appeared to pose no threat to the United States. The 1950s became a rock 'n' roll era for teenagers, who were mesmerized by the likes of Elvis and Chuck Berry.

I grew up in a small Florida town—before the population of the state soared to unanticipated levels. The Christian worldview still prevailed in our overwhelmingly Protestant enclave: a small, stable community marked by a sense of belonging. Ours was essentially a contained world focused on what was happening in our immediate area, though we were aware of national news. The paradigm-changer for me was becoming a Christian during my high school years. Prior to graduation, I began to sense God's call to ministry, redirecting me and reshaping my interests, and I began to follow that path as much as I could discern it.

For a brief stint following college, I lived in Miami—my wife's hometown—where I had the delightful experience of teaching Cubans how to speak English. They were leaving Cuba in droves, seeking a safe haven in the United States. Upon arrival, most of them needed help learning how to adjust to their new life in America, and especially how to communicate. They were grateful to be in Miami, spared from the growing problems in Cuba, where Castro had turned out to be worse than Batista. They wanted to be good citizens until they could return to Cuba.

Circumstances would soon change for all of us. Having lived in Miami during the Cuban Missile Crisis, I clearly remember the American blockade of Russian ships transporting missiles armed with nuclear warheads and other military supplies to Cuba. It was a period of unusually high stress in South Florida, with armed missiles on the beaches, planes droning overhead at night, and global conflict appearing imminent. Life did not feel nearly as stable and secure as it had a few short years prior. To that crisis was soon added the heightened tensions of the Civil Rights Movement, along with mounting concerns about the military conflict in Vietnam.

During the 1960s it seemed everything was coming apart or melting down. President John F. Kennedy—adulated by the rising generation—was assassinated in Dallas, plunging the whole country into shock and mourning. The violence continued when Kennedy's brother Robert and Martin Luther King Jr. were also assassinated. Rebellious youth defined this turbulent era, with collegians practicing free speech and free sex, and defiantly rioting against and dismantling the establishment. The Puritan synthesis that had provided a moral and intellectual foundation for hundreds of years was smashed during this time of social upheaval.

It was a bizarre period for Christianity too. Movies like *A Man Called Peter* and *Ben-Hur* were replaced by the Death of God movement and public rejections of historic Christianity. Some church leaders publicly espoused Communism. The stress on clergy was severe enough that by 1971 about 40 percent of those under age forty seriously considered leaving the ministry.[4] Thankfully, some, like Billy Graham, were a source of strength and hope. Campus Crusade and other campus ministries gained ground during the 1960s and 1970s. Overall, however, it was like watching a wrecking ball smash our heritage. For someone like me, a relatively new Christian, the church seemed to be self-destructing. It was distressing to experience the constant public anti-Christian actions and rhetoric. Although I didn't understand and

4. Robert D. Putnam and Lewis M. Feldstein, *Better Together: Restoring the American Community* (New York: Simon & Schuster, 2003), 95.

couldn't explain why, the glue that held my world together was coming apart.

As the world changed and the one I knew faded away, the real loss that most people began to experience was the disappearance of their sense of community, of belonging. Consequently, the quest for community became the dominant social tendency of that period. According to sociologist Robert Nisbet, the problem had become more urgent than at any other time since the end of the Roman Empire.[5] He argued that for most people, the structure of economic and political life rested upon "and even presupposed, the existence of the small social and local groups within which the cravings for psychological security and identification could be satisfied."[6] The ability to develop a coherent sense of the outside world was tied to close, interpersonal relations in which values became meaningful.[7] That world was quickly melting away, leaving us adrift.

As America bulked up with industrial might and its population migrated to the urban hubs where jobs were rapidly being created, we thought we were moving up and improving our lives. We had no idea that it would mean losing our sense of place, of belonging and community. Someone facetiously remarked that "IBM means 'I've been moved,'" referring to the high mobility that was relocating and dislocating people. As Vance Packard put it, we were fast becoming "a nation of strangers in which people are disturbed by the feeling that they are rootless or increasingly anonymous, that they are living in a continuously changing environment where there is little sense of community."[8] Philip Slater spoke of it as "the pursuit of loneliness,"[9] and Alvin Toffler coined the term "Future Shock" to describe "the shattering stress and disorientation that we induce in individuals by subjecting them to too much stress in too short a time."[10] Nisbet

5. Robert Nisbet, *The Quest for Community: A Study in the Ethics of Freedom* (Oxford: Oxford University Press, 1969), 45.

6. Ibid., 53.

7. Ibid., 49, 51.

8. Vance Packard, *A Nation of Strangers* (New York: David McKay, 1972), ix.

9. Philip Slater, *The Pursuit of Loneliness: American Culture at the Breaking Point* (Boston: Beacon Press, 1970).

10. Alvin Toffler, *Future Shock* (New York: Random House, 1970).

warned that the "towering moral problem of the age" was the problem of lost community, eroded by the rising tide of individualism.[11]

The transition from rural to urban America, accompanied by a high rate of mobility, changed the lives and behavior of many Americans far more than they realized. As Toffler explained, instead of having friends, you became friendly. People moved into sparkling, new suburban neighborhoods but didn't know their neighbors. Soon they didn't try to know them.

As the relational glue from thousands of small communities and families disintegrated, people found themselves rootless and isolated. Critics traced the cause to the emphasis on individualism that had begun to characterize America in the early nineteenth century. Undoubtedly this was a factor, but a major contributor to the loss of community was the rapid growth of urbanism, high tech, and high mobility. The fragmentation of marriages and families followed soon after, compounding the consequences.

The church, swept up in this fast-moving current of change, suffered similar damage to relationships and community. Instead of leading the way into a peaceful, productive era of mutual understanding and cooperation, Christians were equally stunned and disoriented by these rapid changes and found it difficult to respond constructively. Angry, knee-jerk reactions worsened the situation, widening the gap between traditionalists and young reactionaries. Tensions in the major denominations increased as they grappled with this unexpected problem. Ensuing years were spent seeking understanding and trying to catch up.

In *The Homeless Mind*, Peter Berger observes that the arrival of technological, bureaucratic modernity brought with it a loss of identity, a loss of community, and an erosion of values that caused a deepening condition of "homelessness."[12] According to him, it did not fundamentally change the "finitude, fragility, and morality of the human condition" that wants a meaningful center to life in society.[13]

11. Nisbet, *Quest for Community*, 30.

12. Peter Berger, Brigitte Berger, and Hansfried Kellner, *The Homeless Mind: Modernization and Consciousness* (New York: Vintage, 1974), 82.

13. Ibid., 68, 185.

But the church that had provided that meaningful center was no longer the focus of community life. The most devastating effect, in his opinion, was the challenge to religion.[14] The loss of community lifted moral constraints for the affected, but the liberation did not provide the expected results.

The problems associated with the loss of community continued into the twenty-first century, revealing themselves in political dysfunction, culture wars, and polarization over other issues. Yuval Levin recently described the price of the progress we achieved technologically and economically:

> In liberating many individuals from oppressive social constraints, we have also estranged many from their families and unmoored them from their communities, work, and faith. In accepting a profusion of options in every part of our lives to meet our particular needs and wants, we have also unraveled the established institutions of an earlier era, and with it the public's broader faith in institutions of all kinds. . . . We have set loose a scourge of loneliness and isolation that we are still afraid to acknowledge as the distinct social dysfunction of our age of individualism.[15]

The poor, he observes, became more isolated economically, culturally, and socially.[16]

David Brooks, citing Marc Dunkelman's *The Vanishing Neighbor*, recently described this as a "middle-ring" relationship failure.[17] People become adept at bonding with those who are like them but fail to connect with those who are different. Evangelicals easily fall into this pattern, shunning those who hold opposing views and collecting in partisan camps.

14. Ibid., 184, 185.

15. Yuval Levin, *The Fractured Republic: Renewing America's Social Contract in the Age of Individualism* (New York: Basic Books, 2016), 97, 98.

16. Ibid., 126.

17. David Brooks, "How to Fix Politics," *The New York Times*, April 12, 2016, http://www.nytimes.com/2016/04/12/opinion/how-to-fix-politics.html.

Francis Schaeffer

Then, like a voice in the wilderness, Francis Schaeffer appeared in the 1960s as a much-needed modern-day prophet to confront unbelief, showing why Christianity was true and trustworthy and explaining why an unbelieving public was rejecting it in favor of a path to hopelessness and destruction. A Presbyterian missionary in Switzerland, Schaeffer had an unusual ability to address the crises of the day with the biblical message, reminding his audience of the God who is there.

Courageously addressing the challenges of the moment, Schaeffer also issued sage advice to Christians about the nature of true spirituality, including the need to treat other Christians well. This, he insisted, was critical to solving the crisis of the time, though few people back then would have seen any connection between the problems they were trying to solve and the need to treat others well. His point was that the person who truly loves God will also love his neighbor, and when he behaves accordingly, human relationships and society should benefit.

In several major addresses during this turbulent period in American history, Schaeffer stressed the need to seek beauty in human relationships.[18] He insisted that to be effective, an orthodoxy of truth needed to be coupled with an orthodoxy of community.

> The Christian community and the practice of that community should cut across all lines. Our churches have largely been preaching points and activity generators. Community has had little place. In the New Testament church this practiced community was not just a banner but cut all the way down into the hard stuff of the material needs of the members of the community. This was the reason for the appointing of the first deacons.[19]

18. Francis A. Schaeffer, *Two Contexts, Two Realities* (Downers Grove, IL: InterVarsity Press, 1974); ibid., *The Church Before the Watching World: A Practical Ecclesiology* (Downers Grove, IL: InterVarsity Press, 1971); ibid., *The Church at the End of the 20th Century* (Downers Grove, IL: InterVarsity Press, 1970).

19. Schaeffer, *20th Century*, 39.

Surprisingly, Schaeffer would not always have spoken that way. Early in his ministry, he was as feisty as a bantam rooster, sharing a significant role in church squabbles and splits. But he paid a heavy price for his actions, as did others who were involved in church conflict and division. Eventually, that adversarial life caught up with him. At one point he became so discouraged that he contemplated abandoning the Christian faith altogether. But after taking a lengthy period away to think, pray, and heal, he returned to his ministry with a new understanding of the importance of his relationships with God and other people. He embraced his discovery of what he called "true spirituality." True spirituality not only embraced truth, it created a beauty and harmony in human relationships that would appeal to a watching world.[20]

In reflecting on the disagreements, fights, and divisions followed by lasting estrangements that he had participated in, Schaeffer realized how wrong he had been. Tragically, the damage had already been done. As he observed similar patterns emerging among evangelicals in the 1960s, 1970s, and 1980s, he urged them not to repeat the costly mistakes of his generation. Reflecting on the scars of past battles, he implored them to treat others lovingly and considerately, making every effort to maintain friendships and ministry relationships regardless of disagreements.

> I plead with you, therefore, if, or when that moment comes for you, that you find some way to show an observable love among true Christians before the world. Don't divide into ugly parties. If you do, the world will see an ugliness which will turn it off.[21]

Schaeffer became acutely aware of the inextricable link between love for God and for others, as summarized by Jesus when asked to name the greatest commandment. By now, Schaeffer had become convinced that the mark of the Christian was love: love for one's neighbor and for God. Because he had learned from painful

20. Francis A. Schaeffer, *True Spirituality* (Carol Stream, IL: Tyndale, 1971).
21. Schaeffer, *Watching World*, 79.

experience that an unbelieving world was watching, and that the way we treat each other makes a huge difference in our credibility, he urged fellow believers to give greater emphasis to the orthodoxy of community.

> Love—and the unity it attests to—is the mark Christ gave Christians to wear before the world. Only with this mark may the world know that Christians are indeed Christians and that Jesus was sent by the Father.[22]

Schaeffer became so influential because he spoke honestly and directly to the human predicament. We had lost the sense of belonging and community that once characterized rural, small town America—the America I knew as a boy. Schaeffer understood from prior experiences the critical need to restore cohesiveness to human relationships to rebuild a stable society. As he watched alienation spread like a disease, he realized that it was infecting the church, and that the consequences would be devastating. So he called for observable love among Christians, and for compassionate love to non-Christians. There was yet a chance to turn the tide. In Schaeffer's opinion, the price of failure would ultimately be far greater than anyone would guess, and he persisted in urgently advocating his message.

Body Life

During the 1970s, Ray Stedman faced a similar problem in California, where he pastored the Peninsula Bible Church. Addressing the need from a biblical perspective, he coined the new term *Body Life*, which quickly captured the attention of evangelical churches.[23] In doing so, Stedman popularized the importance of believers' relationships to each other, suggesting ways to rebuild their relationships and sense of belonging.

22. Francis A. Schaeffer, *The Mark of the Christian* (Downers Grove, IL: InterVarsity Press, 1970), 35.

23. Ray C. Stedman, *Body Life*, 3rd ed. (Glendale, CA: Gospel Light Regal Books, 1979).

Stedman understood the need only too well because he experienced it growing up. His father deserted his family when Stedman was about six, so he and his mother—an asthmatic with a heart condition—were forced to live with an aunt. Life was tough. Financial difficulties forced him to drop out of college. To make money, Stedman turned to riding Brahma bulls in rodeos. He moved to Chicago, then to Denver, and then to Hawaii to work for Libby Pineapple. When World War II began, he enlisted.

After the war, Stedman attended seminary and then entered the ministry. Soon he was on the staff of the Peninsula Bible Church in Palo Alto, where he remained for forty years. Warm and affable, he developed his ministry by utilizing a growing understanding of the value of relationships and consensus building. Stedman demonstrated the biblical basis for rebuilding community as a way to combat the problem of growing fragmentation in American society. *Koinonia*, a Greek word referring to commonalities or "in common," became a buzzword for community and fellowship. The hippies craved love, and evangelicals such as Ray Stedman offered it through Body Life.

The Communion of Saints

Although they may have seemed fresh and new at the time, terms like *orthodoxy of community*, *Koinonia*, and *Body Life* were merely new ways of referring to the older doctrine of the communion of saints mentioned in the Apostles' Creed and given its own chapter in the Westminster Confession of Faith. The communion of saints, or the fellowship of believers, is based on our common faith in Christ and the fact that all Christians belong to the family of God as a consequence of that faith. As the Westminster Confession states,

> All saints, that are united to Jesus Christ their Head, by His Spirit, and by faith, have fellowship with Him in His grace, suffering, death, resurrection, and glory: and, being united to one another in love, they have communion in each other's gifts and graces, and are obliged to the performance of such duties, public and private,

> as do conduce to their mutual good, both in the inward and outward man.[24]

The communion of saints finds its explanation in the doctrine of the church: specifically, that there is only one church and it is composed of all those throughout human history who genuinely trust in Jesus Christ for their salvation. Through God's grace and mercy, all believers are united to Christ and to one another by faith. They form an exclusive union; no one else belongs to it. Although we may find ourselves describing any number of Christian groups and subgroups, we come to realize that there are essentially only two kinds of people as far as the Christian faith is concerned: believers and nonbelievers.

All believers belong to the one true church and to each other. The oneness of the church leads us to appreciate all the more the wonderful treasure God has given to us as part of his family—brothers and sisters in the Lord. We are part of the one great church that has existed through the ages and will continue until every believer is gathered into his presence in glory. Those who do not believe in Christ as their Savior are excluded, although they may be members of particular Christian congregations and perhaps even hold leadership positions. As Schaeffer put it,

> The real chasm is between those who have bowed the knee to the living God and thus also to the verbal, propositional communication of God's Word, the Scriptures, and those who have not.[25]

Although most people are not aware of it, the denominational experience is actually an acknowledgement that a denomination—as well as a congregation or person—is part of something bigger. That "something bigger" is the church: the diverse community of faith comprising all people who trust in Jesus Christ as Savior. Like family, they belong to each other because they belong to God. If they weren't united to Christ, they wouldn't be part of his family and belong to

24. WCF 26.1.
25. Schaeffer, *Watching World*, 80.

each other. As Hendrik Kraemer put it, "The fellowship (*koinonia*) with and in Jesus Christ and the Spirit is the creative ground and sustainer of the fellowship (*koinonia*) of the believers with each other."[26]

Personally, the older I've become, the more I've grown to appreciate the communion of saints and the common bond we share in Christ. I am happy to be a mere Christian, without further appellation. With the Heidelberg Catechism, I readily confess that my only comfort in life and death is to know that I belong to my faithful Savior, Jesus Christ.[27] Through him I am a part of the family of faith, a Christian community marked by love, faith, and worship.

According to the Westminster Confession of Faith and its statement regarding the communion of saints, Christians are "obliged to the performance of such duties, public and private, as do conduce to their mutual good."[28] That is to say, we are bound together as believers and obligated to help each other as needs arise. We must be considerate of one another's welfare and do whatever is needed for mutual benefit and edification. In addition, the Confession emphasizes an obligation to

> maintain an holy fellowship and communion in the worship of God, and in performing such other spiritual services as tend to their mutual edification; as also in relieving each other in outward things . . . to be extended unto all those who, in every place, call upon the name of the Lord Jesus.[29]

These three stipulations solemnly remind us that the communion of saints obligates all believers to one another. As Paul reminded the Corinthians, "The eye cannot say to the hand, 'I don't need you!'" (1 Cor. 12:21a). Not only do we need each other, we are obligated to do what we can to bless and benefit one another. Elsewhere Paul adds an exhortation to do good to all people, especially to the household of God, as opportunities arise (Gal. 6:10). Many other scriptures

26. Hendrik Kraemer, *A Theology of the Laity* (Philadelphia: Westminster, 1958), 107.
27. The Heidelberg Catechism, question 1.
28. WCF 26.1.
29. WCF 26.2.

underscore believers' obligations to one another—so many that the point cannot be missed. We are obligated to encourage one another, to build one another up, to pray with and for each other; and we are also obligated to do whatever we can to set the right example for others and to provide help where it is needed.

John Winthrop undoubtedly had this in mind when he preached a sermon, "A Modell of Christian Charity," to his fellow Puritans on board the *Arbella* before disembarking in the New World. Knowing that others would observe them carefully to determine the nature of their commitment and the value of their venture, he reminded them that they were like a city set on a hill. As such,

> Wee must be knitt together in this worke as one man, wee must entertaine each other in brotherly Affeccion, wee must be willing to abridge our selves of our superflueties, for the supply of others necessities. . . . wee must delight in eache other, make others Condicions our owne reioyce together, mourne together, labor and suffer together, always having before our eyes our Commission and our Community in the worke, our Community as members of the same body, soe shall we keep the unitie of the Spirit in the bond of peace.[30]

Dietrich Bonhoeffer

Dietrich Bonhoeffer—the well-known Christian martyr in Hitler's Nazi Germany—wrote his doctoral dissertation on *Sanctorum Communio*, or the communion of saints, which he completed at only twenty-one years of age. His professor, Karl Holl, influenced his choice of topic by showing him how Luther's doctrine of justification was combined with a reformed understanding of church that was necessarily understood as a community.[31]

30. H. Shelton Smith, Robert T. Handy, Lefferts A. Loetscher, *American Christianity: An Historical Interpretation with Representative Documents*, vol. 1 (New York: Scribner's Sons, 1960), 1:101–2. See also Perry Miller and Thomas H. Johnson, *The Puritans* (New York: American Book Company, 1938), 198.

31. Dietrich Bonhoeffer, *Life Together and Prayerbook of the Bible*, ed. Geffrey B. Kelly,

Bonhoeffer quickly recognized the importance of Christian community and the fact that it could not be taken for granted. Acknowledging it as God's gift to the church, he wanted to emphasize it and maximize its influence, but he was also realistic enough to realize that those who loved the dream of community more than the reality could easily destroy it.[32] One problem that worried him was Christians who had inaccurate perceptions of a genuine community and were not properly prepared to develop one into what it should become. In this case, their efforts could actually become harmful.

> Precisely at this point Christian community is most often threatened from the very outset by the greatest danger, the danger of internal poisoning, the danger of confusing Christian community with some wishful image of pious community.[33]

In regard to that, Bonhoeffer noted the tendency of people to "observe, judge, and classify" each other as soon as they formed groups. He was simply pointing out the many sinful forces that could destroy genuine Christian community,[34] some of which he knew from personal experience. Therefore, the communion of saints had to be understood as a community of sinners. Sinners create imperfect communities of all sizes; marriage might be seen as the smallest of these.

Years passed before Bonhoeffer was finally able to achieve the experience of Christian community that he had written about and desperately yearned for. During the summer of 1935, he moved to Finkenwalde to fulfill his dream of forming a genuine Christian community based on the Sermon on the Mount. Strengthened and guided by the presence of Christ, he and his students lived together, learning how to share faith, hope, and love as a prayerful, caring community. It was a journey, but an exciting, promising one.[35]

trans. Daniel Bloesch and James Burthess, vol. 5 of *Dietrich Bonhoeffer's Works* (Minneapolis: Fortress Press, 1996), 7.

32. Bonhoeffer, *Life Together*, 24.
33. Ibid., 34.
34. Ibid., 93.
35. Interestingly, on September 15, 2015, Beeson Divinity School faculty, staff, and

As Bonhoeffer began to test his understanding of what he believed the church should be with this small band of brothers, he became completely convinced that the Christian life cannot be lived in the abstract. Faith and communities of faith need concrete forms of living, sharing, and sacrificing together so that God's presence is felt. Bonhoeffer would not, therefore, settle for a superficial experience of Christian community. He led his students into a profound, intimate togetherness, expressed in the unselfish love of humble service and forgiveness—to love others as Christ loved them. He wanted his students to go beyond feeling inconvenienced into a conscious embrace of willing, sacrificial service. They needed to learn not only to be *with* but also to be *for* each other. As Bonhoeffer talked with his students in various venues through the years, he engaged them in conversations about

> how to form authentic Christian communities through a strengthened spiritual life into which would be integrated appropriate forms of service to people in need. Though their beginnings in community life were informal and spontaneous, they formed the creation of the kind of community life that Bonhoeffer felt might be able to reunite the whole church.[36]

Tragically, his quest for authentic Christian community was brought to a sudden end by the Nazis. They imprisoned him in a concentration camp where, at Hitler's express command, Bonhoeffer was executed only days before the war ended. But his discovery of the joy of true Christian community lives on in his writings, especially in *Life Together*.

It is pertinent that Bonhoeffer lived for a time in the United

students celebrated their first Finkenwalde Day. To my knowledge, it is the first such occurrence in a theological school in North America. It is also a tribute to the leadership and longtime emphasis on community of the founding dean, Dr. Timothy George. See *Beeson Magazine* (2016), 20–22. Paul House, a professor at Beeson, recently wrote *Bonhoeffer's Seminary Vision: A Case for Costly Discipleship and Life Together* (Wheaton, IL: Crossway, 2015), providing additional detail and insight.

36. Bonhoeffer, *Life Together*, 10.

States, where he was well-received as a scholar and where he might have safely remained until the war was over, but he insisted that he must return to Germany. He reasoned that if he did not join his people during their crisis and suffer with them, he would lose the credibility to minister to them when the war ended. He belonged to them as their brother, so he returned to them in their time of need. He could not bear for them to endure such suffering without him.

Toward the end of his life, Bonhoeffer expressed in poetry what had become so important to him:

> Distant or near,
> in joy or in sorrow,
> each in the other
> sees his true helper
> to brotherly freedom.[37]

Rodney Stark

Returning to the early church, Rodney Stark's *The Rise of Christianity* analyzes several issues of importance to the first-century believers, and in doing so he provides an unexpected but timely and pertinent reflection on the importance of the communion of saints.[38] I was initially surprised to discover that Stark would write about the early church, since he was a sociologist. However, I soon discovered that he brought a set of tools to the historical task that are often neglected by earlier church historians. His research on Christianity during plagues and epidemics in the ancient world provided a new perspective regarding the lives of believers who were confronted by such adversity.

Stark notes that during that historical era, a surprisingly large number of people died from disease—especially when epidemics struck the high-density, unsanitary urban areas; as many as one-third

37. Dietrich Bonhoeffer, *Letters and Papers from Prison* (New York: Macmillan, 1972), 218–19.

38. Stark, *Rise of Christianity*, 73–94. See also, Susan R. Holman, *The Hungry Are Dying: Beggars and Bishops in Roman Capadocia* (Oxford: Oxford University Press, 2001).

to one-half of a city's population might perish. Disease spread rapidly, and people died quickly—too quickly to receive care. Often bodies were not disposed of because family members were afraid of becoming infected, taking immediate measures to safeguard other family members.

It may be difficult to imagine the psychological and physical impact of such epidemics, but they were among the most feared experiences of that period. The circumstances were terrifying because people didn't know how to protect themselves. With corpses strewn about, stinking and rotting, pagans usually ran for the hills to avoid infection and death.

Many Christians, however, refused to flee with the panicking masses. Courageously, they remained to nurse the sick and tend to one another's needs—in some instances also caring for the health of their unbelieving neighbors at the risk of infecting themselves and meeting death early. The good news is that many Christians who might have died recovered because of the watchful care of their Christian neighbors. Their stories of illness and recovery soon became powerful testimonies to their unbelieving neighbors, demonstrating vividly the true communion of saints in action. Tremendous social credibility was established, and as a consequence, pagan citizens began to view Christians in an entirely different light.

As might be expected, women who were often burdened with caring for such needs responded positively in large numbers. Many of them gladly became Christians, swelling the ranks of believers among the pagans. Eventually the emperor protested the growing influence of these new converts, grousing, "There are too many Christian women!"[39] Such stories remind us of the love that Christians had for one another and the difference it made throughout the Roman Empire. Catastrophic circumstances called for heroic responses, and the Christian community rose to the occasion, motivated by love: loving one another as Christ had loved them and given himself for them.

39. Stark, *Rise of Christianity*, 95.

As Emil Brunner observed, "Man cannot be man by himself; he can only be man in community."[40] That is true, he asserts, because love only operates in community. The rewarding experience of community—the ultimate foundation for human relationships—is also found in the Trinitarian relationship because we have been made in the image of God; we are relational beings who delight in the reciprocal sharing of love. Believers find their identity in Christ and, through him, communion with the Father and Holy Spirit. That relationship becomes the basis of the communion of saints, as we are bound to one another in love.

We are vividly reminded of this as we gather to observe the Lord's Supper in Holy Communion. Through his death, Christ binds us to himself and to each other. The Communion table should be open to all believers as a sign of oneness in Christ, regardless of our different backgrounds. The divine quality of love that is realized in Christ is made visible to outsiders, as well as to fellow believers.

This relational solidarity lies at the heart of Paul's ecclesiology.[41] Gilbert Meilander concluded, "Our task is this: to achieve within human life the love that is a dim reflection of the life of God."[42] When the communion of saints comes to its intended expression and fulfillment, God is glorified.

The benefit of the communion of saints to children doesn't receive the attention it deserves; its neglect probably contributes to weakening moral and social standards, whereas its desired expression contributes to wholeness and happiness. Research has demonstrated that churches and Christian organizations that care about children and what kind of people they will become

> are more likely than many others to offer a shared vision of the good life, communal support for good behavior, a long-term rather than

40. Emil Brunner, *Dogmatics*, vol. 2, *The Christian Doctrine of Creation and Redemption* (Philadelphia: Westminster, 1952), 64. Also see 55–66.

41. Russell P. Shedd, *Man in Community: A Study of St. Paul's Application of Old Testament and Early Jewish Conceptions of Human Solidarity* (Grand Rapids: Eerdmans, 1964), 195.

42. Gilbert Meilaender, *Faith and Faithfulness: Basic Themes in Christian Ethics* (Notre Dame: University of Notre Dame Press, 1991), 48.

> a short-term outlook, and thick networks of relationships that are multi-generational rather than uni-generational.[43]

This attention has a salutary effect on children, making them far more likely to become constructive participants in their communities.

Past Failures

Although it is one of the tenets of our faith, the communion of saints strangely receives minimal attention these days. This is certainly not because evangelicals do not believe in the fellowship of the saints. On the contrary, we incorporate this concept into the very architecture of our churches, often providing "fellowship halls" for believers to gather together for spiritual and social enrichment. We are pleased to belong to the same churches and denominations; we happily discuss mutual acquaintances; we relish reading the same books and listening to the same broadcasts. Yet in spite of this, true fellowship among believers suffers, receiving scant attention or activity.

Why does this happen? It is reasonable to ask why the communion of saints, a fundamental concept, has not received more emphasis. Why haven't we been more successful in achieving the unity that God desires for us? We are often willing to acknowledge the loss of community. If so, why haven't we pressed for improved results? Is it perhaps related to the loss of community in our culture, inclining us to accept far less than we should?

That certain stalwart Christian leaders fiercely championed the gospel and the authority of Scripture is well known, just as it is known that their beliefs caused them to break off relationships with those who denied them. These truths are the *sine qua non* of the

43. Commission on Children at Risk, *Hardwired to Connect: The New Scientific Case for Authoritative Communities* (New York: Institute for American Values, 2003), 30. *Authoritative communities* refers to a specific combination of warmth and structure in which children appear most likely to thrive. See also Robert D. Putnam, *Bowling Alone: The Collapse and Revival of American Community* (New York: Simon & Schuster, 2000), 296–97.

Christian faith; without them, there is no basis for the church. Lose the gospel and the authority of God's Word and you lose Christianity. Acknowledging this gives encouragement to reflect appreciatively on where we might be today without the efforts of those in earlier periods of history who so diligently defended the faith.

The Reformation and the Fundamentalist-Modernist Controversy became, as a consequence, two defining events for the church. Adversity, persecution, sacrifice, suffering, and sometimes death left lasting scars. Europe had more than its share of religious wars. One consequence was to assure an enduring vigilance for doctrinal orthodoxy as a high priority. The mere suggestion of compromise became repugnant to evangelicals, who feared that bending on even the smallest theological points could have a domino effect, leading to the loss of Christianity's most cherished beliefs.

Given these historic circumstances, particularly the gravity of these concerns, it should be no surprise that the fellowship of believers and other matters became far less important. The continued existence of the community of faith had to be protected first and foremost. It was necessary to assure its continuation before attending to an improvement of its health. While suffering often brings believers closer together—making them realize how much they need each other—these experiences engendered a mentality that minimized a concern for unity, with lasting deleterious effects. The suffering and stress were not experiences from which people easily recovered; life seldom returned to normal.

A second insight to be learned from the Fundamentalist-Modernist Controversy as a defining event is that it changed the thinking and behavior of most evangelicals in more ways than have been acknowledged or perhaps even realized. A defining event occurs when a family experiences divorce, a home is destroyed, a person is fired, or a close relative or friend dies. Signal events of this nature often permanently affect the way one thinks about things, makes decisions, and behaves afterward. A person is never the same again.

I clearly recall such a time in my life. It was Christmas, and I was ten years old, suffering alongside my two brothers and sister with the mumps, while my mother was hospitalized with double viral pneumonia. Tragedy struck in the form of illness and accident, leaving behind a trail of sorrow and devastation. During our illnesses we learned that my father, a railroad engineer, had been in a horrible accident. His locomotive had collided head-on with another, killing several railroad personnel, including some of his friends, and leaving him badly injured. His back was broken in seven places, along with other significant physical injury.

My father was hospitalized for six months. Following that, he wore a body brace for two years. He became an alcoholic, growing violent when he drank. As his alcoholism worsened, so did the health of our family. Eventually we lost everything except our home. As a family, we were so busy coping with the issues at hand that we didn't realize the permanent scars that were being inflicted. Looking back now, I realize how that traumatic experience had a huge impact on me, shaping the rest of my life.

Because of what happened to our family, I rejected the life that had imprisoned us and began to look for something better and more hopeful. My search ended when I became a Christian. A new life with a new supportive community of faith brought joy and hope. But I have not forgotten and still think about that Christmas long ago as the defining event that changed my life and those of my siblings.

After the Fundamentalist-Modernist Controversy, a defining event for American Protestants, evangelicals became preoccupied with defending the Christian faith and aggressively evangelizing the world. Another consequence was that they emphatically rejected Modernist programs. They lost interest in working closely together as believers. Of course, they would not have seen it that way, but that is what happened.

Evangelicalism, molded by this negative reactive behavior, morphed into a different kind of Christianity. This traumatic experience shaped its identity for the remainder of the twentieth century. Along the way, values that had been taken for granted—such as compassion for and ministry to the disadvantaged—gradually diminished, including the relational element of the Christian faith:

the sense of community, belonging, and fellowship. Trust had been broken, leaving many evangelicals alienated.

It was not until much later in the twentieth century that we became aware of some of these unintended consequences. David Moberg, a sociology professor at Marquette University, published a fascinating analysis—*The Great Reversal*—to describe the nature of the transformation. He showed how evangelicals abandoned their historical emphasis on addressing social ills because they now identified such activity with the social gospel of the liberals and therefore would have nothing to do with it. Billy Sunday, the baseball player turned Presbyterian evangelist, grabbed attention by denouncing the social gospel as "socialism and sacrilegious, un-American quackery." He warned that "the road to the kingdom is not by the bathtub, nor the gymnasium." To which he added, "We've had enough of this godless social service nonsense."[44]

By contrast, Miroslav Volf provides a wonderful example of forgiveness and reconciliation in the story of the tragic death of his five-year-old brother, Daniel, who slipped away unnoticed to play with friendly soldiers on a nearby military base. The soldiers put him on a bread wagon so he could enjoy the ride. Daniel leaned out as they were passing through a gate, and his head was caught between a post and the wagon. He died on the way to the hospital. Miroslav's parents forgave the soldiers for the careless mistake that resulted in their son's death, refusing to press charges.[45] They might have been angry at the nanny, Aunt Milica, who should have been more observant and prevented Daniel from leaving home unattended. But they forgave her and never said anything about it to Miroslav. Their example helped him understand the love of God revealed in the gospel and how it becomes the foundation for union with God and other believers. Without the willingness to forgive in spite of wrongs or disagreements, we will fail to realize the beauty of the fellowship of believers that God desires.

44. Billy Sunday, "The Fighting Saint" (sermon, Detroit, MI, October 3, 1916).

45. Miroslav Volf, *Free of Charge: Giving and Forgiving in a Culture Stripped of Grace* (Grand Rapids: Zondervan, 2005), 121ff.

Free Market Christianity

At the beginning of the nineteenth century, Christians in America found themselves with a free market for religion. The new nation was founded on the principle that no church would be established as the official or national church and therefore have a monopoly on other religious organizations. There was a free market for business and also for religion. This freedom unleashed an unexpected avalanche of charitable activity. Amid the religious awakenings and sensibilities that became a part of the fabric of the new nation, so many new organizations were formed to address social needs that they were referred to collectively as "The Benevolent Empire." No one would have imagined that so many Christian organizations would be established so quickly to magnanimously address human needs and problems.

Alexis de Tocqueville discovered this unique benefit of voluntary associations that were springing up everywhere for the common good. As justification for this activity, it can be argued that the founders' reference to the "pursuit of happiness" in the Declaration of Independence implied a commitment to seeking the welfare of all citizens, not individual satisfaction. The pursuit of happiness meant pursuing a life of virtue to contribute to the renewal of American culture. This is another example of the communion of saints: the idea that we have a mutual obligation to one another and, therefore, should work for the common good. The Benevolent Empire contributed significantly to the health of the nation, not merely to the well-being of the church.

So, why can't it be this way now? Why don't positive things like this happen more often? One answer is that lots of good things do happen all the time, but most of them never receive much public attention because they are not considered newsworthy. On the other hand, we must also admit that we too often fall short of what God expects of us and what we want for ourselves. In the words of a familiar couplet,

> To dwell above, with the saints we love, that will be glory.
> But to dwell below, with the saints we know, that's another story.

Such is life. But we must accept our share of the blame for the orneriness and contentiousness that has so often harmed the church. When Schaeffer surveyed his experience, particularly following the Fundamentalist-Modernist Controversy (of which he was a belligerent participant), he was grieved and ashamed of the wounds that were inflicted—some by him in his efforts to defend the Christian faith. Schaeffer warned of the devastating effects of forming fractious parties. Strange, isn't it, how we ignore the warnings of those who have already made costly mistakes and proceed to make our own new ones that probably could be avoided if we heeded their warnings?

In 2000, following the presidential balloting, Florida became known as the state where every vote counts, and counts, and *counts*. The situation was tense and emotions ran high, particularly when the vote challenge was referred to the Supreme Court of Florida. During this time I called a friend—who was one of the justices—to encourage him, knowing the pressure he was under. He was occupied with the decision before the court and unreachable by phone, so I left a message conveying my gratitude for his presence on the court, saying that my wife and I were praying for him. Once the court's decision had been made and he was free to talk, he called to thank me for the encouragement, saying: "You will never know how much that call meant to me." Then he related how he had received some of the nastiest, meanest calls you would ever believe—and many of the meanest ones were from Christians! How often that is the case!

During the 1960s and 1970s, hippies, flower children, and radicals revolted against the establishment and decided that they would make the country more acceptable. They were revolting for love and peace. I recall watching news coverage of a huge demonstration at the Democratic Convention in Chicago. The news included a video clip of a Peacenik clubbing a policeman over the head with his sign. As I watched, I thought, "How can he be for peace when he's striking a policeman?" We quickly criticize that kind of behavior by others, then fail to acknowledge how we have often done similar things.

Not only do we, as Paul says, "keep on biting and devouring each another," but we launch unwarranted attacks and make new enemies as a result (Gal. 5:15). Denominations have their share of fractiousness, political maneuvering, and prickliness. Political parties fuel their differences into animosity and partisan recalcitrance rather than seeking what is mutually beneficial. What is worst—much of this happens in the name of the Lord! Too many deadly activities have been cloaked by a façade of piety.

Diversity

So where do we go from here? How can we ensure a better, more hopeful future for the Lord's people? How can we reap the blessings of fellowship in the Lord?

The first step is to acknowledge that the problem exists so that we can do something about it. Surely we can agree on the need to reject negative, reactive responses and take positive, constructive steps toward rebuilding the relationships that have been neglected, bruised, or mangled.

We should reclaim the biblical agenda and let it direct our future together. In America we celebrate our roots as being "Out of many, one"—*E pluribus unum*—but the *unum* is not at the expense of the *pluribus*. Why should unity be at the expense of diversity in the church, or vice versa? Diversity enriches us. If we have a willingness to acknowledge that all who trust wholeheartedly in Christ for salvation are members of God's church, we have every reason to acknowledge our fellowship with all believers.

Once we acknowledge that, we ought to have a commensurate commitment to love and help each other, regardless of our differences. Our varying gifts will serve to benefit us as a whole, as diversity benefits teams and orchestras. It can become one of our greatest strengths when we learn how to maximize it. A team of quarterbacks is unlikely to be a world-beater. A steady diet of ice cream is bad for your health. No wonder it has been said, "Variety is the spice of life!" We should learn to embrace diversity as we celebrate the fellowship of the Spirit; it is the path to enrichment and achievement, and it calls us to a kingdom view. When this happens, the Lord will be glorified.

Tupelo and Wichita

This may be the ideal time to consider fresh efforts toward cooperation and mutual support as an antidote for that which ails us. Robert Putnam's *Bowling Alone* underscores the problems of isolation, alienation, loneliness, and estrangement in American society, resulting in the loss of social capital, trust, and cooperation. He reports:

> For the first two-thirds of the twentieth century a powerful tide bore Americans into ever deeper engagement in the life of their communities, but a few decades ago—silently and without warning—that tide reversed and we were overtaken by a treacherous rip current. Without at first noticing, we have been pulled apart from one another and from our communities over the last third of the century.[46]

However, in *Better Together* Putnam points to Tupelo, Mississippi—the home of Elvis—as a beacon of hope for addressing these concerns.[47] Yet early in the twentieth century, Tupelo was an impoverished community, having fallen on extremely hard times. In 1940 Lee County, where Tupelo was the county seat, was among the poorest counties in America. The situation was so dismal that production was approximately 25 percent of the average of other communities. Tupelo had sunk to the bottom economically, and there was no hope in sight.

But the indefatigable persistence of George McLean—publisher of the local newspaper, *The Tupelo Journal*—became the catalyst for change. McLean was an unlikely and unwanted source of hope for better times, having supported local workers during a textile strike. In doing so, he had earned the dislike of town leaders, who no longer trusted him. But he was possessed with a sincere concern to improve the community for everyone and came up with a seemingly

46. Putnam, *Bowling Alone*, 27.
47. Putnam and Feldstein, *Better Together*, 98–118.

harebrained idea that he thought might work. The problem was that key leaders didn't agree. As a matter of fact, he was almost run out of town for his effort.

Here's how it unfolded. Well aware of the slow decline of cotton farming and its impoverishment of the land, McLean was unique in perceiving the untapped potential of the dairy industry to improve circumstances for Tupelo. His idea: finding some way to pool their funds to buy a prize bull that could be used to improve the livestock, significantly increasing dairy production and bringing economic improvement to their struggling town.

McLean approached several local businessmen with his idea about pooling their money to buy the bull. He argued that if they didn't do it, they would remain mired in the same discouraging poverty. Resistance was strong, especially because businessmen thought that McLean knew nothing about farming or operating dairies. Eventually, through his indefatigable persistence, he persuaded the town leaders to invest fifty thousand dollars in a prize bull. This was a huge sum at the time, especially for a poor town like Tupelo.

But within a short period, and to everyone's surprise, the venture was successful. The first year the cows sired by the prize bull began to produce milk, they generated one million dollars in revenue. Talk about cause for celebration! That total soon rose to more than ten million dollars, and by the 1950s the town was producing more milk in Lee County, Mississippi, than in many Wisconsin counties! It was an amazing achievement. You can imagine how tongues were wagging in Tupelo!

The success of their communal investment inspired these businessmen to take the next step of establishing a community development program that would enable them to bring greater prosperity to Tupelo. Scrapping the Chamber of Commerce, they began an education program for business development. Because of this important decision, they soon achieved another smashing success by establishing or attracting more than two hundred furniture companies, ranking Tupelo second in the country. The founding of a top-notch medical complex, the largest non-urban medical center in the country, came next.

Gradually, Tupelo became a flourishing, exemplary community. Why? Because people started working *together*. Instead of working independently and in isolation, they pooled their resources and efforts. Once they realized the value of their dependence on one another, they became a marvelous example of synergistic community. George McLean continued to provide leadership and wisely contoured his newspaper accordingly. He avoided the usual focus on corruption, crime, and violence because he thought it aroused fear and cynicism. His *Tupelo Journal* became solution-oriented rather than problem-oriented, and its emphasis on social ties and trust contributed greatly toward building a strong community in which some leaders regularly devoted as much as 50 percent of their time.

The Tupelo story is a real sizzler. Research indicates that strengthening families and communities is a helpful step in reducing poverty.[48] The God-given potential in human relationships becomes apparent when you hear it, and the church could learn a lot from their example. Then again, the church should be leading the way as the most uplifting, productive example of community.

Eastminster Presbyterian Church in Wichita, Kansas, offers another remarkable example of the unselfish good that should flow from the fellowship of believers. Some years ago, Eastminster was a growing suburban congregation, bustling with energy. Multiple worship services were required on Sunday mornings because the building was too small for the size of the membership. Meanwhile, the church gradually accumulated a large building fund to provide a more suitable space for worship.

The church was almost ready to begin construction on a new sanctuary when a devastating earthquake hit Central America, riveting the congregation's attention to the widespread destruction and loss of life. They had an interest in this region because of their missionary support. As they followed news of the earthquake, they learned that many of the area's churches had been destroyed. Moved to respond compassionately to this tragedy, the church decided to postpone building the new sanctuary for which they had saved for

48. Children at Risk, *Hardwired to Connect*, 45.

years. Instead of building for themselves, Eastminster gave every dollar of their building fund to help rebuild between seventeen and twenty-one churches in Central America. That is the communion of saints.

As we hear these and other stories, we realize that the Lord is using his people to do far more than we could ever conceive. God is bigger than we are. What he is doing in the world is far bigger and better than anything we could dream. Shouldn't we be asking how we can be a part of his great work as he builds his church? How can we come together and reach out constructively to his people, wherever they are, so that the communion of saints becomes a beautiful reality and a compelling testimony to an unbelieving, watching world?

As psychology professor and author Jonathan Haidt has astutely observed,

> We may spend most of our waking hours advancing our own interests, but we all have the capacity to transcend self-interest and become simply a part of a whole. It's not just a capacity; it's the portal to many of life's most cherished experiences.[49]

49. Jonathan Haidt, *The Righteous Mind: Why Good People Are Divided by Politics and Religion* (New York: Pantheon Books, 2012), 317.

4

ECUMENISM, SCHISM, AND SECTARIANISM

Presbyterianism is born to division as the sparks fly upward.
Matthew Arnold[1]

Ecclesiology has rarely been an evangelical strength.
Kevin J. Vanhoozer and Daniel J. Treier[2]

A broken communion in a broken world.
James K. A. Smith[3]

Union, and not division, is a Christian axiom,
lying at the very root of all our ideas of a Christian Church.
James Bannerman[4]

WE GENERALLY AGREE that schism and sectarianism are sins, but it is often difficult to agree about when those sins occur. People are sinful—even spiritually mature Christians. And sin is the root cause of unbelief, misunderstanding, and division.

1. Silas McBee, ed., *The Constructive Quarterly: A Journal of the Faith, Work, and Thought of Christendom*, vol. 6, *March to December, 1918* (London: Oxford University Press, 1918), 363.

2. Kevin J. Vanhoozer and Daniel J. Trier, *Theology and the Mirror of Scripture: A Mere Evangelical Account* (Downers Grove, IL: InterVarsity Press, 2015), 21.

3. Smith, *Desiring the Kingdom*, 162.

4. James Bannerman, *The Church of Christ: A Treatise on the Nature, Powers, Ordinances, Discipline, and Government of the Christian Church*, vol. 2 (Edinburgh: Banner of Truth Trust, 1960) 335.

Cultural, economic, spiritual, and social differences multiply the possibilites for misunderstandings and separate identities. Once Protestants established separate churches or denominations to eliminate serious doctrinal error and to perpetuate or preserve their faith, it became easier to justify further proliferation and division.

These divisions frequently occurred because of disagreements about doctrine. Admittedly, some of the precipitating doctrinal issues may not have been essential to the Christian faith, the Reformed faith, or even a particular group's beliefs. But the distinctive doctrinal positions or polity issues were sufficiently important to them to justify—perhaps necessitate—a separate identity. Sometimes personalities or politics were the cause; remember, people usually order their lives according to what is most important to them.

Presbyterians are a good example. As they settled in America, they formed congregations and, in time, a denomination. The first presbytery was not organized until 1706, although congregations were scattered throughout the colonies much earlier. Other Presbyterians with similar roots migrated later and decided to establish additional denominations rather than becoming part of the one already present. Was there adequate justification for forming separate denominations in America or for the division of existing denominations? At the time it may have seemed justified to those who made those decisions, such as in the first major division in 1741. Later, after the smoke cleared and the damage caused by separation was revealed, it may have looked quite different. But at that point, it may also have appeared too challenging to repair the breach.

Eventually there were ten or more Presbyterian denominations in the United States. Some resulted from divisions that occurred when the northern and southern churches divided because of the Civil War, failing to reunite after the conflict ended. Theological differences caused other divisions, as with the Old School and New School division of 1837. Other denominations such as the Associate Presbyterians and the Reformed Presbyterians in the United States were the result of Seceder immigrants from Scotland and Ireland, who wanted to retain their identity in a way that best represented their heritage. This led them to establish separate Presbyterian denominations.

Protestants in America generally regarded themselves as members of a family of related religious bodies called denominations. They were heirs of a common faith and saw themselves as part of a larger body called the church. Gilbert Tennent defined it this way:

> All societies who profess Christianity and retain the foundational principles thereof, notwithstanding their different denominations and diversity of sentiments in smaller things, are in reality but one Church of Christ, but several branches (more or less pure in minuter points) of one visible kingdom of the Messiah.[5]

Denominationalism thus understood is the opposite of sectarianism because it doesn't claim an exclusive understanding of or possession of saving truth. Given this definition, it is possible for Christians—regardless of differences or denominations—to live together in love and peace because of the underlying unity they acknowledge in Christ.

Sectarianism

Sectarianism is tied to an exclusive claim to truth. It thrives on the claim of being entirely right, with a superior claim to truth compared to any other religious group. Some critics might refer to those who are sectarian as "narrow-minded" or "bigoted" (cf. Titus 3:9–11). When theological beliefs or confessions are no longer open to revision in the light of Scripture or important new information, a sectarian spirit is present. "Sectarianism denies catholicity," Edmund Clowney pointed out, because in refusing to recognize other communions as true churches of Christ, sectarians deny the fellowship that Christ requires.[6] Humility and openness to God's Word are essential to avoiding the sectarian attitude that moves one from disagreement to division.

Disagreement is one thing; disparagement and division are more

5. Trinterud, *American Tradition*, 132.
6. Clowney, *The Church*, 97.

serious. This is an important distinction because once a relationship has been broken, it is extremely difficult to mend. Separation or division is a serious, painful action. Unintended consequences inevitably follow, often complicating the relationship even more than might have been anticipated prior to the division. After multiple experiences of contentiousness and fragmentation, leaving bruised and broken Christians in their wake, you would think church leaders would be alerted to the potential damage and make every effort to avoid additional fractures. History reminds us that the wounds from church splits heal very slowly, leaving ugly scars. Consequently, Presbyterians who have divided or have strong disagreements often feel greater estrangement and hostility toward one another than toward other denominations with whom they may have less in common.

The way in which denominational and seminary leaders treated Reformed Theological Seminary (RTS) provides a good example of sectarianism. RTS came into existence in 1966 because of doctrinal disagreements within the Presbyterian Church, US (PCUS), often referred to at that time as the Southern Presbyterian Church. A major factor that led to the establishment of RTS was the realization by certain church leaders that all four of the denomination's seminaries no longer held to the inerrancy and authority of the Bible, nor was there fidelity to the Westminster Confession of Faith. After numerous efforts for reform failed, RTS was founded in an effort to preserve the doctrinal heritage of the denomination.[7]

While that was happening, it became apparent that the denominational leadership did not want to embrace historic orthodoxy and did not want fellow Southern Presbyterians to start an evangelical Presbyterian seminary that could become a competitor to existing seminaries.

E. T. Thompson, the noted church historian at Union Theological Seminary in Richmond, observed that Presbyterians had finally freed

7. Ernest Trice Thompson, *1890–1972*, vol. 3 of *Presbyterians in the South* (Richmond: John Knox, 1973), 502, 503; Sean Michael Lucas, *For a Continuing Church: The Roots of the Presbyterian Church in America* (Phillipsburg, NJ: P&R Publishing, 2015), 258–66; John R. Muether, *The First Forty Years, 1966–2006: The History of Reformed Theological Seminary* (Clinton, MS: Reformed Theological Seminary, 2006), 16, 17, 21–23.

themselves from the dead hand of the past[8]; they obviously did not want to return to that past. Not only did denominational leaders not want an evangelical Southern Presbyterian seminary, they launched a concerted effort to prevent it from happening. As events unfolded and it became apparent that there was sufficient support to establish RTS in Mississippi, the hostility of the denominational leadership became public. About three fourths of the presbyteries stated that they would not permit candidates to attend RTS, nor would they employ its graduates.

One reason the presbyteries gave for forbidding candidates to attend RTS was that the seminary was unaccredited. But when RTS sought accreditation, the four Southern Presbyterian seminaries requested a secret meeting with the accrediting association, The Association of Theological Schools (ATS), to discourage them from accrediting RTS.[9] After RTS became accredited, the attitude of the presbyteries toward RTS did not change in any discernible way. In retrospect this was clearly part of a determined, sustained effort to marginalize evangelicals in the Presbyterian Church, US, to implement a liberal agenda. Liberals had gained control, and they were determined not to relinquish it.

Toward the end of the 1970s, King College in Bristol, Tennessee, long associated with the Presbyterian Church, US, faced a financial crisis that had been worsening over a period of years. The problem had been exacerbated by denominational restructuring that affected the support base for the college. It appeared that the college could not survive, so after considering possible alternatives, the denomination offered it to the state as a part of its university system. Although that plan seemed to be an attractive solution, it did not work. Finally, it seemed the only remaining option was to close the school.

Up until this point, the denomination and the public had paid scant attention to the King College crisis. Once every viable alternative had been explored to no avail, five Presbyterians stepped forward

8. Thompson, *1890–1972*, 222–24, 456. See also 273, 329–39, 478–79, 490, 492, 496–500.

9. Jesse H. Ziegler, *ATS through Two Decades: Reflections on Theological Education, 1960–1980* (Worcester, MA: Heffernan Press, 1984), 291.

with a last-minute offer to save the school, provided that the King board agreed to turn the school over to them. These "white knights" made it clear that King would continue as a Presbyterian college, and it would also maintain its relationship with the denomination's synod.

At that point, the denomination's power establishment—which had made no effort to rescue the college during its recent crisis—suddenly became keenly interested in King's future. They quickly hired lawyers with King College funds and launched a major effort to stop what they referred to as a takeover effort by an undesirable group. To stir up resistance, one denominational leader wrote an editorial in a leading unofficial but widely read journal, insisting that it would be better to close the school than to allow this undesirable group to assume control. Why at that late juncture, after other efforts had failed, was there such a virulent, hostile response to this effort to save their historic Presbyterian college?

What makes this story interesting is that the only reason for the hostile response by these denominational leaders was that the group offering to save King College was evangelical.[10] To the power establishment, that was absolutely unacceptable. "Better no college at all than an evangelical college," was their attitude.[11]

Richard Hutcheson—former chair of the Office of Review and Evaluation of the PCUS—who identified himself with the "liberal-ecumenical" wing of the denomination, thoroughly analyzed these developments to ascertain the reason for them. He concluded that because of "the managerial revolution" following World War II, the liberal-ecumenical wing had learned to excel at acquiring and maintaining power in the denomination. After a careful analysis of the facts, his conclusion was one that evangelicals would painfully and repetitively experience in the years that followed: "Mainline establishments are wide open to cultural pluralism, but not to 'liberal-evangelical' pluralism."[12] In Hutcheson's opinion, if the liberals

10. Richard G. Hutcheson Jr., *Mainline Churches and the Evangelicals: A Challenging Crisis?* (Atlanta: John Knox, 1981), 15–17.

11. Ibid., 23.

12. Ibid., 135–36.

allowed evangelicals to grow and prosper, they believed that it would threaten their liberal pluralism.[13] They viewed these two positions as incompatible, and so they determined to stifle and control evangelicals.

Ironically, Hutcheson's conclusion, although for different reasons, echoed that of J. Gresham Machen in his classic *Christianity and Liberalism*. Machen concluded that liberal theology was not orthodox Christianity, and the two could not remain in the same communion.[14]

Note that this sustained hostility and abuse of power deliberately directed toward evangelicals in the Presbyterian Church, US, the UPCUSA, and—following the merger of these two—the Presbyterian Church (USA), led to a series of departures by individual evangelicals and evangelical congregations in subsequent years. As a consequence, the combined denomination lost about 60 percent of its membership during a fifty-year period. Those who departed were accused of schism, but they were actually the victims of virulent sectarianism and schism, as the record clearly demonstrates.

Basically, the denominational leadership became intolerant of evangelical Presbyterianism. Those who left felt that they had no choice if they wanted to perpetuate a Presbyterianism that honored the authority of the Bible and the Westminster Confession of Faith. Those who sympathized with them, but did not immediately leave, remained behind in an effort to reform from within. As time passed, more and more of the evangelical Presbyterians who remained in the denomination became convinced that, in good conscience, they could no longer do so.

Congregational and denominational sectarianism seldom take catholicity and unity seriously. Yet "catholicity means that the Church is Christ's. We cannot exclude those whom he welcomes or welcome those whom he excludes."[15] One's position always has a rationale. For liberals, it is to maintain control so that they can assure

13. Ibid., 138.
14. J. Gresham Machen, *Christianity and Liberalism* (New York: Macmillan, 1923), 6–7.
15. Clowney, *The Church*, 97.

the implementation of their agenda. For evangelicals, it is typically a biblical reason, no matter how minor the issue may be, and that rationale is argued passionately at the expense of unity. The ecclesiastical landscape, strewn with such wreckage, is a formidable reminder that the unity of the church—even as a doctrine—has been relegated to minor status. It is difficult to find any party without guilt.

Schism

When is separation or division to be judged schismatic? What is schism? Essentially, schism is a separation from the organized church without just cause. This is different from sectarianism as described above or from heresy, which is doctrinal deviation from the fundamental truths taught in God's Word.[16] Jeremiah Burroughs equated schism with "an uncharitable, unjust, rash, violent breaking from union with the church or members of it."[17]

Burroughs's definition is true but rather strong, and it exceeds the idea of "without just cause." When the bond between believers or congregations is ruptured without heresy as the principal cause for the separation, schism is the typical outcome. While any separation is serious and usually traumatic, schism is sinful behavior. If there are differences of opinion that lead believers to agree to go in different directions, but with mutual regard and affection, that is not schism. Calvin, referring to Augustine, said, "Heretics corrupt the sincerity of the faith with false dogmas; but schismatics, while sometimes even of the same faith, break the bond of fellowship."[18]

Calvin took a severe attitude toward schism. He did not hesitate to assert that "Those who disrupt the body of Christ and split its unity into schisms are quite excluded from the hope of salvation, so

16. Justin S. Holcomb, "Why You Shouldn't Call That False Teaching a Heresy," *Christianity Today* (October 6, 2015), http://www.christianitytoday.com/ct/2015/october/truth-about-heresy.html. See also Jeremiah Burroughs, *Irenicum to the lovers of truth and peace: heart-divisions opened in the causes and evils of them. . . .* (Morgon, PA: Soli Deo Gloria Ministries, 2003).

17. See also James Durham, *Concerning Scandal*, ed. Christopher Coldwell (Dallas: Naphtali Press, 1990).

18. Calvin, *Institutes*, 4.2.5.

long as they remain in dissidence of this kind."[19] As far as he was concerned, notwithstanding the trauma and conflict of the Reformation, schism was repugnant. Believers should do everything possible to avoid it, including acquiescing on doctrinal matters as long as the doctrine on which the church is founded would still be held with integrity. As he wrote in the *Institutes*,

> For God values so highly the fellowship of His church that he holds as a traitor and an apostate from Christianity a man who separates himself from any Christian company in which the ministry of his Word and of his sacraments is to be found. . . . It follows that whoever secedes from the church denies God and Jesus Christ. We must all the more therefore keep ourselves from the enormity of such a breach.
>
> Does this not sufficiently indicate that a difference of opinion over these nonessential matters should in no wise be the basis of schism among Christians? . . . But I say we must not thoughtlessly forsake the church because of our petty dissensions.[20]

Calvin had lots of company in this belief, including the Puritans. Burroughs, for example, condemned the divisions of his era as against the command of Christ and the very character of Christianity. He ironically warned that "we are divided notwithstanding we are all convinced of the evil of our divisions." Burroughs advocated that Christians should at the very least agree to be of one heart even if they could not be of one mind, reminding his contemporaries that as long as we live in this muddy world, there will continue to be divisions even among the godly.

Schism is usually identified with those who separate from an ecclesiastical body without adequate justification. There are shameful examples of schism that evangelicals must learn from so that they will not repeat them. John Frame has pointed out several of

19. Reid, *Calvin: Theological Treatises*, 256.
20. Calvin, *Institutes*, 4.1.10, 12.

these within twentieth century Presbyterianism. One was a controversy about the "incomprehensibility of God" that pitted followers of the highly regarded scholar Gordon Clark against followers of Westminster Seminary professor Cornelius Van Til in the early days of the Orthodox Presbyterian Church (OPC). The presenting issue was a disagreement on the relationship of God's thoughts to man's thoughts. Although Clark's ordination was not revoked, the nature of the controversy was such that Clark and many of his supporters decided to leave the new denomination.[21] A related factor was the decision of the OPC not to support prominent missionary Floyd Hamilton's return to Korea—because he had supported Clark. Most of those who decided to leave had become disenchanted with the developing identity of the new denomination and its unwillingness to cooperate with other conservative Christian organizations.[22]

Machen, a noted Princeton scholar and founder of Westminster Theological Seminary, ironically thought that he had founded a "true Presbyterian Church" that would be a beacon of truth and significant influence for defending the Christian faith against unbelief. He did not intend to spawn a host of contentious, fractious followers. Members of this new denomination stood firmly against liberal theology, expecting to find acceptance and fellowship with one another as they sought to build a better future for Presbyterianism. But they were soon rattled by one crisis after another. The signs of imminent division were already apparent by the time of Machen's death in early 1937, but who would have guessed the disappointments and troubles that lay ahead?

Frame has described the steady stream of contentious ministers and professors that followed as Machen's "warrior children." Frame concludes that these warriors were theological battlers who—when one battle was over—soon found another, whether justified or not, so that theological battles about one issue or another have continued to the present and often resulted in separation. One division

21. John Frame, "Machen's Warrior Children," Frame-Poythress.org, June 6, 2012, http://frame poythress.org/machens-warrior-children/.

22. D. G. Hart and John Muether, *Fighting the Good Fight: A Brief History of the Orthodox Presbyterian Church* (Philadelphia: Orthodox Presbyterian Church, 1995), 105–19.

was caused by criticism regarding dispensational millennialism. Another was over abstinence from alcoholic beverages. Then another had to do with charismatic gifts. Conflict and division seemed incessant.[23]

But sometimes churches or denominations that remove ministers or congregations are clearly themselves schismatic. The decision of the Presbyterian Church (USA) to suspend Machen for his role in establishing the Independent Board for Presbyterian Foreign Missions is a well-known example. Having fought a multi-year battle against liberal theology in the Presbyterian Church and at Princeton Theological Seminary, Machen was dismayed when the board of Princeton was reorganized and two ministers who had signed the Auburn Affirmation were elected.

Machen's rationale for establishing the Independent Board was to ensure that everyone who was appointed as a Presbyterian missionary was committed to evangelizing unbelievers, not merely doing good works. The Presbytery of New Brunswick said that this was unconstitutional and illegal, regardless of his concern about evangelism on the mission field. They interpreted his action as an attack on the denomination's Board of Foreign Missions. Refusing to transfer him to another presbytery as requested, they suspended him.

Some of Machen's conservative colleagues were concerned about this new development, caused by establishing the Independent Board for Presbyterian Foreign Missions. It was one issue too many. Several resigned from the board of Westminster as a result. Machen taking the lead in founding Westminster Theological Seminary after the denomination reorganized Princeton Theological Seminary affected how his actions were viewed by denominational leaders who opposed him. His personality undoubtedly alienated important Presbyterian leaders and contributed to the actions taken against him.[24]

Machen justified his decision to found the Independent Board of Foreign Missions by saying that he was only attempting to defend historic Presbyterian beliefs and practices as required by his ordination

23. Frame, "Machen's Warrior Children."

24. Marsden, *Understanding Fundamentalism*, 186.

vows. But obedience to the denomination—not to the Bible or its historic confession—was the issue for the Presbyterian church that suspended him. Machen was genuinely orthodox and enthusiastically embraced historic Presbyterian theology; that was never in question. However, obedience to their denomination was of greater concern to them than his conscientious support of an evangelical agency to support foreign missionaries. Ironically, at his death H. L. Mencken, the highly influential journalist, observed that

> It is one thing to reject religion altogether, and quite another to save it by pumping out of it all its essential substance, leaving it in the equivocal position of a sort of pseudo-science, comparable to graphology, "education," or osteopathy.
>
> Now it seems to me that is what the Modernists have done, no doubt with the best intentions in the world. They have tried to get rid of all the logical difficulties of religion and yet preserve a generally pious cast of mind. It is a vain enterprise. What they have left, when they have achieved their imprudent scavenging is hardly more than a row of hollow platitudes. . . . They may be good people and they may even be contented and happy, but they are no more religious than Dr. Einstein. . . . Dr. Machen tried to impress that obvious fact upon his fellow adherents of the Geneva Mohammed. He failed but he was obviously right.[25]

The Kenyon Case of 1975 is another example. Wynn Kenyon, a seminary graduate ordained by Pittsburgh Presbytery, declared his unwillingness to participate in the ordination of women as pastors because he did not believe that women should be ordained. He also said, however, that he would not oppose the ordination of a woman and indicated his willingness to serve compatibly on the same staff with a woman once she was ordained.

For this, his ordination was contested. The Permanent Judicial Committee of the UPCUSA overturned it because they judged that

25. H. L. Mencken, "Dr. Fundamentalis," *Baltimore Evening Sun*, January 18, 1937.

the ordination of women had become an explicit constitutional provision. Because Kenyon's position conflicted with the constitution, he was now unacceptable for service as a minister in the denomination, although he heartily embraced their confessional standards and the authority of Scripture.

Consider that this same denomination received or defended ministers who denied basic biblical truths and major doctrines of the Westminster Confession of Faith that they had vowed to believe and uphold. This action mirrored the way the denomination responded to those who signed the Auburn Affirmation. Clearly the real problem was Kenyon's unwillingness to accept the new position adopted by the denomination because he was convinced that the Bible taught otherwise.

A contrasting example to Wynn Kenyon is that of Mansfield Kaseman of the National Capitol Union Presbytery of the UPCUSA. In 1971 he denied the deity of Christ and his sinlessness, the vicarious atonement, and the bodily resurrection. Kaseman was nonetheless approved and received by that presbytery. That action, following six trials that further clarified Kaseman's position, was upheld by the Permanent Judicial Commission of the denomination in 1981. Kaseman became a minister in good standing in spite of his theological heresy.

Similarly, on March 4, 2012 John Shuck of Holston Presbytery, PC(USA), preached that the Bible is merely the product of human authors. He did not find it to be believable, adding: "I don't preach on it as if it is a book to believe."[26] On an earlier occasion, he said that he did not believe that Jesus rose from the dead or that any supernatural events occurred during his ministry. Nonetheless, Shuck remained in good standing with his presbytery and denomination.[27]

Reviewing these examples, it is apparent that when evangelical pastors have been deposed or pushed out of their denomination for attempting to maintain biblical positions or defend the faith

26. Parker T. Williamson, "Unbelief Unveiled," *The Layman*, April 2, 2012, http://www.layman.org/newsddc5/.

27. Ibid.

as it had been practiced, the actions of the PC(USA) that removed them was schismatic, rather than the action of pastors who held to biblical truth. The denominational leaders who had them removed or created circumstances that forced them to leave have repeatedly attempted to label those who were pushed out or left as "schismatics." But that is a matter of the pot calling the kettle black. Given the PC(USA)'s policy of mutual forbearance for the purpose of maintaining unity regardless of doctrinal and other differences, these actions just don't fit.

Sometimes divisions in the church and among Christians are warranted. Calvin disagreed sharply with those who claimed that any withdrawal broke the unity of the church and was schism.[28] As far as he was concerned, such accusations were like the wolves complaining about the lambs.[29] He cited the example of Ahab accusing Elijah of troubling Israel when Ahab was the one who had disregarded God's commandments and followed Baal (1 Kings 18:16–19).[30] "Is it not monstrous, I ask, that it should seem a slight and venial offense to violate the holy law of God, and that it should be judged an expiable crime to transgress the decrees of men?"[31] Calvin adamantly opposed those who attempted to claim the high moral ground regarding separation from Rome.

When Calvin found it necessary to separate from the Roman Catholic Church, he justified his decision by saying,

> Now this communion is held together by two bonds, agreement in sound doctrine and brotherly love. . . . But it must also be noted that this conjunction of love so depends on the unity of faith that it ought to be its beginning, its end, and in fine, its sole rule. . . . [Paul] means that apart from the Lord's Word there is not an agreement of believers but a faction of wicked men.[32]

28. John Calvin, *The Necessity of Reforming the Church* (Dallas: Protestant Heritage Press, 1995), 124–26.
29. Ibid., 88.
30. Ibid., 88, 89.
31. Ibid., 80.
32. Calvin, *Institutes*, 4.2.5.

Given those facts, it was clear to him that because there was no unity in the faith, there was no justifiable reason to continue united as one organizationally.

> As soon as falsehood breaks into the citadel of religion, and the sum of necessary doctrine is overturned, and the use of the sacraments is destroyed, surely the death of the church follows—just as a man's life is ended when his throat is pierced, or his heart mortally wounded.[33]

Consequences of Separation

When divisions happened because of fundamental disagreements and substantial error or abuse during the Fundamentalist-Modernist Controversy in the early part of the twentieth century, the consequent bruises and scars engendered a lingering, suspicious spirit among Fundamentalists and evangelicals. They remained on guard to protect against a repetition of the huge losses they experienced. They soon became conscious that constant, resolute vigilance was required or the work of a lifetime could vanish. While many of them were compelled to separate from unbelief, the consequences of doing so were more painful and enduring than they had expected. They also lost their identity with major institutions that shaped the culture. Had they clearly understood those consequences in advance, they might have proceeded differently.

Although their intentions were for the good of the church and the glory of God, many of the conflicts regarding the gospel and biblical truths damaged other facets of the church. Scriptural doctrines may have been successfully protected, but frequently at the cost of deep, permanent scars, impairing ministries in many instances. Those damaged parts, moreover, sometimes assumed a new and different doctrinal importance. Consequently, it can be argued that evangelicals, like veterans of fierce military conflict, were transformed far more than they realized by their ecclesiastical conflicts during the early twentieth century.

33. Ibid., 4.2.1.

Evangelicals frequently disagreed among themselves on how to deal with those who held untenable beliefs. They agreed that it was a serious problem. But not everyone agreed that separation was the correct solution or that the time for separation had arrived. As a result, it was not unusual for pastors or congregations that were united against doctrinal error to find themselves disagreeing with one another about whether separation was required.

Following a church split, one unwholesome solution adopted by some factions was double separation: the separation by evangelicals from other evangelicals who would not agree to separate from their denominations with whom there was profound doctrinal disagreement. For example, if an evangelical left a denomination and practiced double separation, he would no longer have fellowship with another evangelical who was unwilling to leave the same denomination. That practice led many to turn against their fellow evangelicals, viewing them as traitors. Former friends and colleagues became the new opposition. Misunderstandings and hurt often led to ugly attitudes and behavior. A critical, judgmental spirit accompanied by withering criticism frequently characterized the parties involved, particularly those who left a denomination.[34] In some instances they cut themselves off from or alienated friends who did not join them in their decisions to separate, leaving ugly, lasting scars.

In such circumstances, suspicion could flare up quickly into additional full-blown controversies with charges and countercharges, as was the case with a different but related issue: the Evangelicals and Catholics Together statement of 1994. What had been intended as an effort for honest, constructive dialogue between Catholics and evangelicals backfired on the conveners. Evangelicals who participated in the discussions and statement came under heavy criticism from other evangelicals, resulting in lasting estrangement and further division in their community.

Reflecting on the bitterness that could come from bad behavior related to divisions, Francis Schaeffer wrote:

34. Schaeffer, *Watching World*, 76–79.

> Invariably it is lack of love—and the bitter things that are said by true Christians in the midst of differences. These stick in the mind like glue. And after time passes and the differences between the Christians or the groups appear less than they did, there are still those bitter, bitter things we said in the midst of what we thought was a good and objective discussion. It is these things—these unloving attitudes and words—that cause the stench that the world can smell in the church of Jesus Christ among those who are really true Christians.[35]

The more one becomes conscious of these historic splits or divisions in churches and denominations, the more worrisome it becomes. Sometimes it seems harsh disagreements and division are inevitable. That is not necessarily so, and perhaps conflict is not as widespread as some have judged, as Mark Noll has thoughtfully observed:

> Evangelicals, in point of historical fact, may never have been as fractious, fissiparous, and sectarian as is commonly thought. To be sure leaders of evangelical groups have indulged in their fair share of back-stabbing, power-mongering, petty minded polemicizing, gratuitous boundary-marking and schismatic devilment. Although I am convinced that lay evangelicals have done better than leaders in preserving the unity of the Body of Christ, there is enough fragmentation in the evangelical world to go around for all.[36]

There is good reason for evangelicals to be vigilant, especially given the many historical examples of doctrinal declension and apostasy. But there is no justification for a mean-spirited, carping criticism of fellow believers with whom you disagree. Unless evangelicals find more constructive ways to deal with disagreements among themselves the damage will be great, impairing any efforts to present themselves

35. Schaeffer, *Mark of the Christian*, 22.

36. Mark Noll, *American Evangelical Christianity: An Introduction* (Oxford: Blackwell, 2001), 272.

more attractively to the broader public. It will also handicap their growth efforts. This is undoubtedly why Paul warned that "if you keep on biting and devouring each other, watch out or you will be destroyed by each other" (Gal. 5:15). As Edmund Clowney so accurately put it, "The sectarian spirit that Paul decried at Corinth . . . has shattered the unity of Christ's body throughout the history of the church."[37] Too frequently, Christians have mastered majoring in the minors to the irreparable harm of the communion of saints. I must admit that I have been surprised and hurt by experiences of this nature. In my younger years, to my regret, I too was guilty of making wrong judgments of others and allowing the judgments to affect my attitude and relationships with them.

It is worth heeding Professor John Murray, who eloquently stated the long overdue need to address our divisions and disunity:

> It is to be admitted that the fragmentation and lack of coordination and solidarity which we find within strictly evangelical and Reformed Churches create a difficult situation, and how this disunity is to be remedied "in the unity of the Spirit and the bond of peace" is a task not easily accomplished. But what needs to be indicated, and indicated with vehemence, is the complacency so widespread and the failure to be aware that this is an evil, dishonoring to Christ, destructive of the edification defined by the apostles as "the increase of the body into the building up of itself in love" (Eph. 4:16), and prejudicial to the evangelistic outreach to the world. If we are once convinced of this evil, the evil of schism in the body of Christ, the evil of disruption in the communion of saints, then we have made great progress. We shall then be constrained to preach the evil, to bring conviction to the hearts of others also, to implore God's grace and wisdom in remedying the evil, and to devise ways and means of healing these ruptures, to the promotion of united witness to the faith of Jesus and the whole counsel of God.[38]

37. Clowney, *Church*, 81.

38. John Murray, *The Collected Writings of John Murray: Professor of Systematic Theology,*

The Ecumenical Movement

Typically, most efforts to merge or unify various churches or denominations have been identified with Ecumenism, or what is referred to as the Ecumenical Movement. This movement envisioned the formation of one great new church and intended to overcome all divisiveness and sectarianism once all existing denominations were eventually folded into it. More than projecting merely a vibrant pluralism, ecumenism envisions the achievement of one church.

One early proponent who wielded great influence in creating a vision for and shaping the movement was the leading missionary statesman of that time, John R. Mott. He presided over the 1910 Edinburgh Missionary Conference that initiated the modern ecumenical movement, as well as the modern missions movement and became unofficially known as "the father of the ecumenical movement."[39] As the leader of both the Student Volunteer Movement for Foreign Missions and the World Student Christian Federation, Mott developed a concern for unity among Christians in order to evangelize the world in his generation. He devoted more of his time and energy to the ecumenical effort, playing a major role in founding the World Council of Churches (WCC). In recognition of his monumental achievement, he was awarded the Nobel Peace Prize in 1946.

Presented as an effort to achieve the highly desirable unity of all Christians to evangelize the world, the movement's driving factor became organic or organizational unity rather than unity of faith or doctrine—although the latter received ample attention. The Ecumenical Movement became identified with the mainline denominations and a theological agenda that minimized biblical and theological concerns in favor of a social, political agenda.

For most of the twentieth century, these organizations were identified with causes that most evangelicals considered wrongheaded.

Westminster Theological Seminary, Philadelphia, Pennsylvania, 1937–1966 (Edinburgh: Banner of Truth Trust, 1977), 2:335.

39. Mark Galli, "Missions and Ecumenism: John R. Mott," *Christian History*, no. 65, accessed November 3, 2016, https://www.christianhistoryinstitute.org/magazine/article/missions-and-ecumenism-mott/.

Founded to bring Christians together, the WCC and the National Council of Churches (NCC) invested huge amounts of time and energy in largely unsuccessful efforts. The meeting of the WCC in 1954 presented a report on "Our Oneness in Christ and Our Disunity as Churches." Beginning in 1975, the emphasis was on visible unity. That emphasis was not directed toward causes that were appealing to evangelicals, and it did not carry the day with most other denominations.

Perhaps the most disappointing aspect of the WCC has been its emphasis on social and political issues to such a degree that Paul Ramsey, noted Princeton professor, flagged its activities as "the worst intrusion of churchmen into political affairs since the Middle Ages."[40] Ernest Lefever, who carefully attended its assemblies and followed its activities, concluded that the WCC

> is influential in perverse ways, primarily as a continuing source of confusion and as an active supporter of revolutionary elites, both religious and secular. Many WCC Leaders participate in international conferences and movements committed to revolutionary and violent change. They are active in a network of radical academics, scientists, journalists, and politicians that provides ideas, training, and money for 'liberation' efforts driven by Marxist-Leninist fervor and frequently supported by the Soviet Union.[41]

Emerging from the influence of the WCC and its counterpart the NCC, the Consultation on Church Union (COCU) was proposed by Eugene Carson Blake in 1960 when he preached at Grace Cathedral in San Francisco at the invitation of Bishop James Pike. During his sermon, Blake advocated forming a Protestant "superchurch."[42]

40. Paul Ramsey, *Who Speaks for the Church? A Critique of the 1966 Geneva Conference on Church and Society* (Nashville: Abingdon, 1967), 25.

41. Ernest W. Lefever, *Nairobi to Vancouver: The World Council of Churches and the World, 1975–87* (Washington, DC: Ethics and Public Policy Center, 1987), 86.

42. "Ecumenism: From Handholding to Engagement," *TIME Magazine*, May 13, 1966, accessed December 10, 2016, http://content.time.com/time/magazine/article/0,9171,835526,00.html.

Subsequently, COCU was formed in 1962 with high aspirations but eventually failed to achieve the desired union that Blake had proposed. Ten denominations entered the discussions to achieve "A Plan of Union" but never made it. Eventually COCU died and in 2002 was reconstituted as Churches Uniting in Christ (CUIC). The emphasis of the succeeding organization is directed to addressing various forms of exclusion and prejudice.

As the twentieth century drew to a close, the ecumenical impulse had weakened considerably and, in the opinion of many, had reached a crisis point that threatened its future. One ecumenical proponent concluded,

> There is a palpable decrease of common interest in ecumenical themes, events, and publications. The underlying loss in ecumenical motivation is connected with a disdain for the ecumenical achievement and an uncertainty of ecumenical orientation.[43]

Essentially, the Ecumenical Movement—as originally conceived and pursued—is dead.

Presbyterian Mergers

Meanwhile, Presbyterians and other denominations successfully completed several mergers during the twentieth century, but the overall effect of these mergers has been discouraging. Research indicates that most mergers resulted in declining membership. An example is the Evangelical Lutheran Church, formed by a merger of three denominations in 1988. Since the merger, membership has declined from 5.2 million to 3.75 million members. Organizational culture differences, combined with a failure to understand them and make appropriate adjustments, were undoubtedly a factor in most situations. Loss of identity and theological declension also influenced the erosion of membership.

43. Harding Meyer, *That All May Be One: Perceptions and Models of Ecumenity* (Grand Rapids: Eerdmans, 1999), 151.

One might have expected different results for Presbyterians. In the late 1950s, twice as many people wanted to become Presbyterian as were already members. Numbering about 4.5 million, Presbyterians might have expected membership to grow to nine or ten million members if they took advantage of the golden opportunity before them. However, this high tide of popularity was soon squandered by the liberal establishment. The pursuit of massive mergers—such as COCU—did not resonate well, and the aggressive advocacy of a left-wing, social-political agenda among historically conservative Presbyterians generated vigorous pushback. Nonetheless, the increased influence of a well-organized bureaucracy that minimized faith and doctrine in favor of a social-political agenda was able to force its agenda on the whole church. This demoralized and numerically diminished evangelicals who were part of the UPCUSA and the Presbyterian Church, US (PCUS).

The result of these ecumenical ventures was a steady defection of church members and pastors, who found the new, broadening emphasis intolerable to their evangelical commitments. The PC(USA) was formed as part of this determined effort to unite all Presbyterians with all Protestants. This merged entity lost about 60 percent of its membership in fifty years, eventually plummeting to 1.7 million by the end of 2014. According to a recent report from the PC(USA) General Assembly office, membership was projected to decline another four hundred thousand by 2020, leaving less than 1.3 million members—many of them in very small churches.[44] Some members joined new evangelical Presbyterian denominations such as the Presbyterian Church in America (PCA), the Evangelical Presbyterian Church (EPC), and the Evangelical Covenant Order of Presbyterians (ECO), but many of them walked away completely disillusioned, never intending to be Presbyterian again. It is likely that many of them became part of other evangelical denominations or independent evangelical congregations.

Regardless, it is a sad story of the dramatic decline of a once-great Presbyterianism, caused by stubborn leaders of a liberal bent

44. Michael Gryboski, "Megachurches Have Less Involved Members than Smaller Churches, Study Finds," *Christian Post*, February 8, 2016.

who were determined to force everyone into their mold, regardless of the consequences. It was at best a form of sectarianism—and in some instances forced schism—that stifled the gospel and prevented Presbyterian evangelicals from flourishing as they had historically.

One exception was the merger of the PCA with the Reformed Presbyterian Church, Evangelical Synod (RPC, ES) in 1983. The action was referred to by the two denominations as "joining and receiving" rather than a merger. By doing so, they avoided the usual merger process. Interestingly, the OPC was also invited to participate but declined to do so. Once united, the two denominations seemed to fit well together with no apparent friction.[45] The PCA grew steadily afterward with no discernible ill effects from the union and has become the second largest Presbyterian denomination in the United States.

Two other evangelical Presbyterian denominations came into existence after 1980 because of theological declension and conflict within the PC(USA). The EPC was established in 1983, and the ECO was formed in 2012. The EPC membership has grown to more than six hundred congregations in recent years, primarily because of an influx of former PC(USA) congregations. That rapid growth from a single source is quite similar to a merger.

The influx of congregations does not appear to have caused the EPC any internal issues of marked significance. To the contrary—both denominations appear to be healthy, with a high level of cohesiveness and vision. The ECO continues to grow and as of 2016 appears to have the strongest appeal to large congregations leaving the PC(USA). Most congregations leaving the PC(USA) now will probably unite with ECO. Inevitably, the questions that arise in conversations about these two denominations are:

What is the biggest difference? Are they significantly different regarding the ordination of women and confessional standards? Will the EPC and ECO be inclined to join together as one denomination after a period of time, following the large number of departures from the PC(USA) to these two denominations? If so, will they find an easy way to combine forces as the PCA and the RPC, as ES did?

45. Lucas, *Continuing Church*, 236, 237.

If they are so inclined, what is the best way for these two evangelical Presbyterian denominations to move into a closer relationship and eventually merge into one? If they were to accomplish that, they would approximate the size of the PCA.

What will their relationship be to the PCA? Will the PCA reach out to other evangelical Presbyterian denominations and attempt to forge a closer relationship? Will they be able to cooperate and strengthen one another, or will their differences be magnified?

All three denominations represent the evangelical heritage of the two major Presbyterian denominations in the United States that became the PC(USA), and they are approaching the three-quarter million mark in total combined membership. Two smaller ones, the OPC and the Associate Reformed Presbyterian Church, have older histories and appear happy to continue as they are, but that could change too.

Currently several of these denominations, as well as others, are members of the North American Presbyterian and Reformed Council (NAPARC) formed in 1974 with the ultimate goal of union into one church. The initial meeting was held in 1975. Since then the six denominations have increased to thirteen. The important question is: What difference has NAPARC actually made? Should these evangelical Presbyterian and Reformed denominations pursue a different future in their relationships to one another? Is there adequate justification for a continued separate existence? Should all the NAPARC denominations pursue closer relationships outside their NAPARC connections?

Another evangelical merger that turned out well was the 1950 merger of the Swedish Evangelical Free Church and the Norwegian-Danish Free Church to form the Evangelical Free Church. It has grown from an initial number of less than three hundred churches and twenty thousand members to about fifteen hundred churches with a weekly attendance of almost four hundred thousand.

Evangelical Reactions

Although there have been a few evangelical merger efforts, such as these, that turned out well, the result of separation among liberal mainline denominations has generally left a bad taste in their mouths. Consequently, most evangelicals tend to react negatively to all ecumenical overtures because, in addition to viewing them as a waste of time, they fear that it would lead to a compromise of their treasured doctrinal commitments. If compromise occurred, the essence of the historic Christian faith for which they have sacrificed so much would be jeopardized. That biblical message, a pattern of sound words, is their reason for existence, so they cannot afford to lose it. Rather, they prize and protect it at all costs.

The undeniable fact is that the liberal theological agenda, including its rejection of biblical authority and its social-political emphases, is so loathsome to evangelicals that they reject it outright. They would resonate with H. Richard Niebuhr's description of liberal theology: "A God without wrath brought men without sin into a kingdom without judgment through the ministrations of a Christ without a cross."[46]

For evangelicals, that kind of theological position is a denial of the gospel and all that unites them to God and one another. They are appalled when they reflect on the damage that has been done to historic Christianity by the ascendancy of church leaders who reject all the central Christian doctrines after gaining power and then become cruelly intolerant of those who espouse biblical orthodoxy. Cooperating with them is deemed equivalent to inviting a fox into the henhouse. Liberal church leaders often return the favor.

But in rejecting liberal social concern, evangelicals often made a tragic mistake and, to make matters worse, they did it for the wrong reasons. They allowed the practices of those churches and ideologues, rather than the Bible, to determine their agenda and priorities. Their mistake was actually similar to the one they condemned. They faulted the social gospel advocates for abandoning the gospel and failing to evangelize. Yet in the early twentieth century they

46. H. Richard Niebuhr, *The Kingdom of God in America* (New York: Harper & Row, 1959), 193.

abandoned their own former ministries of compassion and mercy because they abhorred the Social Gospel movement and didn't want to be associated with what liberals were doing.

Although they failed to realize it at the time, in their immediate context they had become more influenced by those they opposed than by the Bible. Ironically, although they emphasized the authority of the Bible and its message of salvation, they failed to be governed by it as they determined their contrasting agenda. Concern for the truth is legitimate, but there is another side to this polarization that must not be ignored.

When liberal denominations set an agenda or took a position on a social issue, evangelicals were often immediately against it just because it was a liberal position. They should have been asking what the Bible taught about that issue and what God wanted them to do, letting those answers determine their future. Instead, by focusing on their vigorous disagreement with the liberal agenda, they were distracted from their true calling to biblical fidelity. Unfortunately, they became blind to their own mistakes and losses. Too busy pointing a finger at those they opposed and resented, they wandered from their calling without even realizing what had happened to them.

What evangelicals were supposed to be *for* should have been more important than opposing what they were *against*. They could have rejected the mainline ideology and agenda without allowing it to determine their future decisions and ministry priorities, but they couldn't see this at the time. Their mistake stands as a lesson for our future decisions. Referred to as Fundamentalists, they were separationists and anti-liberal. Some were definitely "Fighting Fundamentalists." However, not everyone who was labeled a Fundamentalist thought and behaved that way. Eventually the conflict led to a parting of ways as many Fundamentalists—or "evangelicals," as many of them would later be called—found it necessary to separate from their historic and greatly loved denominations for the honor of Christ and the gospel. Other evangelicals did not separate, although they remained orthodox theologically.

Evangelical Ecumenism

While lauding the good things accomplished by the Reformers and the many benefits of the Reformation enjoyed by Protestants—especially evangelicals—the unintended legacy of a divided Protestantism became a tragic failure that the church has lived with ever since. That is history. We can't change it, but we should learn from it and attempt to improve on it. The same can be said of the Fundamentalist-Modernist Controversy and the rise of new Fundamentalist and evangelical denominations in the twentieth century.

Carl Henry tried to persuade evangelicals to rethink this issue when he wrote *The Uneasy Conscience of Modern Fundamentalism*, published in 1947. Thanks to his bold effort, the tide began to turn on a few issues, but the general trend of doing the opposite of the mainline agenda continued. It is too easy to think about what might have been, had evangelicals capitalized on the opportunities that God provided and not been so reactionary. One thing we should learn is that past failures do not and should not justify the divisions that we live with now.

Henry encouraged evangelicals not to be separatists or legalistic. His influence, along with others like Harold J. Ockenga, led to the formation of the NAE in 1942, which was a major turning point. Ockenga, NAE's first president, insisted that evangelicals seek unity and abandon the isolation and negativism that had been such an impediment following the Fundamentalist-Modernist Controversy. He advocated working with evangelicals in the mainline denominations as well as evangelical organizations and denominations. "It is folly to speak of the union of the true Church and then declare that those who profess to believe in the doctrines of the true Church can never work in unity."[47]

The National Conference for United Action Among Evangelicals convened in St. Louis, and it was an ambitious effort to end factionalism through founding the NAE. In a move that shocked

47. Timothy George and John D. Woodbridge, *The Mark of Jesus: Loving in a Way the World Can See* (Chicago: Moody Publishers, 2005), 136–37.

Fundamentalists, J. Elwin Wright and Ockenga as co-conveners invited Pentecostals, Anabaptists, Holiness, and other Christian denominations to attend, many of whom did. At that historic meeting, speakers stressed the need for unity and love among different evangelical Protestant traditions—for the sake of the gospel and the world.

The founding of the NAE held great symbolic and institutional significance, since it offered an alternative national organization to the Fundamentalists' separatist American Council of Christian Churches (ACCC), formed one year earlier by arch-Fundamentalist Carl MacIntire.[48] The NAE leaders intended to rebuild and unite the evangelical Protestantism that had crumbled and split into acrimonious, resentful factions earlier in the century. Rather than continue to be identified with reactionary separatists, they wanted to proactively engage with one another in a way that was "intellectually respectable, culturally engaged and socially responsible."[49] Through this initial meeting that created a distinct, publicly recognizable, collective identity, they essentially began restructuring the American religious identity.[50] In doing so, they also laid the foundation of what would become a new evangelical ecumenism. As a result, the NAE grew exponentially in subsequent years and remains a major organization of influence for evangelicals who seek "Cooperation Without Compromise."

Not every evangelical concurred and enthusiastically joined the movement. Machen's OPC could have linked arms with other evangelicals who admired and respected them. Together, at that opportune moment historically, they might have developed a formidable witness against liberal theology and led a resurgence of evangelical Christianity during an important time in American history. They chose not to do so, however, and consequently remained a relatively insignificant denomination.

48. Christian Smith, *American Evangelicalism: Embattled and Thriving* (Chicago: University of Chicago Press, 1998), 11.

49. Ibid., 11. See also Joel. A. Carpenter, *Revive Us Again: The Reawakening of American Fundamentalism* (New York: Oxford University Press, 1997), 144–50.

50. Ibid., 14, 15. The OPC declined to join. For an explanation, see Hart and Muether, *Good Fight*, 105–19, 135–45.

Youth for Christ burst onto the scene in the post-World War II years, attracting support from a wider base than the NAE. By 1946 it was remarkably successful, growing to about nine hundred rallies and a million constituents, eventually reaching forty-six countries by 1948.[51] Billy Graham became the first full-time evangelist for Youth for Christ. His increasingly significant evangelistic ministry blossomed dramatically in 1949 because of his Los Angeles crusade. It lasted eight weeks and gained national media attention, giving new popularity and credibility to evangelicals. The founding of *Christianity Today* in the 1950s gave additional impetus to what was called "The New Evangelicalism."

From this small beginning and big vision, evangelicalism flourished during the last half of the twentieth century, benefitting from the open system that encouraged the proliferation of congregations, organizations, and networks—a perfect fit for evangelical entrepreneurism. Carl Henry's vision of a vast evangelical alliance that would coordinate a national strategy for education, evangelism, publications, and social-political action had gained ground. As evangelicalism continued to prosper and grow,

> By 2000 what might be called a New Ecumenism was emerging, re-grounded in classic Christianity and drawing together the biblically orthodox from pre-Reformation, Reformation, and post-Reformation traditions. All these efforts point a way to possible closer consolidation and cooperation, uncompromising, uncompromised and within recognized limits, between conservative Christian constituencies.[52]

Beginning in the 1960s, evangelicals grew rapidly while the mainline denominations lost numbers and influence. Monopolistic, hierarchical systems tend to stifle innovation and spiritual flourishing,

51. Carpenter, *Revive Us Again*, 161–76. See also Joel A. Carpenter, "From Fundamentalism to the New Evangelical Coalition," in *Evangelicalism and Modern America*, ed. George Marsden (Grand Rapids: Eerdmans, 1984), 14–15.

52. J. I. Packer and Thomas C. Oden, *One Faith: The Evangelical Consensus* (Downers Grove, IL: InterVarsity Press, 2004), 25.

which is a terrible fit for evangelicals. Bureaucracy also isn't well suited to evangelicals who have flourished in America because they have had freedom to organize and direct their energies and resources to perceived needs. Denominational control, especially in the hands of liberals, handcuffed evangelicals and stymied such flourishing, leaving them utterly frustrated. In response, evangelicals left the mainline denominations in increasing numbers, especially after the social upheaval of the 1960s. As a result, there was a dramatic decrease in the membership of the mainline denominations. By the end of the 1980s, they had become unexpectedly relegated to the sidelines in regard to membership.

But it is important to understand that the decline of the older, more liberal denominations has not meant the decline of Christianity. It has only meant the steady decline in numbers and influence of the mainline denominations; evangelicals flourished during this same time period. The year 1976 became "The Year of the Evangelical" according to *Newsweek*. Unfortunately, liberal denominations seem to have developed a strong animus toward evangelicals—as if evangelicals are to blame for their hemorrhaging membership and declining revenues. Of course, evangelicals have usually returned the favor in their attitude toward liberal denominations.

Meanwhile, rapid proliferation and dynamic diversity became a hallmark of the burgeoning evangelicalism. Robert Wuthnow, in *The Restructuring of American Religion*, emphasized this transdenominational development as the biggest change in Christianity since the Reformation.[53]

The democratizing of American religion from the early nineteenth century made it possible for evangelicals to grow and prosper tremendously. Freedom of choice was essential to fueling that growth. They could support what they believed to be important, and when it flourished, they found fresh motivation in the good results. During the twentieth century, evangelicals continued to group and regroup in response to changing circumstances and opportunities.

53. Robert Wuthnow, *The Restructuring of American Religion: Society and Faith Since World War II* (Princeton: Princeton University Press, 1988).

Evangelical organizations and ministries of all kinds flourished. Through the years evangelicals have identified with and generously supported parachurch ministries; many of them, like Cru and Young Life, are large and influential now. More recently evangelicals have gravitated to church associations like Saddleback and Willow Creek. Numerous evangelical seminaries were established and grew rapidly during the last half of the century to support the growth of evangelicalism. A dynamic network of evangelical ministries with constant ebb and flow was the result; Acts 29, Together for the Gospel, Desiring God, and The Gospel Coalition are notable examples. The NAE remains as a potential umbrella organization to facilitate communication and cooperation among these diverse evangelical organizations.

Although recent congregational growth among evangelicals has been toward independence rather than denominations, those congregations often find ways to identify with the larger evangelical movement through various evangelical networks. Admittedly, Protestant churches appear to be more fragmented than ever, and for the moment, the independent church movement seems to be the wave of the future.

It is important to remember, however, that this loose network of evangelical congregations, organizations, and denominations has much in common. Moreover, it is an informal network that is flexible and responsive to changing circumstances. The potential for greater cooperation is clear from the formation of new networks and associations. Just as voluntary associations offered the opportunity for Christians of the nineteenth century to cooperate in addressing specific needs, so evangelical networks of fellowship and service offer similar opportunities today. A sense of common identity can grow as evangelicals facilitate such efforts, once there is awareness of a significant reason to do so.

In fact, in recent years, the need to cooperate supportively is becoming clearer as evangelicals face new opposition from many directions, including strong secular pressure. The highly partisan secular situation, especially with political issues, exacerbates that need. Recent research indicates that 70 percent of the Christian community would welcome a more constructive, cooperative approach. Millennials add weight to this need for more effective communication and greater cooperation.

This new evangelical ecumenism has occurred without organizational unity or a center of influence. As a matter of fact, a brief survey of history intimates that a push for organizational unity at this time might actually undermine the achievement of less formal expressions of unity in the Holy Spirit. If cooperative efforts are forced and the organizational cultures don't mesh well enough to create cohesiveness, efforts will likely be counterproductive. It is better for any such efforts to be made in well-thought-out steps that give the greatest promise of success. Recent research demonstrates that money and programs will not assure success unless attention is directed to an organization's culture: the way people work together, their values and expectations.[54] It is preferable to enjoy working together and to strengthen relationships that will endure.

Billy Graham, the best known and most admired of American evangelicals, offers a proven model through his vibrant evangelistic ministry of a half century.[55] As much as any one person or organization, he has contributed to a sense of unity among believers. By consensus, Graham—a genuinely good person who has carefully avoided scandal of any kind—attempted to be inclusive with his evangelistic crusades and other outreach efforts. He refused to be identified with the divisive brand of fundamentalism associated with Bob Jones University and other Fundamentalists. Criticism from conservative Christian leaders as well as liberal church leaders became routine, but the masses revered him and supported him generously. No Christian leader had a greater influence in America during the last half of the twentieth century.[56]

Mark Noll astutely observed of Graham that he "brokered his particularly inoffensive way of reminding people that they are sinners

54. Rachel Mosher-Williams, Sarah Brenner, and Amy Celep, "It's Not Foundation Money but Culture and Talent that Can Change the World," *Chronicle of Philanthropy*, February 10, 2016, https://www.philanthropy.com/article/Opinion-It-s-Not-Foundation/235257.

55. Carpenter, *Revive Us Again*, 211–29.

56. Grant Wacker, *America's Pastor: Billy Graham and the Shaping of a Nation* (Cambridge: Belknap Press, 2014) 12–25, 283–11.

in need of grace into one of the most powerful forces for Christian ecumenicity ever seen."[57] Graham's leadership in initiating various evangelical gatherings—such as the Berlin Congress of 1966, the International Congress on World Evangelism in Lausanne in 1974 and in Manila in 1987, The International Conference for Itinerant Evangelists in Amsterdam in 1983, and another Amsterdam conference in 2000—produced "statements of prime and pioneering significance."[58]

Additionally, Noll observes that hymns were another major unifying force for Christians from all denominations. "Amazing Grace" is the most notable example, but "How Great Thou Art," "Jesus Loves Me," "What a Friend We Have in Jesus," and other hymns all served a similar purpose. For many years, hymns were fairly prevalent in movies too. "Nothing so profoundly defined the *lex credendi* of evangelicalism as the *lex cantandi*, what Evangelicals have believed is what we have sung." So that, in Noll's judgment, evangelical hymnody reveals "an unusually broad, unexpected, gracious ecumenicity."[59]

In recent years, evangelical ecumenism has expressed itself in many places through gatherings, organizations, and statements. Oden and Packer think that there is a "shared view of the Bible and the atonement, of faith and life in Christ, and of the church's life and mission" that "hold them tightly together, more tightly than used to be the case when denominational walls were higher."[60] They see a consensus that clearly appears in some of the evangelical pronouncements, such as the Manila Manifesto, which states:

> Our message that Christ reconciles alienated people to each other rings true only if we are seen to love and forgive one another, to serve others in humility, and to reach out beyond our own community in compassionate, costly ministry to the needy.

57. Noll, *American Evangelical Christianity*, 5.
58. Packer and Oden, *One Faith*, 25.
59. Noll, *American Evangelical Christianity*, 268–69.
60. Packer and Oden, *One Faith*, 161.

> Our challenge to others to deny themselves, take up their cross and follow Christ will be plausible only if we ourselves have evidently died to selfish ambition, dishonesty, and covetousness, and are living a life of simplicity, contentment, and generosity."[61]

In stronger language regarding Christian unity, the DuPage Declaration reads:

> We deplore the scandalous isolation and separation of Christians from one another. We believe such division is contrary to Christ's explicit desire for unity among his people and impedes the witness of the church in the world.[62]

The Chicago Call says,

> Therefore we call Evangelicals to return to the ecumenical concern of the Reformers and the later movements of Evangelical renewal. We must humbly and critically scrutinize our respective traditions, renounce sacred shibboleths, and recognize that God works within diverse historical streams. We must resist efforts promoting church union-at-any-cost, but we must also avoid mere spiritualized concepts of church unity. We are convinced that unity in Christ requires visible and concrete expressions. In this belief, we welcome the development of encounter and cooperation within Christ's church. While we seek to avoid doctrinal indifferentism and a false irenicism, we encourage Evangelicals to cultivate increased discussion and cooperation, both within and without their respective traditions, earnestly seeking common areas of agreement and understanding.[63]

Given these observations, it seems appropriate to ask: Shouldn't we find fresh motivation to prioritize the unfulfilled Protestant

61. Ibid., 27.
62. Ibid., 27.
63. Ibid., 115.

mission to achieve greater visible unity in the aftermath of the Reformation? Given the Protestant experience in America, shouldn't we learn to capitalize on our common faith and work closely together to advance the gospel? When organizational unity is unrealistic for the immediate future, shouldn't we find new ways to cooperate and affirm one another as evangelicals so that our sense of unity is perceived publicly? Shouldn't we at least try this within our subgroups?

The apparent answer is that it is preferable to find worthwhile projects on which it is possible to enjoy working together constructively. That is what the voluntary Christian associations did so successfully during the early nineteenth century. They demonstrated a working unity that was directed toward the achievement of goals such as evangelism and education. Organizations were established and supported only as needed to carry out the mission.

But shouldn't it also be a biblical mission to work toward a united evangelical Protestantism to the greatest degree possible? Of course. But pressing for the organic union of evangelical organizations without a mature understanding of the issues involved is foolish—a quick way to do more harm than good. It seems wiser by far to develop good relationships through good communication, cooperation, and building trust. If that is successful, it can lead to even closer relationships that demonstrate a unity in the Holy Spirit.

What should that ecumenical evangelical Protestantism look like? How could the efforts to mutually affirm one another publicly and work together cooperatively become more important than institutional survival or emphasizing doctrinal distinctives? Isn't the greater goal to reach everyone with the gospel and maximize resources constructively for the greatest good?

Is it possible to answer no to these questions and still have a clear conscience before the Lord?

G. C. Berkouwer argued that "the Bible demands a deep concern for the unity of the church, a concern that can hardly be stressed too strongly. And the ecumenical movement has alerted us to this biblical concern."[64]

64. G. C. Berkouwer, "What Conservative Evangelicals Can Learn from the Ecumenical

What constructive steps should now be considered? We will explore that question in the final chapter. We should begin to think of it as building bridges to true Christian community rather than erecting walls of resistance or moats of isolation. Integrity, as we honor the Lord and attempt to be faithful to his call, may sometimes lead us to do the unexpected, but our great goal remains the same: to honor him and advance his work wherever we can.

Movement," *Christianity Today*, May 27, 1966, 18.

5

CHALLENGES AND CONCERNS

The mandate for unity is clear but putting it into practice is another matter.
Charles Colson and Ellen Vaughn[1]

The hard-edged schismatic tendency of the evangelical right is matched by the wooly-minded irenics of the evangelical left.
Gabriel Fackre[2]

To our great loss, the idea of unity in diversity in the Christian community is often talked about as a nice theory, but rarely put into practice.
Marva J. Dawn[3]

Church unity is more than a pragmatic goal; it is a doctrinal imperative.
Kevin J. Vanhoozer[4]

GIVEN THE PLURALISTIC shape of American Christianity, it should be readily apparent that any effort to achieve large-scale organizational unity would be overwhelmingly difficult, if not

1. Charles Colson and Ellen Vaughn, *One Body* (Nashville: W Publishing, 2003), 77.
2. *Pro Ecclesia: a Journal of Catholic and Evangelical Theology*, vol. 6, edited by Joseph L. Mangina (Washington DC: Rowan & Littlefield, 1997), 15.
3. Marva J. Dawn, *Truly the Community: Romans 12 and How to Be the Church* (Grand Rapids: Eerdmans, 1997), 77.
4. Kevin J. Vanhoozer, *The Drama of Doctrine: A Canonical-Linguistic Approach to*

impossible to achieve. If history offers any guidance, the prospect is not encouraging nor are evangelicals prepared to engage constructively. From its inception, Protestantism has moved in the opposite direction, resulting in a continuous multiplication of denominations, organizations, and independent congregations. Most evangelicals show minimal motivation to move toward any kind of organizational unity.

Additionally, the flow of people in recent years has been toward independency, and many of those independent churches have become megachurches with memberships in the thousands. Denominations, especially the mainline denominations, are in a slow decline—some more rapidly. For example, the United Church of Christ (UCC) recently projected an 80 percent decline in membership during the next thirty years. Some evangelical denominations are now struggling to grow, while others are barely maintaining membership levels or losing ground. Meanwhile, efforts to unite small denominations have proved far more daunting than most onlookers might have surmised.

Most of the twentieth century mergers of large mainline denominations failed to produce significant growth or happy operations. Optimistic projections for future growth have been abandoned. Some mergers, as with the PC(USA), have been disastrous failures. Of course, there are various reasons for the discouraging results, but most of the mainline denominations hemorrhaged members during the last half of the twentieth century. Problems such as the clash of organizational cultures or loss of heritage and identity added to the merger woes and concerns about membership retention. At this juncture, there appears to be no compelling success story that would motivate any major denomination to deem merger efforts a necessity or even appealing.

While attempting to achieve greater organizational unity through mergers may be too formidable a challenge for most denominations, greater cooperation—including an acknowledgment of belonging to one catholic or universal church comprised of all believers—is a different matter. Unfortunately, no one can declare enviable progress on this front either. There are realistic alternatives, however, that

Christian Theology (Louisville: Westminster John Knox, 2005), 422.

can lead to greater cooperation and mutual esteem as brothers and sisters in Christ.

Earlier generations embraced a functional catholicity, recognizing a unity in Christ that transcended the diversity of their various ecclesiastical structures and doctrines. Their experience underscores the importance of analyzing the current situation to consider alternatives that could contribute to more hopeful, beneficial results, enabling evangelicals to work together more happily and effectively. So far the most successful efforts have been through parachurch organizations such as Cru (formerly Campus Crusade for Christ), InterVarsity, The Gospel Coalition, World Reformed Fellowship, and NAE. Willow Creek and Saddleback have also built impressive networks that continue to shape evangelicalism, which is notable for the development of such networks for ministry. These networks create a sense of common identity and unity.

When considering the current landscape, it should be apparent that failure to address the matter of unity more forthrightly—especially organizational unity—and neglecting to look for ways to break through the impasses will be a mistake. As a smaller percentage of the population claims to be Christian each year, it becomes that much more important for evangelicals to work together to enable others to see how Christianity contributes to the common good. A great deal is accomplished daily by Christian organizations that have not been concerned to draw public attention. The situation will probably worsen without the development of a more united effort that recognizes the challenges of a culture becoming less and less accommodating to evangelical Christianity.

The current fragmentation of evangelicalism—combined with unwise actions or critical comments, often made to justify continued separation—doesn't give encouragement for the prospect of a healthy, united evangelical and Reformed church. No one seems to be giving it that much attention, yet failure will be costly. Respected figures of the past would remind us how true this is. Bavinck lamented that,

> We cannot be humble enough as Christians about the disruption and the discord that have existed in the Church of Christ through

> all the ages; it is a sin against God, in conflict with the prayer of Christ, and caused by the darkness of our mind and the lack of love in our heart.[5]

Richard Baxter asked, "Has anything in the world done more to lose our authority and disable us for God's service, than our differences and divisions?"[6] Frame adds to the argument by asserting that denominationalism is an offense against God and that it has weakened the church's witness.[7] Carl Henry, while editor of *Christianity Today*, addressed this issue on more than one occasion. In 1962, he wrote about the importance of "Recasting the Ecumenical Posture," saying:

> Evangelical failure to delineate Christianity in a positive way should trouble our conscience and provoke evangelicals to exemplary leadership. If unity based on theological concession is undesirable, disunity alongside theological agreement is inexcusable. Evangelicals suffer from divisive internal competitions. To deplore the theological inclusivism that tries to overcome the fragmentation of Protestantism as a whole without earnestly seeking to overcome the proliferated witness of the evangelical segment is to remain spiritually vulnerable. It is time for evangelicals to find their ecumenical posture, and to set forth the doctrine of biblical unity which will preserve the vitality of the Gospel without compromising the witness of the Church."[8]

Several years later, Henry escalated his concern with a series of six articles on "Evangelicals in Search of Identity." He was disturbed about the self-centered attitudes of various evangelical groups that had resulted in multiple accusations and misunderstandings. They were

5. Bavinck, *Dogmatics*, 47.

6. Richard Baxter, *The Reformed Pastor*, 2nd rev. ed. (London: Epworth Press, 1950), 124.

7. John Frame, *Systematic Theology: An Introduction to Christian Belief* (Phillipsburg, NJ: P&R Publishing, 2013), 1022. For a more detailed analysis of his views on this matter, see also his *Evangelical Reunion: Denominations and the One Body of Christ* (Grand Rapids: Baker Books, 1991).

8. *Christianity Today*, October 26, 1962.

damaging to all involved, and the evangelical movement was sacrificing potentially significant gains as a consequence of the strife. He addressed the problem in his final article, "Vision of a Uniting Task," lamenting that some evangelicals were not on speaking terms with each other, and asking how it could be possible for them to say that they were indispensable to one another when they disowned one another and drifted apart. He concluded with this sharply worded comment:

> While we supposed leaders champion our special interests and assure our followers that the evangelical prospect was never brighter because of what we represent, more and more discerning Christians are asking what has happened to comprehensive, coordinated leadership that stimulates not only evangelical initiative but also evangelical reconciliation. It is time that the evangelical movement sees itself for what it is: a lion on the loose that no one today seriously fears.[9]

Rather than moving closer together, evangelicals have tended to ignore advice like that offered by Carl Henry and go their separate ways, depending on the passions that they pursued or the disagreements that divided them. Expending vast quantities of energy, effort, and other resources, evangelicals became a numerically large force in the latter part of the twentieth century; their rapid growth was seemingly slowed by the aftereffects of the culture wars. Marked by their deep convictions and overwhelming commonalities, they were nonetheless unable to develop institutionally in such a way that they would have the lasting impact on American culture that many of them desired. As Christian Smith observed,

> They have failed to understand how the social world actually works and develop the necessary social structures that would give them the influence in the public square they desired so much.[10]

9. Carl Henry, "Vision of a Uniting Task," *Christianity Today*, October 8, 1976, 40–41.

10. Christian Smith, *American Evangelicalism: Embattled and Thriving* (Chicago: University of Chicago Press, 1998), 202.

Impediments to Unity

Far more was possible—in terms of cooperation and unity among churches and denominations—than has been achieved during the last hundred years, especially by evangelicals. The actual accomplishments are embarrassingly minimal. The biblical case for church unity is compelling. But unless the speed bumps and roadblocks are more carefully examined and viable pathways seriously sought, the landscape will remain unaltered, and insipid excuses will continue to justify the status quo. Some of the impediments will be mentioned below, followed in the next chapter by suggestions for constructive steps to help improve relationships.

Commonalities are impressive, especially among mainline denominations, but also among evangelical ones. But the various heritages, organizational cultures, and disagreements are more than enough to keep them apart. Evangelical churches certainly appear to hold much in common, yet their disparate identities are heightened by seemingly minor differences that typically provide them with ample justification for their continued separate existences. This is particularly true for pastors, church leaders, and academicians. It is less true, however, of church members and seekers who are not well informed about theological or ecclesiastical matters and see little significant difference.[11] Given the relative ease they experience in transitioning to other congregations or denominations when they relocate to another city, labels seem less and less important to the average church member. They are more interested in finding a church where they are comfortable and make friends.

When disagreements persist and tensions heighten in a congregation or denomination, individual members can become restive and inclined to move where they feel more comfortable and are a better fit. Our consumer-oriented society seems to encourage mobility to match personal preferences, reducing any sense that there is a need to unify. It appears that everyone should be able to pursue their dreams separately and thrive. In addition, a high degree of marital and family

11. Putnam and Campbell, *American Grace*, 539–40.

mingling and matching has resulted in a relatively fluid situation for religious affiliation, making almost any change of church membership acceptable to most Americans. If it is true that denominational affiliations are declining in importance for most laity, you would expect it to foster openness toward greater unity and stability. However, it should be noted that while that seems to be true for laity, it is not for the clergy, who are much more attuned to theology, polity, and power issues.

Here is the sobering thought that must not be avoided: If the unity of the church is as important as the Bible says it is, aren't we are obligated to attempt to surmount all impediments to its achievement to the greatest degree possible? If we are unwilling to do this, shouldn't we honestly admit that the goal of Christian unity is relatively unimportant to us?

An unwillingness to seriously acknowledge and pursue unity is difficult to reconcile with an expressed desire to obey the commands of Scripture, regardless of the excuses we may offer. Yet the rapid proliferation of American Christianity, with its multiple facets and fragments, has encouraged many Christians to give up on the possibility of achieving a greater degree of unity and reluctantly accept the status quo. Greater unity may not be mission impossible, but attitudes and priorities will need to greatly change before there can be significant progress.

Benign Neglect

Regarding cooperation and union, benign neglect has been the prevailing pattern among evangelicals. On the one hand, the importance of seeking the unity of the church is affirmed, while on the other, nothing much is done about it.

This pattern is reminiscent of churches that enthusiastically endorse evangelism as a major priority but invest minimal time and money in actual evangelism, with unsurprising results. Not only do they usually fail to acknowledge their lack of success in seeing people converted, they attempt to justify it. Sometimes they do this by pointing to what others are doing. Sometimes they emphasize their constraints. When this happens, it is not because evangelism is perceived to be unimportant; rather, it is because once they have affirmed it, pastors and congregations experience some measure of satisfaction, perhaps complacency, enabling them to go about their regular business and assume that evangelism will occur. If success is minimal, any guilt is mitigated by the mere fact that the church identified evangelism as a priority. In most instances, when there *is* evangelistic activity, it is not planned and well executed.

Unless initiatives such as evangelism are high priorities—with goals in place to measure activity and results, allowing churches to adjust efforts and plans accordingly—nothing will change. Recent history validates this. That is why few established congregations are successful in reaching people with the gospel. It is also why the most successful evangelism occurs in church plants.

Again, if it is a high priority to build relationships with other Christians, a commensurate level of activity will follow. The same is true of relationships between denominations. If it is a high priority that has been decided and affirmed by the denomination, denominational leaders will give appropriate attention to it. They will map a strategy to align interests, cooperate, and if possible, merge. They will then begin to implement it. If not, the priority will die of neglect.

Other Priorities

Because matters other than unity usually dominate the agenda of evangelical churches, the likelihood of them making any significant progress toward achieving it is effectively minimized. Under such conditions, unity will occur by accident, if at all. The tyranny of the urgent tends to drive decision-making because most people are busy and have difficulty getting everything done. Dealing with budgets, growth goals, worship preferences, social agendas, and people problems easily dominates a congregation's attention most of the time. Internal health and flourishing usually take precedence over reaching out to other congregations or denominations. All these responsibilities and needs divert interest and attention away from seeking unity, which is perceived as less important, certainly less urgent. One factor that can get attention and change behavior is a pressing problem or project that is bigger than one congregation or denomination can handle, requiring cooperation to assure success.

In general, factors such as worship preferences, social issues (such as the definition of marriage), and missional interests may become occasions to perpetuate division rather than furthering the elusive goal of unity. Ethnic differences have continually raised barriers, as have cultural factors. Very small differences can pose huge obstacles. The differences may be real, but they do not justify division or remaining separate. They should be viewed as providing opportunities for new understanding and enrichment.

Recently, while chatting with a denominational leader, I mentioned the seemingly apparent appeal of a merger with a similar denomination. In my opinion, the differences between them were minimal and the potential synergy and influence seemed overwhelming, so I was encouraged to suggest that they consider it seriously. His response was essentially to say he couldn't be bothered, although he did not state it in those terms. He offered several reasons, such as the way the other denomination seemed to view his denomination. He was passing the blame for any failure to the other denomination, attributing the impediments to them. As far as he was concerned, they were the problem. He was convinced that his denomination was doing the right thing by ignoring the other one. Issues would have needed to be overcome, but it became an opportunity lost. This is not an unusual occurrence.

When I was a pastor in Miami, I was keenly interested in reaching the growing Hispanic population and urged other church leaders to consider multiple services in English and Spanish or to plant Hispanic churches. Hispanics were open to the gospel and responsive to attention; I knew this from my earlier experience teaching Cubans how to speak English. It was disappointing to discover the repeated indifference and total disinterest that led churches to do almost nothing. The leaders' interest levels were minimal, however, and churches essentially did nothing. A great opportunity was missed.

Organizational Dynamics

Organizational dynamics can certainly be the root of misunderstanding and division, although it does not usually make the list of top problems to be wary of in ecclesiastical circles. As an example, many older, smaller congregations on the fringes of growing cities may experience rapid growth as the city encroaches on their area. It lasts until the church has a major crisis, possibly leading to a split.

The scenario unfolds this way. Typically, new attendees are welcomed heartily, since small fringe churches tend to have a meager existence because of their low numbers and limited resources. But as the number of new attendees and church members increases, the older membership discovers that their church has changed so much, they don't like what it has become. The new members, who are gradually gaining influence, want to make changes and eventually gain the power to execute them. The old-timers now find themselves in a minority position in what seems to be a very different church, resenting the new people who have changed the culture of "their church." There is an inevitable clash, after which a number of those dissatisfied with the results withdraw.

Major shifts in organizational culture can be devastating, as many businesses can readily attest. Three-fourths of business mergers and plans fail because of organizational culture issues of which they were unaware or unprepared to handle. Unfortunately, most congregational and denominational mergers have paid scant attention to this matter that is so essential to a successful experience.

The Cumberland Presbyterian Church provides an instructive example. Its genesis during the Second Great Awakening of the early nineteenth century—particularly in Tennessee and Kentucky—has often been attributed to theological differences. But a good case can be made that personal and organizational dynamics played a far more significant role in the emergence of the new denomination than is usually acknowledged.

The roots of the denomination are found in the thousands of people who gathered in protracted camp meetings for evangelistic preaching that resulted in dramatic spiritual experiences and conversions. They were soon gathered into area churches. Christianity on the American frontier was dramatically different from the Christianity of the older, settled towns with their established congregations and regular pastors—some of whom served for many years.

Historian Gordon Wood refers to the early 1800s as the time of greatest religious chaos and originality in American history. Clergy from both ends of the social spectrum wanted authority, but the upstarts from the frontier areas who had the common touch seized the advantage, resulting in a huge, profoundly democratic upheaval.[12] The older Presbyterian denomination lost power and control; several new denominations emerged. This account is not intended to minimize the theological issues, but rather to create a larger frame of reference for understanding what transpired in that part of the country amid tremendous spiritual developments.[13]

Disagreements

Sometimes it seems impossible to avoid disagreements. As long as people are sinful, this is certain to be true, and the range of disagreements varies from insignificant to substantial. Changing times and circumstances have a way of causing misunderstanding and division. A rising generation often looks at things differently than an older one would. One person's level of spiritual maturity and understanding of the Scriptures can differ from another's and also contribute to disagreement. The same may be said of education and cultural influences. Let me offer a wide range of illustrations with varying degrees of importance.

I was recently reminded of the way these disagreements occur when I became engrossed in a conversation about same-sex marriage and gays with a young Christian under twenty. I was somewhat surprised when the teen, an evangelical, said that gays should not be condemned but accepted. No biblical basis was offered in

12. Hatch, *Democratization*, 220, 226.

13. See also Ben M. Barrus, Milton L. Baughn, and Thomas H. Campbell, *A People Called Cumberland Presbyterians* (Memphis: Frontier Press, 1972), 64ff.

support of this assertion. When the Bible was mentioned, the reference was disregarded and the issue was clearly not open for serious discussion. I was reminded how, within a span of less than twenty years, opinions regarding this issue have changed significantly, especially among younger age groups. Other moral practices are rapidly changing too, and scant attention is given to biblical instruction in evaluating them.

An example of a different nature is music at worship services. This is a source of frequent disagreement because attitudes and preferences are influenced generationally as well as theologically and educationally. Few congregations are devoted to exclusive psalmody anymore, and most congregations would be surprised to discover that any churches are. Praise bands have replaced choirs and organs in many churches, but not without strong resistance.

On another matter, scholarly researchers may uncover new information offering insight about a biblical text that other people are reticent to accept because they have always thought and believed differently. This occurred some years ago when archaeological discoveries revealed information about ancient suzerainty treaties that led to a new understanding of covenant as it was practiced in the ancient Near East. It soon became obvious that these ancient treaties were a model for biblical covenants and redefined the way covenants were to be understood. One scholar even argued that these treaties provided a basic model for the structure of the whole Bible. It wasn't long before this new information forced a change in the way Old Testament covenants were understood. Although widespread acceptance was not immediate, there was a gradual shift in the understanding of the meaning of covenant, which benefitted from the archaeological discoveries.

On other occasions, new interpretations of Scripture have led to disagreement and division, as was the case when dispensational millennialism became popular and when many evangelicals disassociated themselves from it. Some of the cults, such as the Jehovah's Witnesses and Christian Science, also arose this way through the introduction of new or additional scriptures and new interpretations. In other instances, personalities figured prominently in disagreements and consequent divisions, as seems to have occurred with the origin of the Cumberland Presbyterian Church and the Bible Presbyterian Church.[14]

Many of the disagreements that occur may be seen positively as an expression of the diversity that is always present in the church. People will not agree on everything, and it would be foolish to expect such. When you consider all the economic, social, cultural, and intellectual variations, and the differences in understanding of what the Bible teaches, it is a wonder that we agree as much as we do. However, most disagreements need not disqualify a person as a Christian or as a member of Christ's church. Their differences may be questionable, perhaps incapable of a strong defense, but if their commitment to Christ is clear, then that is paramount.

Admittedly, there are sectarian extremes such as congregations that practice handling poisonous snakes as an essential demonstration of faith, as was the case with Jamie Coots of Kentucky, who was featured on National Geographic Television.[15]

Disagreements should not necessarily lead to pejorative attitudes or disrespect between believers, which can become divisive although it easily occurs. Pride, insensitivity, and stubbornness can unnecessarily isolate believers from one another. Disparaging comments about other Christians, sister congregations, or denominations that arise from disagreements almost inevitably lead to harmful consequences too. The fact is we will not agree on everything and shouldn't expect to, but we should still care for and respect one another. This should guide our attitudes and speech. Disagreement as an expression of diversity can be a great benefit. It can enlighten and enrich those who think differently. Occasionally, a person is disagreeable as well as persistently disagreeing, and such a person should not be permitted to control or determine group decisions because it will usually have a destructive effect on the group.

14. Barrus, Baughn, and Campbell, *Cumberland Presbyterians*, 62 ff.

15. Vincent Funaro, "Kentucky Snake Handler Bit During Church Service Refuses Medical Treatment and Dies," *The Christian Post*, July 29, 2015, accessed February 3, 2016, http://www.christianpost.com/news/kentucky-snake-handler-bit-during-church-service-refuses-medical-treatment-and-dies-142061/.

Theological Differences

For many years, theological differences have provided the principal justification for those divisions or perpetuating separate identities—especially among evangelical denominations. And theology continues to be a major identifying factor of conflict and an impediment to closer relationships among evangelical denominations and organizations. Because evangelicals believe so strongly, any conflicts about doctrinal matters are taken seriously, and feelings run deep. The more important the theological issue, the greater the intensity of feeling. Any semblance of disagreement with or departure from the Bible makes unity difficult to accept.

Can you imagine Southern Baptists suggesting that a formal union with any group of evangelical Paedobaptists would be highly desirable? Of course not, because doing so would destroy their identity that is so closely tied to this fundamental doctrine. Similarly, baptism by immersion not only justifies but necessitates a separate existence for those who are convinced that anyone who has not been immersed has not been baptized. When an identity is so wrapped up in historic theological beliefs, any proposed change is threatening. For Episcopalians, episcopacy—or the succession of bishops—is integral to the identity of the church. And, as you can imagine, self-consciously Reformed churches chafe at any suggestion of merging with Arminian churches, though they might have high esteem for them otherwise.

In evangelical circles, holding certain doctrines may trigger strong criticism or ostracism from those who deem those doctrines unbiblical and therefore unacceptable. Consider, for example, the response of some evangelicals to N. T. Wright's position on justification—often referred to as the New Perspective on Paul—and the reciprocal response by Wright and his followers. When you add to this mix strong disagreements about liturgy, music, and social/moral issues, you realize how many and how formidable the obstacles to unity may be.

Doctrines are so important to evangelicals because, dating back to the Reformation, they are deeply rooted in their commitment to the authority of Scripture. The Bible is the ultimate authority for what evangelicals believe and how they are supposed to live. The very origin, heritage, and identity of evangelical Protestantism are tied tightly to the authority of the Bible. For anyone to slight this commitment is a serious matter. The stronger the commitment, the harder it is for any change—any *thought* of change—to occur. Given the history of religious struggles related to the authority of Scripture and the damage that has been done to many Christians and denominations because of it, their reluctance to change is easy to understand and justify.

As an example, Robert Wuthnow, a well-known professor of sociology at Princeton University who has given a large share of his time to producing valuable research regarding Christianity in America, described his observations of some evangelicals and liberals within the UPCUSA who were of different minds about the church and its agenda. One of his observations was that the turmoil within the UPCUSA had been more notable in its magnitude and the consequences have been more profound than in other denominations struggling with similar issues. Consequently, tensions escalated, resulting in vitriolic conflict, attrition, and decline. Given his well-researched opinion, it is worth taking a closer look at that development.

Often, Wuthnow says, efforts seek to bring opposing parties together to bridge a growing chasm. Meetings are usually designed to bring these opposing groups together with activities and conversations designed to develop relationships and perhaps even friendships that are rewarding. Generally, after some time together, dialogue begins and barriers slowly fall, opening the door for more constructive relationships. But that was not what happened with these Presbyterians, as Wuthnow quickly learned. They vigorously disagreed about doctrinal and social matters. "The more each side came into contact with the other, and the more knowledge it gained about the other, the less it liked the other."[16] Reading Wuthnow's account is, in some ways, reminiscent of descriptions about escalating

16. Wuthnow, *Struggle for America's Soul*, 24, 68–69.

hostility between spouses in a divorce. By the time that stage has been reached, it is difficult to remove the emotional barriers and proceed to a constructive discussion.

For these Presbyterians, the unresolved theological differences that worsened with time coupled with an increasing balance of power in the hands of liberal church leaders has resulted in a precipitous decline of membership in the PC(USA). Evangelicals who found themselves strongly disagreeing with denominational actions and positions yet unable to effect acceptable changes moved their membership to more compatible congregations. Evangelical pastors, who increasingly found themselves out of step with the denomination, made similar decisions.

As the differences became more pronounced and unacceptable, it became apparent that evangelical congregations had to accept the new conditions and live with them or leave. Many of those congregations decided that they could no longer remain in their old denomination, so they left—with or without their property. Some ministers, who could not agree to the changes pressed on them, lost their jobs or were pushed out of the denomination. This sad, century-long process of estrangement and separation continues into the present. A once great, nationally prestigious denomination—that during the nineteenth century was the greatest missionary force in the modern world—slowly slid toward numerical and cultural irrelevance.

Where to Draw the Line

Commonalities among evangelicals are far greater than the differences, although the critical comments evangelicals make regarding those differences may not always give that impression. Typically the differences result from differing interpretations of the Bible, not a rejection of biblical authority. They may also be from different emphases in their traditions. Nevertheless, these differences exist and must be dealt with. Theological differences, as noted above, have often been the root of disunity and division, and it is easy to understand why.

The real problem, however, often lies not in the differences themselves as much as in the seeming inability of evangelicals to determine the degree of importance of matters on which they disagree. Surprisingly, this discrepancy receives far too little attention, as if all doctrines are of equal importance. When disagreements occur they can quickly assume disproportionate importance. This happens because many times evangelicals often have difficulty knowing where to draw the line between what is essential and what is not, or what is of primary, secondary, and tertiary importance. Long ago, A. A. Hodge addressed this matter by saying:

> The gospel is a logically consistent system of truth, some of whose principles are essential to its integrity, while others are essential only to its symmetry and perfection. . . . A fundamental doctrine, then, is either one which every soul must apprehend more or less clearly in order to be saved, or one which, when known, is so clearly involved with the knowledge and belief of which is essential to salvation, that one cannot be rejected while the other is really believed.[17]

For evangelicals, one of those primary and essential doctrines is the atonement, sometimes called the substitutionary atonement. A person cannot be part of the church unless he or she believes that Jesus, the incarnate Son of God, died on a cross and suffered the punishment for human sin, and that sincere repentance for one's sins and faith in Christ is essential for forgiveness and eternal life. Other doctrines such as the bodily resurrection, justification by faith and not works, the Trinity, and the authority of Scripture are also primary.

Some denominations and organizations no longer make such distinctions. In their opinion, it is not essential to believe that Jesus is the incarnate, sinless Son of God who died on the cross to atone for sins. Typically, they find it difficult to work with evangelicals who insist that salvation is only through Christ, as described above. To

17. Archibald Alexander Hodge, *Outlines of Theology* (Grand Rapids: Eerdmans, 1957), 475–76.

them, that doesn't make sense in our modern world. They are more concerned about a social agenda.

A case in point occurred at Wheaton College in 2015. Larycia Hawkins, an associate professor of political science, was placed on leave and a termination process was initiated after she began wearing a headscarf during Advent. She was expressing her concern for and solidarity with Muslims because of their suffering, adding that we "worship the same God." The Wheaton College administration said that it had no issue with her decision to wear the headscarf as an expression of care or compassion for Muslims. But it was clear in communicating Wheaton's position that salvation is through Christ alone, and that there are fundamental differences between the two religions that cannot be disregarded.[18]

As might be expected, given the wide media attention, the Hawkins case stirred strong reactions outside the Wheaton community as well as within it—especially after the administration initiated termination procedures. The Faculty Council unanimously expressed their disagreement with the action of the administration and asked that her leave and notification of termination be withdrawn. Eventually the administration and Hawkins reached an agreement that "with a mutual desire for God's blessing" they would part ways.[19] The theological issue regarding whether both religions worship the same God was a major issue to the college, but not to Professor Hawkins and many of her supporters. Professor Hawkins perceived herself to be an upstanding evangelical Christian who loved Wheaton and embraced its Statement of Faith, so she was surprised and dismayed by the action of the college administration.

Part of the problem was the confusion caused by her indiscriminate mingling of compassion for suffering Muslims with belief in a

18. "Wheaton College Statement Regarding Christian Engagement with Muslim Neighbors," December 11, 2015, accessed December 11, 2015, http://www.wheaton.edu/Media-Center/Media-Relations/Statements/Wheaton-College-Statement-Regarding-Christian-Engagement-with-Muslim-Neighbors.

19. Manya Brachear Pashman, "Wheaton College reverses efforts to fire professor, but she won't return to teach," *Chicago Tribune*, February 6, 2016, accessed February 8, 2016, http://www.chicagotribune.com/news/local/breaking/ct-wheaton-college-professor-firing-reversal-20160206-story.html.

major Christian doctrine. In addition, as events unfolded, it appeared that the issue could and probably should have been handled more wisely by both parties. The Hawkins issue clearly underscores the challenge of knowing where and how to draw the lines. It also raises the question of the most constructive way to address and resolve such matters when they occur. In addressing differences, the method of resolution can become as equally determinative of the outcome as both sides' actions. A wisely implemented process is important to a good outcome.

Somewhat similar to the Wheaton College situation was the crisis that confronted the Council of Christian Colleges and Universities (CCCU) in 2015 when two of their member institutions, Eastern Mennonite University and Goshen College, announced publicly that they would accept faculty who were engaged in same-sex marriages. In doing so, they became the first CCCU member institutions to declare a willingness to retain or hire non-celibate faculty and staff who were married to other gays or lesbians. Eventually, it became apparent that there would be a large-scale exodus of member schools from CCCU should these schools be permitted to remain without rescinding their new policies, and Eastern Mennonite and Goshen withdrew.

This issue was exacerbated by the public attention that had already been directed toward Gordon College because of its stance, based on the Bible, that homosexuality was a sin and that sex outside of marriage was wrong. After surviving strong media criticism and a challenge to its accreditation, Gordon was able to continue with its position regarding same-sex marriages but took steps to assure that none of their LGBT students would be bullied, assuaging external concerns from accreditors.

In evaluating these two situations, clearly the key issue for Wheaton College centered on the gospel and whether or not it is necessary to believe in Christ for salvation, which is a primary issue. Does someone who does not believe in Christ worship the same God as evangelical Christians? What about someone who denies the Trinity? The standard evangelical answer is an unequivocal no. Muslims, of course, reject the doctrine of the Trinity.

By comparison, the CCCU and Gordon issues were centered on moral issues, not a doctrine essential to salvation. But the moral issues they confronted were clearly tied to what the Bible requires—or perhaps permits—regarding such behavior. Interestingly none of the institutions involved claimed that the deviation by faculty or staff meant that they were not Christians. Rather, it was a matter of what conformed to the expected faith and practice position of the institutions in the light of Scripture.

How does a Christian organization decide what moral transgressions merit separation or expulsion? What is the nature of the moral failure? How serious is it? Can expulsion or separation be justified biblically? Is it required? How does a Christian organization determine what is a primary doctrine that should be required of every member? As is well known, religious institutions may require adherence to statements of faith and approved moral standards. Evangelical organizations usually address these issues by requiring adherence to a statement of belief and a moral code. Usually, these are clearly based on what the Bible teaches.

Some doctrines, such as the method of baptism—by sprinkling, pouring, or immersing—may be important as part of a denominational identity but are not essential to salvation. Therefore, should they become a barrier to fellowship in the Holy Spirit or unity? The same could be asked of ordaining officers in the church, such as bishops, elders, and deacons. Should one be Presbyterian, Episcopalian, or Congregational in church polity to be accepted?

Once again, the principal question is where and how to draw lines. It may seem simple and clear, but lines in the sand have a way of moving in both directions, becoming stricter or looser. For example, some Christian institutions have required employees, students, and board members to refrain from drugs, alcohol, tobacco, movies, dancing, etc. Others require chapel attendance. While morality is an appropriate concern, how a denomination or Christian institution confidently draws lines that everyone must observe is a serious matter with significant consequences. What are the consequences for failure to comply? How is that determined? Moreover, unintended consequences can be severe.

Some doctrinal positions are absolutely unacceptable. One of the early Christian heresies was the claim that Jesus was not God, but a man whom God adopted. Those who thought that way did not believe that Jesus could suffer and die for the sins of others. A modern cult, the Jehovah's Witnesses, also believes that Jesus is not God. This is a primary or essential doctrine, and evangelicals are right to insist that one must believe that Jesus is God to be accepted.

Other positions can cause difficulty in arriving at a consensus. For example, Cru uses the Four Spiritual Laws as an evangelistic tool. One of those laws is, "God loves you and has a wonderful plan for your life." Although it has worked well for evangelizing non-Christians, some evangelicals have argued that God does not have a wonderful plan for everyone's life, only for Christians.

Some Christians say the Bible teaches that Jesus will return to establish a literal thousand-year (or millennial) reign on earth before the final judgment; others contend that the millennium occurs between Christ's ascension and his return. Some denominations ordain women; others do not. Some denominations disallow instrumental music in worship while most others are more concerned about what kind of music will be used. These are not primary doctrines, nor are they all of equal importance.

Many other such differences could be described. Are they sufficient to break fellowship with one another or to require separate denominations? Unless they are primary doctrines, they do not justify breaking fellowship. The problem comes when lesser doctrines are determined to be primary or essential and are used as justification for separation from those who are not in agreement.

Emo Phillips decided to joke about the way these seemingly small differences can be magnified out of proportion. He used the following narrative to make his point.

> I was walking across a bridge one day and I saw a man standing on the edge, about to jump off. So I ran over and said, "Stop! Don't do it!"
>
> "Why shouldn't I?" he asked.
>
> "Well, there's so much to live for."

"Like what?"

"Well, are you religious?"

He said yes.

I said, "Me too. Are you Christian or Buddhist?"

"Christian."

"Me too. Are you Catholic or Protestant?"

"Protestant."

"Me too. Are you Episcopalian or Baptist?"

"Baptist."

"Wow, me too. Are you Baptist Church of God or Baptist Church of the Lord?"

"Baptist Church of God."

"Me too. Are you original Baptist Church of God or are you Reformed Baptist Church of God?"

"Reformed Baptist Church of God."

"Me too. Are you Reformed Baptist Church of God, reformation of 1879, or Reformed Baptist Church of God, reformation of 1915?"

He said, "Reformed Baptist Church of God, reformation of 1915!"

I said, "Die, heretic!" and pushed him off.[20]

Another example comes from an RTS professor who, in 1975, was attempting to correct the thinking of some overzealous seminary students. The following is excerpted from his chapel message:

He who is not with me is against me. (Matt. 12:30)

Whoever is not against us is for us. (Mark 9:40)

In our Scripture reading, the disciples were embarrassed because Christ caught them arguing about who was the greatest. Nobody here seriously questions, Who is the greatest? We *know*. We are. We

20. Christena Cleveland, *Disunity in Christ: Uncovering the Hidden Forces That Keep Us Apart* (Downers Grove, IL: InterVarsity Press, 2013), 32–33.

are *Reformed.* We thank the Lord that we are not as other men are. We are not Papists. We are not Pietists. We are not Pelagians, semi-Pelagians, Arminians, Amyraldians, Fundamentalists, Neo-Fundamentalists, Evangelicals, Neo-Evangelicals, or Neo-Orthodox.

We are *Reformed.* Not semi-Reformed, pseudo-Reformed, neo-Reformed, moderate Reformed, ultra-Reformed, hyper-Reformed, sub-Reformed, or extra-Reformed.

And we are not just Reformed, mere Reformed, run-of-the-mill Reformed. We are *thoroughly* Reformed, Covenant theology, infralapsarian, Old School, Sabbatarian, Van Tillian, Paedo-Baptist, double Predestinarian, Puritan, true Blue, House of Orange, five-point, Thornwellian, Presbyterians of the South, Reformed; Calvinists of the Calvinists; as touching the confessions, strict subscriptionists; concerning zeal, putting down the almost Reformed; and, touching the righteousness which is in theological formulation, I do not say we are infallible, but I have a hard time imagining on what points we might be fallible.

Somehow we have managed to become heirs of all the right divisions in the history of the Church, which (as everybody knows) is a history of divisions. We have inherited the valid structures. Comparing the theological systems, we find them all lacking but the one which we have inherited or to which we have lately become converted. Our studies have sharpened our ability to discern what is right with our positions and what is wrong with those of others. Orthodoxy is our doxy.

We can proclaim, expound, apply, and defend the Reformed Faith. We have learned and committed ourselves to a great deal. We can deduce, systematize, synthesize, and debate our theology.

But we are not without a little problem. How are we going to deal with those others? While we wait for the final stroke of doom to fall on their systems, how are we going to treat the ignorant and

> deluded victims of those systems? We don't exactly know what to do with the 4½ point Calvinist, the general redemptionist, the mere Evangelical, the Fundamentalist, and the Pietist. To what extent can we tolerate those who can tolerate the ignorant, the imperfect, and the irregular theologians? I am not talking now about the out-and-out heretics and infidels. For the moment I am concerned with Christian brethren.[21]

The professor's concern was to show future ministers the folly of such shameful categorizing and behavior by learning to respect and appreciate Christians who think differently. Drawing all kinds of theological distinctions in a prideful way is harmful. Whoever trusts in Christ, as he pointed out, cannot be excluded and must not be treated badly or spoken of disrespectfully. The fact is: every believer has theological and moral weaknesses. Disagreement is no cause for disparagement.

An alternative to this seemingly never-ending challenge of drawing lines was posed by missions scholar Paul Hiebert, who suggested a "centered set" model as an alternative to the "bounded set" that is preoccupied with setting boundaries.[22] While others have weighed in with their own approaches to solving the problem of definition, Kevin Vanhoozer and Daniel Treier have suggested the term "anchored set." As they put it,

> An anchor is like a center in that it is a fixed point whose purpose is to restrict a vessel from drifting. The church is not the anchor but the vessel . . . there are indeed limits on the surface as to how far a vessel can drift.[23]

The bounded set is concerned with drawing lines or establishing boundaries rather than core commitments. One of the problems with

21. Rev. Albert H. Freundt Jr., "Who Is My Adversary?" (sermon preached at Grace Chapel, Reformed Theological Seminary, Jackson, MI, May 2, 1975).

22. Paul G. Hiebert, "Conversion, Culture and Cognitive Categories" in *Gospel in Context* 1, no. 4 (October 1978), 24–29.

23. Vanhoozer and Treier, *Theology and the Mirror of Scripture*, 51.

this approach is that the lines can be drawn too tightly, excluding those who should be accepted. Or they can be moved in the opposite direction, accepting those who should be excluded. The lines can be moved at any time as new expectations are added and old requirements are dropped. When they change, you may find yourself outside rather than inside. Or everything inside may be considered of equal importance because it is inside the boundary. Examples are plentiful in liberal and evangelical organizations. Moreover, once a group becomes focused on setting boundaries, there is a tendency to lapse into legalistic patterns of behavior to monitor the established standards or boundaries.

Presbyterians, as a confessional tradition in which ministers and officers subscribe or agree to confessional documents, have been aligned with this bounded-set model. The confessional (secondary) standards, based on biblical teaching, express a reformed theology. Ministers were expected to subscribe to the system of doctrine. That would be understood as including all primary doctrinal teaching and, in addition, all reformed theology or doctrines. Anything else would be considered tertiary or nonessential. Ministers who could not agree to the confessional standards would not be accepted. For years this was the practice of Presbyterians.

However, the PC(USA) has been inconsistent regarding compliance. Many pastors who have rejected important confessional doctrines have been accepted while some others, who were faithful to historic doctrines, were disciplined. Recently, the PC(USA) denomination, in a politically charged and highly publicized action, changed its position regarding same-sex marriage. They said they would not require all ministers and churches to comply but now that it has been approved, they could begin to require it at a given point, as they did regarding the ordination of women. If they began to require all pastors and churches to comply with the recent revision, those who objected would at that point be outside the accepted boundary.

This actually occurred in December 2015 when Thomas Morgan filed a complaint against the First Presbyterian Church of Ashboro, NC, regarding their policy on marriage. The Permanent Judicial Commission (PJC) of the Presbytery of Salem soon ruled that,

> A categorical decision by the session not to permit any marriage by a couple of the same-sex on church property without consideration of their commitment to each other, their understanding of the nature of the marriage covenant and their commitment to living their lives together according to its values is inconsistent with the process required by W-4.9001–9006.

The PJC added that this is not optional; it is required. In this instance the lines have suddenly been redrawn.[24] Although the denomination has not taken this position, it could do so, and then anyone not willing to comply would be subject to disciplinary action.

Another case in point is that of Wynn Kenyon, mentioned earlier, who was denied ordination because of his position regarding the ordination of women. He said that he would not participate in ordaining a woman but added that he would not oppose the ordination of women and that he was willing to work on the same staff with ordained women. Nonetheless, after a long process his denomination—the UPCUSA—did not permit him to be ordained. Kenyon did not view the issue as one requiring separation from the denomination, but his denomination took the opposite point of view and expelled him.

The PCA, on the other hand, when receiving ministers, has historically allowed flexibility regarding three basic positions on the days of Genesis 1 and the age of the earth: 1) calendar day; 2) day-age; and 3) framework hypothesis.[25] A growing number of PCA ministers, however, have embraced the twenty-four-hour-day interpretation of the first six days of creation and a young earth. Some of them have become adamant about their position and view it as the only way to interpret the Bible. Is it possible that this group could gain sufficient numbers to require all PCA pastors to accept their position? If so, all new pastors would be obligated to agree or they would not

24. Paula R. Kincaid, "PJC Ruling: One Man and One Woman Marriage Policies Are Discriminatory," *The Layman*, May 12, 2016, accessed November 7, 2016, http://www.layman.org/pjc-ruling-one-man-one-woman-marriage-policies-discriminatory/.

25. PCA 28th General Assembly, "Report of the Creation Study Committee," PCA Minutes (2000), 119–212.

be accepted, and any current pastors that could not agree might be forced to leave the denomination.

Yet another example of redrawing the lines is the initial openness to charismatics in the PCA that was later abandoned so that charismatic pastors were not accepted. This position, however, appears to have softened somewhat in recent years. Tim Keller presented an analysis of current PCA divisions that he titled "The Cultures of the Presbyterian Church in America." He delineated three major groups that he called Reformed historical, Reformed conservative, and Reformed evangelical, and offered constructive suggestions for working together rather than allowing differences to push them apart, as could easily occur.[26]

These are a few examples of denominations redrawing lines without consideration for the difference in primary and secondary doctrines. Again, primary doctrines are essential to being a Christian. The secondary doctrines could be those that are essential to being Presbyterian or Reformed. Examples could be provided regarding other denominations since most of the older mainline denominations have patterns similar to Presbyterians in accommodating to the secular culture. When they do so, they intensify feelings about the issues involved and increase the likelihood that the disagreeing parties will feel constrained to go in separate directions.

The EPC, at its inception, tacitly recognized these categories. Accordingly, they attempted to accommodate differences among themselves in the most charitable way possible. While clearly distancing themselves from the liberalism of the PC(USA) that had caused them to separate from it, they graciously acknowledged that the differences among themselves were insufficient to require separation. Some of them affirmed women officers as biblically acceptable while others believed the Bible did not permit it. They took a similar approach to charismatics, unwilling to require or restrict one another regarding existing differences. They were convinced that their unity in Christ and as confessional Presbyterians transcended these and

26. Tim Keller, "The Cultures of the Presbyterian Church in America (PCA)" (unpublished paper, 2003).

other differences. They were mutually supportive and enriched by their diversity.

In taking these actions, the EPC staked out for itself a moderate, more inclusive Calvinism in contrast to the PCA and OPC. They perceived themselves as being evangelical first and Reformed second. For them, the lines did not have to conform to those of other Presbyterian denominations on the left or the right. In their judgment, these other matters were tertiary issues on which they could accept differences without prejudice.

It should be apparent that the centered-set approach is more concerned with focusing on central convictions and mission rather than an ongoing process of drawing and redrawing lines on the periphery. One person put it this way: the closer you are to Christ, the more some issues fade in importance. To explain it another way, if I am secure in my relationship to Christ and certain about bedrock biblical truths, I can relate to other Christians who may not share my convictions without being threatened by the differences between us.[27] I am firm in my faith and do not feel obligated to try to change them.

This reminds me of John Wesley, who said, "Is your heart as my heart? Then give me your hand." If another person loves the Lord and honors his Word, we should be able to build bridges and work together on matters that may be of mutual benefit to the kingdom. I don't have to be concerned about that person agreeing with me on details about the faith. Nor do I have to be concerned that if I don't agree with him on every single item we can't cooperate productively. Those who are comfortable and secure in their faith are easier to work with. That is the beauty of the centered-set approach. Another way of describing this might be to say that if we are agreed on the primary doctrines of the Christian faith as found in the historic ecumenical creeds, we should be able to hold one another in high esteem as fellow believers.

There are, however, what might be called secondary and tertiary differences too. There can be a lack of clarity about what doctrines belong in each group. For Presbyterians, the confessional standards

27. John Frame, "Certainty," Frame-Poythress.org, May 6, 2012, http://frame-poythress.org/certainty.

such as The Westminster Confession of Faith define what is essential to being Reformed and Presbyterian represent those secondary differences. Other doctrinal positions that are not essential to being Christian or Presbyterian ought to be considered tertiary and do not require the same level of adherence.

It is one thing to courageously defend the unchanging truths of the gospel and another thing to "charitably acknowledge the interpretative diversity of nonessential truths."[28] Of course, the big question is, when are these differences significant enough to justify disassociation or continued separation? And, we might add, who makes that decision? Are there other spiritual, character, and timing factors that should influence how and when such decisions are made? When drawing theological lines trumps the spiritual and relational or character concerns, shouldn't the boundary need adjustment? These critical questions illustrate the need for the spiritual maturity and wisdom that enables a person to determine how biblical truths converge to shed light on given matters.

> The evangelical failure to address ecclesiology and theological authority in tandem—not just to address the intricacies of particular traditions but also to acquire shared principles for ecumenical collaboration—leaves decisions about "community" to individual whim and maybe institutional principles. The result is frequent chaos. In former days, Evangelicals did not linger over the ecclesiological rationale for activism. They may not have had the luxury. Times having changed, there is no longer luxury to neglect the fullness of the church as the context and aim of evangelical fellowship. As the company of the gospel, the church is both the creature of the Word and the fellowship of the Spirit—the primary end of the most dramatic divine action.[29]

James K. A. Smith also appears to have put his finger on a sensitive spot when he observed that perhaps the center of gravity should

28. Vanhoozer and Trier, *Mirror of Scripture*, 123.
29. Ibid., 40.

be shifted away from a fixation on thinking, ideas, and doctrines and located in the affective.[30] While clearly not saying doctrines are unimportant, he called attention to the importance of the heart and of that which is spiritual. His emphasis is more holistic.

Smith's observation and plea for balance makes sense. In Protestantism to a great degree, especially in Reformed circles, doctrine is often emphasized to the neglect of the spiritual. Having spent most of my life in ministry and theological education, I have frequently been disappointed by the lack of attention given to what is genuinely spiritual. I have observed many a ministerial examination that gave significant attention to knowledge but floundered in addressing the spiritual life or pastoral aptitude and competence. Paul's admonition to the Galatians (5:25) to live by the Spirit and stay in step with the Spirit is especially pertinent regarding those characteristics that contribute to Christian unity or the fellowship of the Spirit. A genuine love for the Lord and a humble desire to walk faithfully can overcome many imposing obstacles.

Resources

The biggest burden on a congregation separating from its denomination or planting a new congregation is generating sufficient resources to become self-sustaining, especially if new property and buildings are required. If there is a provision of funds by a sponsoring group or another congregation, the burden is lightened. If not, it can be stressful for a small group to form, grow, and sustain the new ministry. The generous support of a sponsoring congregation or congregations—or perhaps the denomination—can not only be a great source of encouragement but can also bond the new congregation to its supporters.

The power of some denominations to claim all real property—regardless of circumstances—has deterred many ministers and congregations that want to change denominations. This has been especially true of the established mainline Protestant denominations

30. Smith, *Desiring the Kingdom*, 63.

that have tended to aggressively seize all assets whenever possible. The basic tactics have been to intimidate, punish, and destroy. At one point, the Presiding Bishop of the Episcopal Church said that she would rather see Muslims have the church building than the evangelical Episcopalians who wanted to leave the denomination to join the Anglican movement in the United States.

Although property can become leverage to control pastors and churches, the inability of a denomination to control its membership through a claim to its property is clear when you observe the major shift of the religious population from the mainline denominations to evangelical ones during the twentieth century. The claim to assets has not significantly enriched the older denominations, but it has left a bitter taste in the mouths of evangelicals who already experienced a loss of their theological heritage and felt forced out. Because of bad experiences with church hierarchies, it is no surprise that the major trend in evangelical church membership growth during the last thirty years has been toward independent churches.

The responsibility for a careful stewardship of resources should probably lead some churches that are not financially sustainable to consider merging with other churches or encouraging members to attend other similar evangelical congregations. In some instances, this may result in a wiser use of resources for ministry purposes rather than the cost of construction and maintenance on one more building.

Mobility

The last half of the twentieth century was one in which social mobility increased tremendously. One negative effect of that mobility was described by Alvin Toffler as "Future Shock." As cities grew in number and size, the older sense of neighborhood identity and rootedness faded, freeing people to try new or other churches without social pressure to remain in their former congregations. The same was true of the flood of young talent moving from small towns to cities to find promising careers. Society became fluid, individualistic, and consumer-oriented. Consequently, most people now not only expect freedom of choice but abundance of choice—whether in clothing, food, entertainment, or religion.

As the American market-driven consumer culture shapes the way people think about church, multiple choices—like multiple products on the shelf—are seen as a benefit. It enables people to find a church that fits them best with their kind of people. Independence—without control by or obligation to a larger organization—has become highly desirable.

Given the relative ease of transitioning to another group when disagreements persist or tensions heighten, individuals, pastors, and congregations are inclined to move to where they are more comfortable. The very nature of Christian voluntary associations in America facilitates this. The longstanding pluralistic experience has also minimized any motivation to unify or merge denominations because there is no stigma attached to a separate existence to preserve one's heritage and distinctiveness. In addition, for those congregations that are independent, there is freedom from unwanted interference or coercion by a denominational hierarchy.

The revivalist tradition undoubtedly contributed to this mind-set with its emphasis on reaching everyone in the world with the gospel. The modern missionary movement has also contributed by endeavoring to reach everyone by a certain time. But it must also be granted that competition and entrepreneurism are built into the fabric of American life. This has worked to the benefit of evangelicals, even if it has not brought them closer together.

Church Growth Emphasis

Over time, especially in the nineteenth century, growth and size became major indices by which to judge the success of congregations and denominations. If the Lord blessed a ministry, people responded accordingly and the ministry flourished. During the first half of the nineteenth century, Baptists and Methodists benefitted most from their identity with Revivalism. Presbyterians initially did the same but soon became divided over issues associated with the revivals, with the Cumberland Presbyterian Church as one consequence. That put pressure on churches to evangelize and grow, and to develop helpful, appealing ministries to which the masses would flock. This became especially true of evangelical churches, eventually spawning a school of thought called "Church Growth" and "the Church Growth Movement," which was championed by the faculty of Fuller Theological Seminary.

When the pressure to grow becomes a major priority, what happens to churches? They tend to focus on what contributes to that growth. Apart from the selection of a pastor (the most significant factor), the three most prevalent means of church growth are evangelism, transfers, and the birth of children. The baby boom was a major contributor. With rapid population growth post–World War II—particularly in urban areas—and a high level of mobility, it gradually became easier to attract new members from other church backgrounds because of the large percentage of the population that was Protestant. Once it became accepted practice to transfer church membership, a competitive dynamic flourished, with adverse effects for encouraging unity. Some pastors and congregations that were threatened by membership transfers to other churches groused about the evils of proselytizing.

Congregations that rapidly grew into megachurches threatened smaller ones, just as a Wal-Mart might threaten Mom and Pop stores in a local community. When certain congregations became popular and experienced rapid growth, they forced other churches to find ways to remain healthy and appealing in their communities; otherwise, the tendency was to turn inward, becoming protective or reaching out aggressively to attract new members. The larger churches typically had minimal concern for the problems they caused for smaller congregations. As cities grew, the number of large churches grew also, offering more and better programs to attract members.

Such competitiveness easily breeds self-centeredness, and self-centered churches breed resentment, mistrust, and estrangement. They create an atmosphere that militates against cooperation or trust, distancing them from other churches and often reducing the level of commitment within their own congregations.

Rather than analyzing the reasons for such changes and learning from them to improve their ministries, churches that were losing members often blamed other churches for their losses. They were unwilling to acknowledge their own shortcomings; consequently, their walls became higher and stronger. Upon reflection, it could be argued that this problem tended to be an internal one, because when people are happy they do not look for alternatives. If people are happy and involved in their church, they are unlikely to leave to find a better church.

Entrepreneurism

Another somewhat similar impediment to fuller expressions of unity is what might be described as the entrepreneurial spirit and competition, which are closely tied to the ongoing development and robust growth of evangelicalism. The roots of this independent-minded competition are entwined in the self-conscious decision of our Founding Fathers to disestablish religion rather than have a national church. This created an opportunity for all churches and religious organizations to flourish and function according to their ability and God's provision. A yearning to worship God according to their consciences—and escape persecution—brought many of the earliest colonists to this country. They willingly faced many hardships to do so, then threw off the king's yoke when it threatened their freedom. Once established in America, the colonists felt the spirit of independence blowing across the land—a spirit that would not be restrained.

This free-market approach to religion and business fit the American spirit because it permitted people to identify, support, and participate in causes that were important to them. The Founding Fathers' decision unleashed tremendous religious energy that was directed to many needs, including starting churches. The result was a vast array of religious organizations helping orphans, addressing drunkenness, easing poverty, and much more. Christianity was caught up in the rapid growth of the voluntary societies that sprouted everywhere in this fertile soil of need and opportunity.

The overall effect was so dramatic that it has been referred to as "The Benevolent Empire." Individual Christians and congregations had the freedom to choose, organize, and marshal resources to address particular needs—whether drunkenness, orphans, evangelism, poverty, or a lack of Bibles. They did exactly what appealed to them most, creating a huge number and variety of religious organizations.

The result of their freewheeling pluralism, as has been aptly noted by Nathan Hatch, is that American evangelicalism evolved "like a supermarket, a consumer-oriented, highly fragmented, religious marketplace." Evangelicals are, in his estimation, "entrepreneurial, decentralized, and given to splitting, forming and reforming."[31] Faced with so many opportunities and choices, progress—not unity—was the priority. Getting things done was paramount. Action and results were driving motivators.

This fluid, diverse, dynamic evangelicalism essentially had no organizational center, as Hatch observed. Big organizations or bureaucratic denominations with central controls were viewed as counterproductive—a hindrance to getting the job done. By contrast, this robust Christianity, marked by voluntary societies through which Christians were organizing everywhere to address needs, is what so impressed Tocqueville during his visit to America.

This great strength of evangelicalism, which continues to fuel its sense of mission and growth, need not be an impediment to unity. Missions organizations are an excellent example of how the desire to reach people with the gospel can bring greater collaboration and cooperation.

Is it possible that, in our age of bureaucratization, the same motivation could spur cooperation among evangelicals who face an increasingly secular population and opposition to biblical moral standards? A myriad of Christian and Christian-sponsored nonprofits continues to multiply and address human needs. Many of them already communicate about important developments and collaborate as it makes sense to do so. Congregations that work together in their communities accomplish far more than they could individually. Denominational labels become secondary to the joint mission they share.

31. Nathan O. Hatch, "Evangelicals in the New Millennium," unpublished paper, 5.

Such efforts, however, must be mission-driven to be successful. As long as the vision is clear and everyone agrees on the importance of achieving it, they have a basis for working together.[32]

Other challenges and concerns exist besides the ones listed above, but these make it clear that the path to greater love, understanding, fellowship, and unity is a long and arduous road, made more treacherous by the sins that so easily beset us.

32. Phil Butler, *Well Connected: Releasing Power, Restoring Hope through Kingdom Partnerships* (Waynesboro, GA: Authentic Media, 2005), 9, 93ff.

6

CONSTRUCTIVE STEPS TOWARD UNITY AND COMMUNITY

In essentials—unity; in nonessentials—liberty;
and in all things—charity.
Richard Baxter[1]

Anything that binds people together into dense
networks of trust makes people less selfish.
Jonathan Haidt[2]

Community, I am beginning to understand, is made through a skill I have never learned or valued: the ability to pass time with people you do not and will not know well, talking about nothing in particular, with no end in mind, just to build trust. . . . A community is not something you have, like a camcorder or a breakfast nook. No, it is something you do. And you have to do it all the time.
Wendell Berry[3]

THE MOST IMPORTANT step in building bridges toward unity and community is to grow closer to God. The process of

1. Popularized in English by Richard Baxter, the quotation's origins are uncertain. Some credit it to Marco Antonio de Dominis (c. 1617).

2. Haidt, *The Righteous Mind*, 360.

3. Alan Thien Duming, *This Place on Earth: Home and the Practice of Permanence* (Seattle: Sasquatch, 1996), 264.

spiritual maturation draws us closer to God and to one another. We may not perceive it immediately, but it will occur; as we are conformed to the image of God in Christ, the strength of those ties to one another will be impressed upon us. We discover that when others belong to Christ, we have a kinship with them that overshadows all differences of nationality, culture, or denomination. The realization that we are brothers and sisters in the Lord, one family, is the key to that sense of belonging. Accordingly, the Lord expects us to express affection and goodwill toward other believers on individual, congregational, and denominational levels, demonstrating our spiritual transformation. We need not always agree, but we must always acknowledge the ties that bind. The following pages provide a few suggestions regarding ways in which we may seek a greater expression of unity and fellowship.

Love One Another

On a personal level, one easy place to begin is by considering all guidance the Bible offers regarding relationships. Foundational to all biblical guidance is our obligation to love one another as God has first loved us (1 John 4:7–19). Jesus summarized the commandments in response to a question from the Pharisees who were trying to trap him, saying: "'Love the Lord your God with all your heart and with all your soul and with all your mind.' This is the first and greatest commandment. And the second is like it: 'Love your neighbor as yourself'" (Matt. 22:37–39).[4] When love for others guides our personal interactions, we are following God's example and expectation.

The Bible encourages Christians to love one another and warns that without love, faith is suspect. It also describes the behavior of love so that we can more clearly understand what God expects of us. Love exudes kindness and caring; it doesn't retaliate when treated badly. It isn't easily angered or self-seeking. Love is patient (1 Cor. 13). When genuine love and concern for the wellbeing of others are

4. See also Matt. 19:18, 19; Rom. 13:8–10; Gal. 5:13, 14.

clearly demonstrated, they become the fertile soil in which trust can take root and grow. It requires "bearing with one another in love" (Eph. 4:2) and being "devoted to one another in brotherly love," honoring "one another above yourselves" (Rom. 12:10).

By contrast, dealing with people who are obnoxious is a challenge, as is relating to those with whom you have little in common. To demonstrate love and concern to another party and establish rapport, patience, and persistence may easily be stretched to the limit. But without a willingness to pay that price, the next step becomes an almost insurmountable barrier to progress.

James K. A. Smith insists that this is basic Christianity because we should first think of ourselves as lovers:

> Being a disciple of Jesus is not primarily a matter of getting the right ideas and doctrines and beliefs into your head in order to guarantee proper behavior; rather, it's a matter of being the kind of person who loves rightly—who loves God and neighbor and is oriented to the world by the primacy of that love.[5]

There are numerous "one another" verses that can be helpful to someone seeking biblical direction for relationships. Believers are encouraged to pray for one another (Jas. 5:16), bear one another's burdens (Gal. 6:2), build one another up (1 Thess. 5:11), serve one another (Gal. 5:13), forgive one another (Eph. 4:32), and the list continues. Verses also state what believers should not do, such as do not judge one another (Matt. 7:1, 2) and do not speak evil of one another (Jas. 4:11).

To these verses many others can be added, such as:

> If it is possible, as far as it depends on you, live at peace with everyone. (Rom. 12:18)

> Do not repay evil with evil or insult with insult, but with blessing. (1 Peter 3:9)

5. Smith, *Desiring the Kingdom*, 32, 33.

> Remind the people . . . to slander no one, to be peaceable and considerate, and to show humility toward all men. (Titus 3:1, 2)
>
> Let us not become conceited, provoking and envying one another. (Gal. 5:26)
>
> Do to others as you would have them do to you. (Luke 6:31)
>
> Let us consider how we may spur one another on toward love and good deeds. (Hebrews 10:24)

These and similar verses can easily be applied to groups such as congregations or denominations. The fundamental idea of love and concern for the welfare of others is essential to developing a context in which people can flourish. They need to feel safe and supported. In that regard, it is worth noting that the Old Testament addresses social concerns to protect individuals, with an underlying message of love and obligation to one's neighbor.[6]

Build Trust

Trust is foundational to building strong relationships among individuals, and it is no different in the church. For this reason, it is important to learn what is required to build that trust. The possibilities are myriad, but all require a willingness to reach out to others at an appropriate time with genuinely kind and appreciative gestures or good deeds. A kind word or thoughtful encouragement offered in a timely, sensitive manner may become the first step in building a strong relational bridge. Initiating personal, private expressions of goodwill may also be a place to start, but public expressions of appreciation and support are likely to accomplish even more because of their public nature.

Once a genuine concern for the good of the other person has

6. See Richard L. Pratt Jr., ed., "Major Social Concerns in the Covenant," *The Spirit of the Reformation Study Bible* (Grand Rapids: Zondervan, 2003), 283.

been established, it becomes possible to take the next step and begin a fruitful conversation. This requires a willingness to listen carefully to the other person to understand—*before* speaking. It requires give and take. Questions are asked for clarification, and observations are offered in return. Stories and impressions may (and probably should) be shared. Jonathan Haidt says that you first have to take time to understand how the other person views matters if you want to change their thinking.[7]

Good listening, however, is more than gathering facts. It is empathetically listening to the other person's heart, not merely their words, and discovering the story of how that person has been shaped by various experiences. Seeing with *their* eyes and feeling with *their* heart—or, as was once said, "walking in their moccasins for a few miles"—enables you to identify and understand the basic building blocks for establishing trust.

Some congregations are reaching out to others that are different to cooperate and to exchange pulpits occasionally. A number of primarily black and primarily white congregations have found this to be helpful. Tim Keller established an excellent model through Redeemer Presbyterian Church, planting more than one hundred churches in the New York metro area, of which about fifteen are Presbyterian.

Trust also requires a willingness to talk about issues honestly but sensitively, explain your point of view and why you hold it, and listen carefully to the other person. What are the reasons that you are persuaded of this position? How did you arrive at this conviction? What have been the turning points in your thinking along the way? Are there uncertainties that you are wrestling with now? The search for truth and goodness also demands openness to questions and challenges that are presented in good faith. This is not arguing for your position or against the other's position; it is honest, constructive interchange directed toward understanding and learning for mutual benefit.

Serious, sustained discussions seeking a clearer understanding of differences also offer another way for believers to learn from one

7. Haidt, *Righteous Mind*, 58.

another. When a polemical spirit is absent and believers endeavor to listen carefully to one another with sincerity, the results can be surprisingly constructive. Why should any Christian be reticent to enter into such a conversation, especially if the other person has a similar intent?

Obviously, a level of trust must be developed before conversations of this nature can occur. Without mutual trust, defenses go up and the conversation fails to build cohesiveness. Both parties become too concerned with making their points, focusing on weaknesses in the opposing position, and persuading the other person to capitulate or agree; information about the other party, whether accurate or not, may be circulated to undermine their influence. When discovered, such actions destroy trust. Negative perceptions prevail and progress stalls.

The next step in establishing trust is to ensure predictability or dependability. People need to know that they can count on you for certain behavior in all circumstances. It means you will do and not merely say the right thing. Typically this relates to character and integrity, but competence is a factor too. For example, they must know that you will not violate given moral standards. You will not cheat or steal. You will not lie and undermine them. You will have their best interests at heart and not put yourself first. You will not let them down, even if it costs you to do what is needed.

Seek Understanding

Jim Belcher deals with the difficulty of talking to others to assure accurate understanding in his book *Deep Church.* He relates the experience of two leaders of the emerging church movement, Tony Jones and Doug Pagitt, who reached out to John Piper since they all lived in the Minneapolis metro area. Following a lunch meeting to discuss differences and commonalities, they each wrote about the experience, coming away from that lunch discussion with quite different understandings. As an example, Piper stated that it would be impossible to work together unless they agreed on essential doctrines such as the atonement. As Belcher relates the conversation, it went this way:

> Because Pagitt and Jones don't hold to Piper's view of the atonement, they are "rejecting the gospel *in toto*, and so, by logical extension, [they] are not . . . Christian." When Jones pushed back that through the millennia billions of Christians have not had the same view of atonement that Piper holds today, "The pastor paused, looked at me, and said, 'You should never preach.'" Jones tried to explain that for him the gospel was mainly about reconciliation. It is more than a "fixed point of doctrine that is the litmus test of all ministry," he said. . . . "In fact," Jones concluded, returning Piper's slight, "I'm not sure it's even possible to be an orthodox Christian if you're not living a life of reconciliation."[8]

Viewing this conversation from the sidelines—observing the difficulties in communication and consequent distrust—makes you shake your head in wonder and frustration. These are highly respected, good pastors. Well-intended, they nonetheless had difficulty understanding one another and concluded the conversation with reservations about each other.

Belcher asks if there could be a middle way that would resolve such difficulties. He proposes an answer modeled after the *Mere Christianity* of C. S. Lewis that he calls "Deep Church." He describes it in his book after having listened carefully to each point of view. In doing so, Belcher demonstrates the need for a willingness to listen to others in order to understand, rather than merely talking past one another in regard to differences.

Often Christians who disagree fail to hear accurately beyond the words themselves and arrive at a genuine understanding of what is meant. They certainly do not intend to do this, but it happens as they analyze both what is said and the actions accompanying the conversation. The same can occur between married couples who discover that they need the aid of counselors to improve their ability to communicate in order to strengthen or heal their relationships. Communication, especially when discussing important matters about

8. Jim Belcher, *Deep Church: A Third Way Beyond Emerging and Traditional* (Downers Grove, IL: InterVarsity Press, 2009), 11–12.

which there may be disagreement, requires absorbing body language, inflection, tone, etc.

One important discovery couples make is that they need to keep loving and talking—regardless of disappointments or hurts—because talk alone usually will not solve their problems. When people have different ways of perceiving reality or different frames of reference, it challenges their relationships. Part of the problem is that they fail to grasp the other person's reasoning and may attribute wrong ideas or motives to them. Meaning will be assigned, whether it is accurate or not. When that occurs, it is necessary to find ways to bridge the gap and overcome misunderstandings or different views of reality to preserve the relationship. That is difficult to achieve.

This is the way we attempt to make sense of ambiguity or confusing circumstances so that we can make informed choices and control our lives. We always assign meaning to circumstances; the challenge is to be sure it is accurate. As Peter Berger has observed, "Reality can be perceived and lived differently from what one had thought of as the only way."[9] But, he adds, if people keep on talking to each other, they will influence each other.[10]

Engage Differences

In his series of articles "Gospel Polemics," Tim Keller demonstrates how prominent Christian leaders such as John Newton, George Gillespie, and Archibald Alexander were concerned to avoid any misunderstandings and possible alienation when explaining their positions and attempting to persuade others.[11] When humility and love are the priority for such interactions, a good outcome is far more likely. After all, the pursuit of truth and a good relationship are paramount—not demolishing an argument or making another

9. Peter L. Berger, *The Many Altars of Modernity: Toward a Paradigm for Religion in a Pluralist Age* (Boston: DeGruyter, 2014), 3.

10. Ibid., 2.

11. Timothy J. Keller, "Gospel Polemics, Part 1," The Gospel Coalition, September 20, 2011, accessed March 2, 2016, https://www.thegospelcoalition.org/article/gospel-polemics-part-1.

person look bad. Refraining from pejorative comments about a person or a position they hold, even when such comments appear to be justified, can aid in eliminating barriers to understanding and cooperation.

I recall Francis Schaeffer describing his participation in a highly anticipated and publicized debate with Episcopal Bishop James Pike, who had become well known for his liberal views, having been charged with heresy on three separate occasions. Commenting on this experience at a later date, Schaeffer said that at one point during the debate it became apparent to Pike that Schaeffer had exposed a weak position in Pike's argument. Had he pressed his advantage with his line of attack, he could have embarrassed Pike quite badly. Schaeffer, however, made a quick decision to refrain from doing so, carefully directing his comments elsewhere rather than going for the jugular and demolishing Pike's argument—and Pike—publicly. After the debate ended, Pike asked to add something and proceeded to state publicly that he was appreciative of the kind way he was treated—the first time on such an occasion that he felt he had been treated as a human being.

Following the debate, Schaeffer made an effort to be kind to Pike, who privately acknowledged his awareness of what had happened and expressed his appreciation to Schaeffer for his charitable response. Pike then unexpectedly confessed that his own theological education had provided him with little more than what he described as "a handful of pebbles" rather than the spiritual and theological substance he had sought. This conversation provided Schaeffer with an unexpected opportunity to develop a warm relationship with Pike and offer a beneficial spiritual influence.

The Pikes invited the Schaeffers to visit them at their home in California, which they did. The Schaeffers reciprocated with an invitation to visit L'Abri and the Pikes accepted, planning to stop over on a return trip from Israel. (Sadly, Pike died in the Judean Desert when his vehicle got stuck and he ran out of water.) Pike's friendship with Schaeffer only happened because Schaeffer demonstrated that his regard for Pike as a person was more important than winning the debate.

Tim Keller notes that on an earlier occasion Dr. Martyn Lloyd-Jones pleaded with Toronto pastor T. T. Shields to cease his contentious, censorious attacks on liberals. Shields's usual method was to publicly stigmatize and therefore marginalize his opponents. He tried to destroy them logically so that no one would respect their point of view. He was quite effective at it, humiliating and marginalizing those whom he attacked.

Lloyd-Jones found his methods objectionable, however, and warned Shields that what he was doing was actually unwise and would be harmful to his own ministry if he continued to speak of those he disagreed with so negatively. He warned Shields, "You can make mincemeat of the liberals and still be in trouble in your own soul,"[12] and urged Shields to abandon his harsh polemical spirit and preach the gospel positively so that he would win people to the Christian faith.[13]

Research on social identity theory sheds light on this kind of behavior. When group membership is involved, we tend to do four things to maintain positive self-esteem:

> (1) We gravitate toward and form groups with similar others; (2) once the group is formed we engage in group-serving biases that defend the group's positive identity; (3) we try to increase our status by associating with higher-status groups and distancing ourselves from lower-status groups; and (4) if all else fails we literally disparage other groups because in doing so we elevate our own group.[14]

Richard Mouw, who has experienced more than his share of such situations, wisely suggests that "God is not honored when we are unfair to people with whom we disagree." Mouw makes a timely, convincing case for "Christian Civility in an Uncivil World."[15] Who

12. Iain Murray, *David Martyn Lloyd-Jones: The First Forty Years, 1899–1939* (Edinburgh: Banner of Truth Trust, 1982), 271.

13. Keller, "Gospel Polemics."

14. Cleveland, *Disunity in Christ*, 84–85.

15. J. Mouw, *Uncommon Decency: Christian Civility in an Uncivil World*, rev. ed. (Downers

knows how much damage has been done by Christians who are unfair to those with whom they disagree?

Most of us are willing to admit that we've been wrong about a decision we made, a position we held, or actions we took—but usually not until much later. When we finally see the light, so to speak, our attitudes change and we can deal with the problem, perhaps wishing that it hadn't taken us so long to come around. These experiences remind us that we can learn from and help each other if we want to. But unless we have open, receptive attitudes, it is unlikely to happen, and we will probably continue to go our separate ways. Our egos and opinions influence us far more than we are aware of and are willing to admit, thwarting better relationships with others. John Armstrong in his insightful book *Your Church Is Too Small* candidly admits his sectarian past, his repentance, and a subsequent pursuit of the unity of the church. His description of his change of direction that led to his passionate call to a new ecumenism is compelling.[16]

Be Kind

I recall instances when I wanted or needed to build a relationship with someone who was from a different background or organization—perhaps a somewhat adversarial one. I preferred to keep my distance, and I admit the absence of a "warm glow" when I thought about him. It was easy to persuade myself that I had enough problems without adding another one.

In one instance, I had an opportunity to extend an unexpected kindness to a pastor in the same city, though the relationship between our two congregations would have been described as somewhere between estranged and hostile. He was surprised, but that one kind act—followed by a slow dance of several tentative, reciprocal moves—eventually led to a lasting friendship and trust. It also

Grove, IL: InterVarsity Press, 2010), 140.

16. John H. Armstrong, *Your Church Is Too Small: Why Unity in Christ's Mission Is Vital to the Future of the Church* (Grand Rapids: Zondervan, 2010).

opened the door to improving the relationship between our congregations. To be honest, that relationship did not develop quickly, nor did we resolve all differences. It could have dissolved on a number of occasions because it was tentative and fragile. But reciprocal goodwill and perseverance paid off with benefits for everyone, including the community. For it to happen, though, someone had to make the first move.

On another occasion I became involved with an organization that included participants from various backgrounds and different theological commitments. I quickly realized that, theologically and politically, I was in a minority position. As such, I realized that I was—although received politely—probably considered of marginal importance to the group. Nonetheless, I did my best to cooperate with everyone and worked hard to advance the organization. I served carefully, with integrity. After a period of time, I was selected to serve in several important roles and did so happily. An unpromising beginning became a surprisingly rewarding experience.

To my additional surprise, the leader of that group, following his retirement and employment elsewhere, recommended me for a position as CEO of an important organization. I was surprised that he had recommended me so highly because we were so very different. As a matter of fact, I was surprised that he would recommend me for anything! Though I declined the opportunity, I immediately called him to express my surprise and appreciation. He was delighted to receive my call, conveying gratitude for our past working relationship and his confidence in me to successfully handle that daunting opportunity. Experiences like these have convinced me that we can do far more to overcome differences and build good relationships than we may realize. Admittedly, it is more difficult with congregations and denominations than with individuals, but the basic principles remain valid. With congregations and denominations, the leaders are the key. If the leadership is willing and takes the right approach, progress is possible.

A relationship, once established, must be nurtured and protected. This means continually reinforcing goodwill toward the other party. Thoughtful gestures are important. Offer help when it is needed, not when it is convenient for you. Negative or critical comments about others should be avoided because they tend to be repeated, sometimes inaccurately. It is essential to protect and even improve a person's reputation with others. Confidences must be honored. Take whatever extra steps may be needed to help and you are likely to strengthen the relationship, even if it is not immediately apparent.

Good things can come from expressing appreciation, supporting and encouraging other Christians. Tim Keller suggests nine biblical practices for building community that require sharing, serving, and affirming.[17] When done in a timely, sensitive manner, such practices can contribute significantly to improved relationships and building trust. This should motivate evangelicals to discuss issues of common interest in order to learn from one another. These discussions can lead to collaboration on projects of mutual interest, another way to build bridges between disaffected parties.

There are many ways to do this in any given community, from providing food and shelter to those without, to attending to those in hospitals and nursing homes, to helping with worthwhile community improvement projects. If a project has not been selected, the first step is to ascertain what is most appropriate. Reaching out to help youth, especially those who are troubled or disadvantaged, usually has broad appeal. The same can be said for helping the elderly or those who are very ill. Deepening relationships and greater common understanding are often enduring byproducts of such cooperative efforts. Tangible results stimulate repetitive acts of goodness, since serving others brings out the best in people and makes them want to do more good things. David Brooks reminds us that, "Gracious leaders create a more gracious environment by greeting the world openly and so end up maximizing their influence and effectiveness."[18]

17. Timothy Keller, *Gospel in Life Study Guide: Grace Changes Everything* (Grand Rapids: Zondervan, 2010), 59–72.

18. David Brooks, "The Art of Gracious Leadership," *The New York Times*, August 26, 2016, accessed October 25, 2016, http://www.nytimes.com/2016/08/26/opinion/the-art-of-gracious-leadership.html.

Former senator and ambassador John Danforth argues in *The Relevance of Politics: How Faithful People Can Change Politics*, as well as his book on this subject, that civility can open the door to progress in solving problems and overcoming hostile resistance. He points to an example from his hometown of St. Louis. Loretto Wagner—a Catholic and major pro-life advocate—responded to an invitation from pro-choice advocate and director of Missouri's largest abortion clinic, B. J. Isaacson-Jones, to create collaborative relationships. Typically, the two organizations would have been adversaries, thinking bad thoughts about each other. But long conversations led to a friendship and trust that enabled them to discuss their differences constructively. They bridged relational, not ideological, barriers in doing so and called themselves Common Ground. The abortion clinic even opened adoption services on site for those who decided not to abort. As Danforth put it, "In the grand scheme of the long raging debate over abortion, none of these achievements were earth shaking, but each showed that people who seek common ground can find it, and in finding it they can change the culture of a community." The practical, constructive results they achieved would have been impossible without collaboration.[19] They now stand as a model for knocking down walls and building bridges.

Small Groups

In *American Grace*, Robert Putnam and David Campbell highlight the synergy that comes from the connectedness of a religious group to a community. One of the most powerful examples of cooperation that forged a strong, lasting community is the Clapham Sect, assembled by William Wilberforce at the beginning of the nineteenth century. Its name came from Holy Trinity Church on Clapham Common, the village a few miles outside of London where their close-knit group of families and friends spent weekends discussing what they could do for the Lord together. Over a period of forty years, they developed

19. Jake Meador, "John Danforth: I'm Not Absolutely Right and You're Not Absolutely Wrong," *Christianity Today*, October 26, 2015; John C. Danforth, *The Relevance of Religion: How Faithful People Can Change Politics* (New York: Random House, 2015), 46–47.

and implemented a strategy that would bring widespread blessing, including one of the most famous: the cessation of the slave trade. Together, through their vast networks with all kinds of leaders, they were able to change England for the better. Their sustained efforts as a group accomplished far more than any of them could have achieved individually. They remain a powerful example worthy of emulation.

Without experiences like these, bonding is difficult to achieve. Working, eating, and playing together strengthens relationships as people get to know one another. The familiarity and sharing facilitates bonding. There can also be cooperation in evangelistic outreach efforts, similar to what transpired during the Billy Graham Crusades. Motivation for continued cooperation and coordination usually faded after these evangelistic events concluded, however, and was soon forgotten as churches returned to their usual way of operating. Typically, cooperation does not become a high priority until the benefits are considered valuable enough to motivate sustained effort.

Small groups have been important to building and strengthening community, particularly in the church. The small group movement that emerged in the 1960s offered a serious way of combating fragmentation and anonymity while reuniting spirituality with its roots in community.[20]

Christians became involved early; one of the first books was Clyde Reid's *Groups Alive—Churches Alive: The Effective Use of Small Groups in the Local Church*.[21] The influence of Lyman Coleman and others was soon felt. Today it is estimated that at least 40 percent of the population is involved in small groups, and at least half of those groups are religious in nature. A Barna survey detected a larger percentage of small group participation in churches with more than five hundred adult members.[22] Large churches are typically in urban

20. Robert Wuthnow, *Sharing the Journey: Support Groups and the Quest for a New Community* (New York: Free Press, 1996), 40.

21. Clyde Reid, *Groups Alive—Churches Alive: The Effective Use of Small Groups in the Local Church* (New York: Harper & Row, 1969).

22. Barna Group, "Who is Active in Group Expressions of Faith? Barna Study Examines Small Groups, Sunday School, and House Churches," Barna, June 28, 2010, https://www.barna.com/research/who-is-active-in-group-expressions-of-faith-barna-study-examines-small-groups-sunday-school-and-house-churches/.

settings, so small groups should be valued for their help in building community in that urban world. They provide accountability and help people stick with a church. Unless a person develops at least six somewhat close relationships within six months of attending, they usually don't remain. Small groups can provide the glue needed to hold the church's fabric together.

Members of small groups are exposed to networks of care and support that emphasize and strengthen relationships while providing spiritual benefits that many would claim could not be discovered elsewhere. As Wuthnow observes, "Small groups make a difference to the spiritual lives of their members mostly by demonstrating love, by nurturing intimate relationships, and by giving people an opportunity to tell their stories."[23] Storytelling provides an excellent way for participants to begin to understand one another, bonding them much more closely together than teaching could achieve. It may be one of the most powerful ways to bond individuals and groups.

Small groups also help people deal with stress and crises more effectively. As Simon Sinek notes,

> Ask anyone who has made it through any sort of setback—depression, loneliness, failure, getting fired, a death in the family, the loss of a relationship, addiction, legal conflict, victimization by crime, anything—how they made it through. In nearly 100% of the cases, they will say something to the effect that 'I could not have done it without the support of ________' as they go on to say the name of a family member, close friend, or sometimes even a giving stranger.[24]

Not only are small groups a testimony to the ongoing quest for community in our urban world, those who are involved tend to become more active in their local communities, helping others in need and thinking more deeply about social and political issues.[25]

23. Wuthnow, *Sharing the Journey*, 346.

24. Simon Sinek, *Leaders Eat Last: Why Some Teams Pull Together and Others Don't* (New York: Portfolio, 2014), 206.

25. Wuthnow, *Sharing the Journey*, 346.

Pastoral Relationships

It is strange but true that pastors have often underestimated the importance of relationships and their influence on every area of the church. Yet for quite a few years we have heard that the inability to establish strong relationships has been the greatest single cause of ministerial ineffectiveness.[26] Perhaps one of the reasons for this is that pastors often think of themselves primarily as preachers, teachers, and leaders. They focus on preaching as the way they are responsible to lead and help people change, giving scant attention to the ways people relate to one another—and even to themselves—except as needed to implement programs. Consequently, the relational aspect of ministry receives minimal attention. In time, this usually extracts a painful price.

Moreover, the typical seminary education is heavy on cognitive development but usually weak in addressing ministry skills, such as developing relationships. Yet more is required than getting the right ideas and doctrines in one's head to assure proper behavior. A wise step toward progress would be to improve educational development for this area of ministry. Otherwise, the lesson is learned later, if at all.

Richard Halverson is the former senior minister of Fourth Presbyterian Church in Bethesda, Maryland, and later was chaplain of the Senate. One of the most important lessons he learned about ministry was that people are far more important than programs. He was forced to admit that early in his ministry he had been wrong in his thinking, and he resolved to change his mind-set and pastoral behavior. In reflecting on past experiences, he confessed,

> Our tendency is to presume upon our personal relationships, expect them to work out of their own accord. Often we learn far too late that indifference and neglect of a relationship allows it to disintegrate. Far too easily we capitulate to difficulty . . . and lose the relationship, however important.[27]

26. Alvin J. Lindgren, *Foundations for Purposeful Church Administration* (New York: Abingdon, 1965), 135.

27. Richard C. Halverson, *How I Changed My Thinking about the Church* (Grand Rapids: Zondervan, 1972), 115.

From numerous stories related by others regarding his remarkable ministry, I know the enduring, formative effect of his pastoral concern for all his church members and friends. Many of those who were touched by his ministry still talk about the difference it has made in their lives.

Seek the Unity of the Spirit

We most naturally pray for those who are close to us or with whom we have the strongest identity, but why should we restrict our prayers to these few? Shouldn't we be praying for all Christians since we are all members of God's family? How can brothers and sisters not love and pray for one another? Shouldn't genuine caring and goodwill be channeled into fervent prayer for one another?

Additionally, won't caring for and helping one another be rewarded in time? Isn't it true that if we aren't willing to pray for all God's people, we are unlikely to take other steps that will draw us closer to the rest of the Lord's people?

An essential part of our agenda must be to pray for God's people everywhere, especially in our local communities where we know each other best but not excluding those who are more distant (Gal. 6:10). Fervent prayer and expressions of goodwill should in time be rewarded. We know this to be true.

The question is: *How* should evangelicals responsibly seek the unity of the Spirit? It is one thing to agree that it should be pursued; it is an entirely different matter to achieve it. Anyone who tries to cultivate the fellowship of the Spirit quickly realizes that no sooner have you begun than you encounter obstacles.

Without experiencing the work of the Holy Spirit in conversion, such fellowship cannot begin (John 3:5–8). Following conversion, the Holy Spirit begins to knit us together so that our diverse gifts can be mutually beneficial. It follows that there must be a daily reliance on the Holy Spirit for assurance, guidance in understanding God's Word, and knowing how to live with one another selflessly (Phil. 2:1; 2 Cor. 13:14). As the Holy Spirit gave direction to the church leaders at the Jerusalem Council, so we may expect helpful guidance as we attempt to discern God's will and live obediently.

Of the many friends and acquaintances I have made through the years, many of whom are wonderful examples of spirituality, one person more than any other epitomized the fellowship of the Spirit in his daily life—Dallas Willard. Self-effacing, kind, and humble, Dallas immediately put you at ease and let you know that he cared for you. He was Professor of Philosophy at the University of Southern California, teaching there for forty-eight years. His expertise was Edmund Husserl, the founder of phenomenology; Dallas translated a number of his writings into English for the first time. But Dallas's greatest impact sprang from his devout Christian faith. He guided a generation into a deeper understanding of spirituality through his speaking and writing ministry. He emphasized those things that would help a person grow in the fruit of the Spirit (Gal. 5:22, 23). For those who wish to cultivate the fellowship of the Spirit, he remains a model worthy of emulation.

Whither Evangelicalism?

As noted above, it is essential to develop relationships of understanding, trust, and goodwill if efforts toward unity are to be successful. Not everyone will be cooperative, and some expressions of unwillingness or distrust are to be expected. But that doesn't preclude serious discussion and genuine change if we sincerely care enough to pursue it. Entering into serious, sustained discussions of differences with other believers for the purpose of deepening understanding, resolving disagreements, and promoting unity certainly is a spiritual obligation. Evangelicals—specifically Reformed evangelicals—should act accordingly. Pastors and denominational leaders need to accept their responsibility to set a positive direction and tone.

If love and trust mark our relationships, there is good reason to humbly, respectfully, and hopefully begin to engage in constructive conversations. Those who have demonstrated that they are untrustworthy or have malicious intent should be avoided. Wherever possible, cooperative efforts should be initiated with a desire for mutual blessing and a closer relationship. Although it seems natural and appropriate to defend one's position and challenge those who think differently, honest discussion can lead to a deeper understanding and perhaps even agreement. Disagreements need not deter us from building closer relationships. I can't recall a single congregation or denomination of which I have been a member in which I was in agreement with everyone. There were always areas of disagreement and times of frustration, but we accepted one another and worked together in spite of them.

What about organizational unity? Should we aggressively pursue that too? As noted above, organizational unity has less appeal to many evangelicals who generally have a different set of priorities, with unity lower on their list. But it may be time for evangelicals to confess that too often they have been too sensitive about differences, occasionally making mountains out of molehills. There has also been a tendency to develop unwarranted negative sentiments regarding those who are not part of their particular circle. Given the experiences of the last five hundred years, this is understandable but far from desirable. Greater organizational unity among evangelical Reformed churches is desirable and worthy of serious exploration.

A maturation of spiritual leadership among these denominations should produce opportunities to move beyond a preoccupation with defending the faith or growing churches and denominations. Those concerns are important and will remain so. But Reformed evangelicals should endeavor to achieve a constructive, creative approach to enthusiastic collaboration, with an emphasis on more substantial expressions of unity. This is happening in various settings intermittently, but a broader, more consistent expression is needed, along with a willingness to deal with prickly or problem people who are impediments to that process. They should not be allowed to frustrate the desires of the larger body.

The process of seeking greater organizational unity may require a candid acknowledgment of the influence of American culture on the excessive proliferation and fragmentation of the church, as well as fresh engagement with biblical expectations. Yet if there is a willingness to rethink and reprioritize, there is an opportunity to rise above the failure of our Reformed predecessors—including Reformation leaders—and to achieve a new level of unity. This may become more important than has been acknowledged when it comes to attracting Millennials.

Unity and Organizational Culture

Evangelicals have tended to overlook the importance of organizational culture, especially as it relates to cooperative efforts or mergers. They are not alone in this. Secular organizations have behaved similarly; consequently, three-fourths of all corporate strategies and mergers fail because of issues with the organizational culture. If there is to be any hope for success, we cannot afford to ignore our own organizational cultures and must ascertain how they align with Scripture and how they differ. Many congregations in decline would benefit from paying attention to this. As Patrick Lencioni puts it, "The single greatest advantage any company can achieve is organizational health. Yet it is ignored by most leaders even though it is simple, free, and available to anyone who wants it."[28]

My work experience in theological education taught me a similar lesson. Seminaries concentrate on faculty, theology, students, and curricula; but a hidden curriculum is often ignored: the institutional culture. If the way people behave—especially the leaders—is contrary to published theology or values, that will have a greater influence on student outcomes than what is taught in the classroom. Peter Drucker once said, "Culture eats strategy for breakfast."[29] I am unaware of a broad effort among educational institutions to address and improve their institutional cultures. It has been done among many businesses to great benefit, just as it has been ignored by others, with undesirable results.[30]

28. Patrick Lencioni, *The Advantage: Why Organizational Health Trumps Everything Else in Business* (San Francisco: Jossey-Bass, 2012), 1.

29. Attributed to Drucker by Martin Fields, president of Ford Motor Company. See Torben Rick, "Organizational Culture Eats Strategy for Breakfast, Lunch, and Dinner," Meliorate, June 11, 2014, https://www.torbenrick.eu/blog/culture/organisational-culture-eats-strategy-for-breakfast-lunch-and-dinner/.

30. Sinek, *Leaders Eat Last*, 127–47.

Recent research regarding philanthropy has demonstrated that money and programs do not assure success unless attention is directed to an organization's culture: the way people work together, their values and expectations.[31] The conclusion that issued from that research merely underlines the importance of organizational culture for the future of any group. The church is no exception.

Some businesses are unpleasant places to work because of the way people are treated and the way mistakes and underperformance are handled. Some churches can be similar in that any disagreement with leadership is not tolerated, and those who are not in lockstep may be ignored, shunned, or made unwelcome. In some cases, all direction is from the top down while in others there is a willingness to listen to members of the congregation and respond accordingly. While some congregations are welcoming, some are cool to those who are new. Invariably, organizations are a reflection of their leadership.

This translates to denominational cultures and experiences too. I have belonged to four Presbyterian denominations during my life and become familiar with others. One of them caught my attention early in its existence: the Evangelical Presbyterian Church. I visited many EPC congregations and consecutively attended every general assembly for about twenty years before missing one. Almost immediately I was struck by a realization that this was an unusually loving, affirming group of churches at all levels. The culture of the EPC was different from that of every other Presbyterian denomination with which I had any familiarity. For an outsider like me, it was beautiful and desirable. There were fine people in the other Presbyterian denominations, of course, but the cultures were different and not as welcoming and affirming.

While the EPC was not free from disagreements, it became apparent to me that they handled them differently. Problems were addressed in a loving, patient, accommodating way that appealed to someone like me who was observing from the outside. The disagreements that occurred revealed no damage to relationships that I could detect.

31. Mosher-Williams, Brenner, and Celep, *Chronicle of Philanthropy*.

This was not the case with some other denominations I had observed, where the nature of disagreements and the ways in which they were addressed left people bruised and sometimes even estranged. Partisanship developed a foothold, as it has in our country. In some instances, one had to be careful not to make mistakes or react to an issue in less-than-approved terms. Mistakes could be very costly. These denominations revealed cultures that shaped the way their ministers related to one another and reduced both their level of happiness and, in some instances, their commitment to the denomination. Pluralism easily migrated to polarization. Consequently, some of those ministers preferred to avoid denominational involvement altogether and focus on their own congregations.

Did disagreement and unhappiness provide sufficient reason for these ministers to break fellowship? No, and it would have been difficult for them to justify doing so. But neither were they enthusiastic participants with a high level of ownership. In some instances, ministers have considered making a change or even leaving the pastoral ministry.

Rethinking the relationships of evangelical Presbyterian denominations, organizational culture factors such as these cannot be ignored. Some are more compatible than others. On the other hand, how can these differences justify continued separation for those evangelical Reformed denominations that are so similar? One answer lies in the fact that we have a hard time knowing where and how to draw lines or determine the relative importance of areas of difference. There is no apparent willingness or desire to address these differences and work for a satisfactory resolution. But there should be. Progress is needed—and soon. The shrinking number of evangelical Presbyterians church members and congregations is sufficient motivation.

Building bridges of communication and cooperation will be a critical step toward strengthening relationships. When we spend time getting to know Christians outside our immediate circles—listening to their stories and discovering what God has done in their lives—we find ourselves enriched and our horizons enlarged. Our own identities are strengthened as we tell stories of our history that are dear to us. I have noticed how true this is of my family history during periodic gatherings.

It was also true of the two congregations that I served. People loved to tell stories that were meaningful to them—many of them quite humorous. In doing so, they were bound that much more closely to their congregation. Recently, I attended a reunion of a congregation I had served as pastor years earlier. Most of the former pastors during the last forty-five years were present. It was an enriching, uplifting experience for all those who were present and strengthened our sense of belonging. We embraced and enjoyed the time together, relating shared memories from the past. In doing so, we celebrated the narrative of God's work in that place.

If we only listen to those who think like we do, our circle of learning and influence will be quite limited, but if we are willing to step outside that circle, we can experience fresh stimulation and insight that is mutually beneficial. Listening to and learning from others in the Christian community, we can begin to view our peers with new esteem, causing us to ponder the value of such friendships and alliances and perhaps even develop unexpected ones. We learn more about our past and the things that happened to make us who we are. These experiences build lasting relationships and trust.[32]

Conclusion

The history of God's people reminds us of the love and patience of God in preserving and blessing his church through the centuries. The church of Jesus Christ continues today because, by his sovereign grace, He has sustained it. Through many tests and trials, as well as exhilarating experiences, the church continues its ministry by protecting and proclaiming the gospel. Believers today are justified, as were the Reformers, in separating from those who deny the gospel and refuse to place themselves under the authority of God's Word.

32. Children at Risk, *Hardwired to Connect*, 39.

It is justified because, when church leaders self-consciously reject the gospel, they no longer appear to be part of his church. We should, however, care for them no less.

It should be equally apparent that the fragmented church of the modern period is a tragic expression of human sinfulness, and greater priority should have been given and should be given to achieving the oneness for which Jesus prayed. Far more important than the future of any denomination or parachurch organization is the future of the church itself. That should be the paramount concern of all God's people.

Evangelicals have no legitimate excuse for failing to emphasize and seek the unity of believers; we must learn to acknowledge and express it genuinely and enthusiastically. Organizational unity should be sought among those of similar commitment. Public expressions of support and acceptance, as well as cooperation, can foster goodwill and respect. As Miroslav Volf wrote, "To the extent that theology is able to shape broader society at all, it will be able to do so largely to the degree that it is able to shape the life of Christian communities."[33]

The time has come for repentance, healing, and fresh uniting initiatives among evangelicals so that, while we remain diverse and benefit from it, we may also become a true communion of saints who faithfully and honestly represent God's image to an unbelieving world. Imperfect though our communion as saints may be now, we look forward to the more glorious day that is coming.

> For all the saints who from their labors rest
> Who thee by faith before the world confessed,
> Thy name, O Jesus, be forever blessed.
>
> O blest communion, fellowship divine!
> We feebly struggle, they in glory shine;
> Yet all are one in Thee, for all are thine.

33. Miroslav Volf, *Captive to the Word of God: Engaging the Scriptures for Contemporary Theological Reflection* (Grand Rapids: Eerdmans, 2010), 10.

But lo! There breaks a yet more glorious day;
The saints triumphant rise in bright array;
The King of glory passes on his way.

Alleluia! Alleluia!

—William Walsham How (1864)

BIBLIOGRAPHY

"Apostles' Creed." Theopedia. Accessed February 23, 2016. http://www.theopedia.com/apostles-creed.

Armstrong, John H. *Your Church Is Too Small: Why Unity in Christ's Mission Is Vital to the Future of the Church*. Grand Rapids: Zondervan, 2010.

Augustine. *The Trinity*. Vol. 45 of *The Fathers of the Church*, translated by Stephen McKenna. Washington, DC: Catholic University of America Press, 2010.

Aulen, Gustaf. *Reformation and Catholicity*. Edinburgh: Oliver & Boyd, 1962.

Banks, Robert. *Paul's Idea of Community: The Early House Churches in Their Historical Setting*. Grand Rapids: Eerdmans, 1980.

Bannerman, James. *The Church of Christ: A Treatise on the Nature, Powers, Ordinances, Discipline, and Government of the Christian Church*. Vol. 2. Edinburgh: Banner of Truth Trust, 1960.

Barna Group. "Who is Active in 'Group' Expressions of Faith? Barna Study Examines Small Groups, Sunday School, and House Churches." Barna, June 28, 2010. https://www.barna.com/research/who-is-active-in-group-expressions-of-faith-barna-study-examines-small-groups-sunday-school-and-house-churches/.

Barrus, Ben M., Milton L. Baughn, and Thomas H. Campbell. *A People Called Cumberland Presbyterians*. Memphis: Frontier Press, 1972.

Barth, Markus. *The Broken Wall: A Study of the Epistle to the Ephesians*. Chicago: Judson Press, 1959.

Bavinck, Herman. *Reformed Dogmatics*. Vol. 4 of *Holy Spirit, Church, and New Creation*, edited by John Bolt and translated by John Vriend. Grand Rapids: Baker Academic, 2008.

Baxter, Richard. *The Reformed Pastor*, 2nd rev. ed. London: Epworth Press, 1950.

Belcher, Jim. *Deep Church: A Third Way Beyond Emerging and Traditional*. Downers Grove, IL: InterVarsity Press, 2009.

Berger, Peter L. *The Many Altars of Modernity: Toward a Paradigm for Religion in a Pluralist Age.* Boston: De Gruyter, 2014.

Berger, Peter L, Brigitte Berger, and Hansfried Kellner. *The Homeless Mind: Modernization and Consciousness.* New York: Vintage, 1974.

Berkouwer, G. C. "What Conservative Evangelicals Can Learn from the Ecumenical Movement." *Christianity Today.* May 27, 1966.

Best, Ernest. *One Body in Christ: A Study of the Relationship of the Church to Christ in the Epistles of the Apostle Paul.* London: SPCK, 1955.

Bonhoeffer, Dietrich. *Letters and Papers from Prison.* New York: Macmillan, 1972.

———. *Life Together and Prayerbook of the Bible.* Vol. 5 of *Dietrich Bonhoeffer's Works*, edited by Geffrey B. Kelly and translated by Daniel Bloesch and James Burthess. Minneapolis: Fortress Press, 1996.

Bromiley, Geoffrey W. *The Unity and Disunity of the Church.* Grand Rapids: Eerdmans, 1958.

———, ed. *Zwingli and Bullinger.* Vol. 24 of *The Library of Christian Classics.* London: SCM, 1953.

Brooks, David. "The Art of Gracious Leadership." *The New York Times*, August 26, 2016. http://www.nytimes.com/2016/08/26/opinion/the-art-of-gracious-leadership.html.

———. "How to Fix Politics." *The New York Times*, April 12, 2016. http://www.nytimes.com/2016/04/12/opinion/how-to-fix-politics.html.

Brown, Robert McAfee. *The Ecumenical Revolution: An Interpretation of the Catholic-Protestant Dialogue.* Garden City, NY: Doubleday, 1967.

Brown, William Adams. *Toward a United Church: Three Decades of Ecumenical Christianity.* New York: Scribner's Sons, 1946.

Burroughs, Jeremiah. *Irenicum to the lovers of truth and peace: heart-divisions opened in the causes and evils of them. . . .* Morgon, PA: Soli Deo Gloria Ministries, 2003.

Butler, Phil. *Well Connected: Releasing Power and Restoring Hope through Kingdom Partnerships.* Waynesboro, GA: Authentic Media, 2005.

Calvin, John. *Calvin: Institutes of the Christian Religion.* Vol. 21 of *The Library of Christian Classics*, edited by John T. McNeill and translated by Ford Lewis Battles. Philadelphia: Westminster, 1960.

———. *The Necessity of Reforming the Church.* Dallas: Protestant Heritage Press, 1995.

———. "Writings on Pastoral Piety." In *Classics of Western Spirituality*, edited and translated by Elsie Anne McKee. New York: Paulist Press, 2001.

Carey, George. *A Tale of Two Churches: Can Protestants and Catholics Get Together?* Downers Grove, IL: InterVarsity Press, 1985.

Carpenter, Joel A. "From Fundamentalism to the New Evangelical Coalition." In *Evangelicalism and Modern America*. Edited by George Marsden. Grand Rapids: Eerdmans, 1984.

———. *Revive Us Again: The Reawakening of American Fundamentalism*. New York: Oxford University Press, 1997.

Carroll, Colleen. *The New Faithful: Why Young Adults Are Embracing Christian Orthodoxy*. Chicago: Loyola Press, 2002.

Center for the Study of Global Christianity. "Christianity in its Global Context, 1970–2020: Society, Religion, Mission." Gordon-Conwell Theological Seminary, June 2013.Clement of Rome. 1 Clement.

Cleveland, Christena. *Disunity in Christ: Uncovering the Hidden Forces That Keep Us Apart*. Downers Grove, IL: InterVarsity Press, 2013.

Clowney, Edmund P. *The Church*. Downers Grove, IL: InterVarsity Press, 1995.

Commission on Children at Risk. *Hardwired to Connect: The New Scientific Case for Authoritative Communities*. New York: Institute for American Values, 2003.

Cyprian. *The Unity of the Church*.

Danforth, John C. *The Relevance of Religion: How Faithful People Can Change Politics*. New York: Random House, 2015.

Dawn, Marva J. *Truly the Community: Romans 12 and How to Be the Church*. Grand Rapids: Eerdmans, 1992.

Donahue, Bill. *The Irresistible Community: An Invitation to Life Together*. Grand Rapids: Baker Books, 2015.

Duffield, G. E., ed. *John Calvin*. Appleford: Sutton Courtenay Press, 1966.

Dulles, Avery. *Models of the Church: A Critical Assessment of the Church in All Its Aspects*. Garden City, NY: Doubleday, 1974.

Durham, James. *Concerning Scandal*. Edited by Christopher Coldwell. Dallas: Naphtali Press, 1990.

Frame, John M. "Certainty." Frame-Poythress.org, May 6, 2012. http://frame-poythress.org/certainty.

———. *Evangelical Reunion: Denominations and the One Body of Christ*. Grand Rapids: Baker Books, 1991.

———. "Machen's Warrior Children." Frame-Poythress.org, June 6, 2012. http://frame-poythress.org/machens-warrior-children/.

———. *Systematic Theology: An Introduction to Christian Belief*. Phillipsburg, NJ: P&R Publishing, 2013.

Freundt, Rev. Albert H., Jr. "Who Is My Adversary?" Sermon preached at Reformed Theological Seminary, Jackson, MS, May 2, 1975.

Funaro, Vincent. "Kentucky Snake Handler Bit During Church Service Refuses Medical Treatment and Dies." *The Christian Post*, July 29,

2015. http://www.christianpost.com/news/kentucky-snake-handler-bit-during-church-service-refuses-medical-treatment-and-dies-142061/.

Galli, Mark. "Missions and Ecumenism: John R. Mott." *Christian History*, no. 65. Accessed November 3, 2016. https://www.christianhistoryinstitute.org/magazine/article/missions-and-ecumenism-mott/.

Garrison, Winfred Ernest. *The Quest and Character of a United Church.* Nashville: Abingdon, 1957.

George, Timothy and John D. Woodbridge. *The Mark of Jesus: Loving in a Way the World Can See.* Chicago: Moody Publishers, 2005.

Gillies, Donald. *Unity in the Dark.* London: Banner of Truth Trust, 1964.

Gordon, Bruce. *Calvin.* New Haven: Yale University Press, 2009.

Grenz, Stanley J. *The Social God and the Relational Self: A Trinitarian Theology of the Imago Dei.* Louisville: Westminster John Knox, 2001.

———. *Theology for the Community of God.* Nashville: Broadman & Holman, 1994.

Gryboski, Michael. "Megachurches Have Less Involved Members than Smaller Churches, Study Finds," *Christian Post*, February 8, 2016. http://www.christianpost.com/news/megachurches-less-involved-members-than-small-congregations-duke-study-finds-157080/.

Haidt, Jonathan. *The Righteous Mind: Why Good People Are Divided by Politics and Religion.* New York: Pantheon Books, 2012.

Halverson, Richard C. *How I Changed My Thinking about the Church.* Grand Rapids: Zondervan, 1972.

Hart, D. G. and John R. Muether. *Fighting the Good Fight: A Brief History of the Orthodox Presbyterian Church.* Philadelphia: Orthodox Presbyterian Church, 1995.

Hatch, Nathan O. *The Democratization of American Christianity.* New Haven: Yale University Press, 1991.

———. "Evangelicals in the New Millennium." Unpublished paper.

Henry, Carl. "Recasting the Ecumenical Posture." *Christianity Today*, October 26, 1962.

———. *The Uneasy Conscience of Modern Fundamentalism.* Grand Rapids: Eerdmans, 2003.

———. "Vision of a Uniting Task." *Christianity Today.* October 8, 1976.

Hiebert, Paul G. "Conversion, Culture and Cognitive Categories." *Gospel in Context* 1, no. 4. (October 1978): 24–29.

Hillerbrand, Hans J., ed. *Oxford Encyclopedia of the Reformation.* Vol. 1. Oxford: Oxford University Press, 1996.

Hodge, Archibald Alexander. *Outlines of Theology.* Grand Rapids: Eerdmans, 1957.

Hoge, Dean R. *Division in the Protestant House: The Basic Reasons behind Intra-Church Conflicts.* Philadelphia: Westminster, 1976.

Holcomb, Justin S. "Why You Shouldn't Call That False Teaching a Heresy." *Christianity Today*, October 6, 2015. http://www.christianitytoday.com/ct/2015/october/truth-about-heresy.html.

Holman, Susan R. *The Hungry Are Dying: Beggars and Bishops in Roman Capadocia.* Oxford: Oxford University Press, 2001.

Hoogstra, Jacob T. ed. *John Calvin: Contemporary Prophet.* Grand Rapids: Baker Books, 1959.

Hudson, Winthrop S. *Religion in America: An Historical Account of the Development of American Religious Life.* 3rd ed. New York: Scribner's Sons, 1981.

Hutcheson, Richard G., Jr. and Peggy Shriver. *The Divided Church: Moving Liberals & Conservatives from Diatribe to Dialogue.* Downers Grove, IL: InterVarsity Press, 1999.

———. *Mainline Churches and the Evangelicals: A Challenging Crisis?* Atlanta: John Knox, 1981.

Irenaeus. *Against Heresies.*

Isserman, Maurice and Michael Kazin. *America Divided: The Civil War of the 1960s.* 3rd ed. New York: Oxford University Press, 2008.

Jenkins, Philip. *The Lost History of Christianity: The Thousand-Year Golden Age of the Church in the Middle East, Africa, and Asia—and How It Died.* New York: HarperCollins, 2008.

Johnson, David Enderton, ed. *Uppsala to Nairobi: 1968–1975 Report of the Central Committee to the Fifth Assembly of the World Council of Churches.* New York: Friendship Press, 1975.

Karkkainen, Veli-Matti. *An Introduction to Ecclesiology: Ecumenical, Historical & Global Perspectives.* Downers Grove, IL: InterVarsity Press, 2002.

Keller, Timothy J. "The Cultures of the Presbyterian Church in America (PCA)." Unpublished paper, 2003.

———. *Gospel in Life Study Guide: Grace Changes Everything.* Grand Rapids: Zondervan, 2010.

———. "Gospel Polemics, Part 1." The Gospel Coalition, September 20, 2011. Accessed March 2, 2016. https://www.thegospelcoalition.org/article/gospel-polemics-part-1.

Kik, J. Marcellus. *Ecumenism and the Evangelical.* Philadelphia: Presbyterian and Reformed, 1958.

Kincaid, Paula R. "PJC Ruling: One Man and One Woman Marriage Policies Are Discriminatory." *The Layman*, May 12, 2016. http://www.layman.org/pjc-ruling-one-man-one-woman-marriage-policies-discriminatory/.

Kraemer, Hendrik. *A Theology of the Laity*. Philadelphia: Westminster, 1958.

Lefever, Ernest W. *Nairobi to Vancouver: The World Council of Churches and the World, 1975–87*. Washington, DC: Ethics and Public Policy Center, 1987.

Lencioni, Patrick. *The Advantage: Why Organizational Health Trumps Everything Else in Business*. San Francisco: Jossey-Bass, 2012.

Levin, Yuval. *The Fractured Republic: Renewing America's Social Contract in the Age of Individualism*. New York: Basic Books, 2016.

Lincoln, Andrew T. *Ephesians*. Vol. 42 of the WBC. Dallas: Word, 1990.

Lindgren, Alvin J. *Foundations for Purposeful Church Administration*. New York: Abingdon, 1965.

Lowrie, Walter. *Problems of Church Unity*. London: Longmans, Green, 1924.

Lucas, Sean Michael. *For a Continuing Church: The Roots of the Presbyterian Church in America*. Phillipsburg, NJ: P&R Publishing, 2015.

Machen, J. Gresham. *Christianity and Liberalism*. New York: Macmillan, 1923.

Mackay, John A. *Ecumenics: The Science of the Church Universal*. Englewood Cliffs, NJ: Prentice-Hall, 1964.

Marsden, George M., ed. *Evangelicalism and Modern America*. Grand Rapids: Eerdmans, 1984.

Marsden, George M. *Understanding Fundamentalism and Evangelicalism*. Grand Rapids: Eerdmans, 1991.

Marty, Martin E. *Church Unity and Church Mission*. Grand Rapids: Eerdmans, 1964.

McNeill, John T. *Unitive Protestantism: The Ecumenical Spirit and Its Persistent Expression*. Richmond: John Knox, 1964.

Mead, Sidney E. *The Nation with the Soul of a Church*. New York: Harper & Row, 1975.

Meador, Jake. "John Danforth: I'm Not Absolutely Right, and You're Not Absolutely Wrong." *Christianity Today*, October 26, 2015.

Meilaender, Gilbert. *Faith and Faithfulness: Basic Themes in Christian Ethics*. Notre Dame: University of Notre Dame Press, 1991.

Mencken, H. L. "Dr. Fundamentalis." *Baltimore Evening Sun*, January 18, 1937.

Meyer, Harding. *That All May Be One: Perceptions and Models of Ecumenity*. Grand Rapids: Eerdmans, 1999.

Middleton, J. Richard. *The Liberating Image: The Imago Dei in Genesis 1*. Grand Rapids: Brazos Press, 2005.

Miller, Perry and Thomas H. Johnson. *The Puritans*. New York: American Book Company, 1938.

Mosher-Williams, Rachel, Sarah Brenner, and Amy Celep. "It's Not Foundation Money but Culture and Talent that Can Change the World." *The Chronicle of Philanthropy*, February 10, 2016. https://www.philanthropy.com/article/Opinion-It-s-Not-Foundation/235257.

Mouw, Richard J. *Uncommon Decency: Christian Civility in an Uncivil World.* Rev. ed. Downers Grove, IL: InterVarsity Press, 2010.

Muether, John R. *The First Forty Years, 1966–2006: The History of Reformed Theological Seminary.* Clinton, MS: Reformed Theological Seminary, 2006.

Murray, Iain H. *David Martin Lloyd-Jones: The First Forty Years, 1899–1939.* Edinburgh: Banner of Truth Trust, 1982.

———. *Evangelicalism Divided: A Record of Crucial Change in the Years 1950 to 2000.* Edinburgh: Banner of Truth Trust, 2000.

Murray, John. *The Collected Writings of John Murray: Professor of Systematic Theology, Westminster Theological Seminary, Philadelphia, Pennsylvania, 1937–1966.* Edinburgh: Banner of Truth Trust, 1977.

Neill, Stephen. *The Church and Christian Union.* London: Oxford University Press, 1968.

Niebuhr, H. Richard. *The Kingdom of God in America.* New York: Harper & Row, 1959.

Nisbet, Robert A. *The Quest for Community: A Study in the Ethics of Freedom.* Oxford: Oxford University Press, 1969.

Noll, Mark A. *American Evangelical Christianity: An Introduction.* Oxford: Blackwell, 2001.

———. *America's God: From Jonathan Edwards to Abraham Lincoln.* New York: Oxford University Press, 2002.

NPNF[2]. Vol. 3.

Nugent, Donald. *Ecumenism in the Age of the Reformation: The Colloquy of Poissy.* Cambridge: Harvard University Press, 1974.

Oberman, Heiko A. *Luther: Man between God and the Devil.* New Haven: Yale University Press, 1982.

———. *The Reformation: Roots and Ramifications.* Grand Rapids: Eerdmans, 1994.

Owen, John. *The Works of John Owen.* Vol. 2 of *Of Communion with God the Father, Son, and Holy Ghost*, edited by William H. Goold. Edinburgh: Banner of Truth Trust, 1965.

Packard, Vance. *A Nation of Strangers.* New York: David McKay, 1972.

Packer, J. I. and Thomas C. Oden. *One Faith: The Evangelical Consensus.* Downers Grove, IL: InterVarsity Press, 2004.

Parker, T. H. L. *John Calvin: A Biography.* Oxford: Lion Publishing, 1975.

———. *Portrait of Calvin.* London: SCM, 1960.

Pashman, Manya Brachear. "Wheaton College reverses efforts to fire professor, but she won't return to teach." *Chicago Tribune*, February 6, 2016. http://www.chicagotribune.com/news/local/breaking/ct-wheaton-college-professor-firing-reversal-20160206-story.html.

PCA 28th General Assembly. "Report of the Creation Study Committee." PCA Minutes, 2000. Accessed November 4, 2016. http://www.pcahistory.org/creation/report.html.

Pelikan, Jaroslav. *Obedient Rebels: Catholic Substance and Protestant Principle in Luther's Reformation*. New York: Harper & Row, 1964.

Pratt, Richard L., Jr., ed. "Major Social Concerns in the Covenant." In *Spirit of the Reformation Study Bible: New International Version*. Grand Rapids: Zondervan, 2003.

Putnam, Robert D. *Bowling Alone: The Collapse and Revival of American Community*. New York: Simon & Schuster, 2000.

Putnam, Robert D. and David E. Campbell. *American Grace: How Religion Divides and Unites Us*. New York: Simon & Schuster, 2010.

Putnam, Robert D. and Lewis M. Feldstein. *Better Together: Restoring the American Community*. New York: Simon & Schuster, 2003.

Ramsey, Paul. *Who Speaks for the Church? A Critique of the 1966 Geneva Conference on Church and Society*. Nashville: Abingdon, 1967.

Reid, J. K. S., ed. *Calvin: Theological Treatises*. Vol. 22 of *The Library of Christian Classics*. London: SCM, 1960.

———. *Groups Alive Churches Alive: The Effective Use of Small Groups in the Local Church*. New York: Harper & Row, 1969.

Reid, J. K. S. *Presbyterians and Unity*. London: Mowbrays, 1962.

Rouse, Ruth and Stephen Neill, eds. *1517–1948*. Vol. 1 of *A History of the Ecumenical Movement*. London: SPCK, 1954.

Runciman, Steven. *The Eastern Schism: A Study of the Papacy and the Eastern Churches During the Eleventh and Twelfth Centuries*. Oxford: Clarendon, 1955.

Rupp, Gordon. *Protestant Catholicity: Two Lectures*. London: Epworth, 1960.

Rycroft, W. Stanley. *The Ecumenical Witness of the United Presbyterian Church in the USA*. Philadelphia: Board of Christian Education of the United Presbyterian Church in the USA, 1968.

Schaeffer, Francis, A. *The Church at the End of the 20th Century*. Downers Grove, IL: InterVarsity Press, 1970.

———. *The Church Before the Watching World: A Practical Ecclesiology*. Downers Grove, IL: InterVarsity Press, 1971.

———. *The Mark of the Christian*. Downers Grove, IL: InterVarsity Press, 1970.

———. *True Spirituality*. Carol Stream, IL: Tyndale, 1971.

———. *Two Contexts, Two Realities.* Downers Grove, IL: InterVarsity Press, 1974.

Shedd, Russell P. *Man in Community: A Study of St. Paul's Application of Old Testament and Early Jewish Conceptions of Human Solidarity.* Grand Rapids: Eerdmans, 1964.

Sinek, Simon. *Leaders Eat Last: Why Some Teams Pull Together and Others Don't.* New York: Portfolio, 2014.

Slater, Philip E. *The Pursuit of Loneliness: American Culture at the Breaking Point.* Boston: Beacon Press, 1970.

Smith, Christian. *American Evangelicalism: Embattled and Thriving.* Chicago: University of Chicago Press, 1998.

Smith, H. Shelton, Robert T. Handy, and Lefferts A. Loetscher. *American Christianity: An Historical Interpretation with Representative Documents.* Vol. 1. New York: Scribner's Sons, 1960.

Smith, James K. A. *Desiring the Kingdom: Worship, Worldview, and Cultural Formation.* Grand Rapids: Baker Academic, 2009.

———. *Introducing Radical Orthodoxy: Mapping a Post-Secular Theology.* Grand Rapids: Baker Academic, 2004.

Spitz, Lewis W. and Wenzell Lohff, eds. *Discord, Dialogue, and Concord: Studies in the Lutheran Reformation's Formula of Concord.* Philadelphia: Fortress, 1977.

Stackhouse, John G., Jr., ed. *Evangelical Ecclesiology: Reality or Illusion?* Grand Rapids: Baker Books, 2003.

Stark, Rodney. *The Rise of Christianity: A Sociologist Reconsiders History.* Princeton: Princeton University Press, 1996.

Stedman, Ray C. *Body Life.* 3rd ed. Glendale, CA: Gospel Light Regal Books, 1979.

Sunday, Billy. "The Fighting Saint." Preached in Detroit, MI, October 3, 1916.

Tertullian, *Apology.*

Thompson, Ernest Trice. *1890–1972.* Vol. 3 of *Presbyterians in the South.* Richmond: John Knox, 1973.

Toffler, Alvin. *Future Shock.* New York: Random House, 1970.

Trinterud, Leonard J. *The Forming of an American Tradition: A Re-Examination of Colonial Presbyterianism.* Philadelphia: Westminster, 1949.

Vanhoozer, Kevin J. *Biblical Authority after Babel: Retrieving the* Solas *in the Spirit of Mere Protestant Christianity.* Grand Rapids: Brazos Press, 2016.

Vanhoozer, Kevin J. and Daniel J. Treier. *Theology and the Mirror of Scripture: A Mere Evangelical Account.* Downers Grove, IL: InterVarsity Press, 2015.

Volf, Miroslav. *Captive to the Word of God: Engaging the Scriptures for Contemporary Theological Reflection.* Grand Rapids: Eerdmans, 2010.

———. *Free of Charge: Giving and Forgiving in a Culture Stripped of Grace.* Grand Rapids: Zondervan, 2005.

Wacker, Grant. *America's Pastor: Billy Graham and the Shaping of a Nation.* Cambridge: Belknap Press, 2014.

Westminster Assembly. The Westminster Confession of Faith.

Wheaton College. "Wheaton College Statement Regarding Christian Engagement with Muslim Neighbors." December 11, 2015. http://www.wheaton.edu/Media-Center/Media-Relations/Statements/Wheaton-College-Statement-Regarding-Christian-Engagement-with-Muslim-Neighbors.

Williamson, Parker T. "Unbelief Unveiled." *The Layman*, April 2, 2012. http://www.layman.org/newsddc5/.

Wuthnow, Robert. *The Restructuring of American Religion: Society and Faith Since World War II.* Princeton: Princeton University Press, 1988.

———. *Sharing the Journey: Support Groups and the Quest for a New Community.* New York: Free Press, 1996.

———. *The Struggle for America's Soul: Evangelicals, Liberals, and Secularism.* Grand Rapids: Eerdmans, 1989.

Ziegler, Jesse H. *ATS through Two Decades: Reflections on Theological Education, 1960–1980.* Worcester, MA: Heffernan Press, 1984.

INDEX OF SCRIPTURE

INDEX OF SUBJECTS AND NAMES

Luder Whitlock is the executive director of the CNL Charitable Foundation, president of Excelsis, and minister at large for First Presbyterian Church in Orlando.

Under his leadership as president of Reformed Theological Seminary (RTS) from 1978–2001, the seminary grew to become one of the ten largest seminaries in North America.

He served as president of the Fellowship of Evangelical Seminary Presidents for eight years and on the executive committee of the Association of Theological Schools (ATS) for ten years, including a two-year term as president.

He has served on the boards of the National Association of Evangelicals (NAE), the Lausanne Committee for World Evangelization, Greater Europe Mission, Desire Street Ministries, and the Barna Institute. He was director of strategic development for Redeemer City and is on the board of the Langham Partnership, formerly John Stott Ministries.

He cofounded and was first chairman of the Church Planting Center. He was also cofounder and copresident of the International Reformed Fellowship before helping to establish the World Reformed Fellowship.

He served as executive director of *The New Geneva Study Bible* and a major revision, published as *The Spirit of the Reformation Study Bible*. He is the author of *The Spiritual Quest* and has contributed to more than forty volumes and periodicals.

He is a graduate of the University of Florida, Westminster Theological Seminary, and Vanderbilt University. He and his wife, Mary Lou, have three children and eleven grandchildren.